"NO PLACE FOR A GIRL"

"NO PLACE FOR A GIRL"

How One Female Jockey Broke into an Exclusive Men's Club

KAREN WILTSHIRE

with
Nick Townsend

First published by Pitch Publishing, 2024

Pitch Publishing
9 Donnington Park,
85 Birdham Road,
Chichester,
West Sussex,
PO20 7AJ
www.pitchpublishing.co.uk
info@pitchpublishing.co.uk

© 2024, Karen Wiltshire with Nick Townsend

Every effort has been made to trace the copyright.
Any oversight will be rectified in future editions at the
earliest opportunity by the publisher.

All rights reserved. No part of this book may be reproduced,
sold or utilised in any form or transmitted in any form or by
any means, electronic or mechanical, including photocopying,
recording or by any information storage and retrieval system,
without prior permission in writing from the publisher.

A CIP catalogue record is available for this book
from the British Library.

ISBN 978 1 80150 992 3

Printed and bound in the UK on FSC® certified paper in line
with our continuing commitment to ethical business practices,
sustainability and the environment.

Typesetting and origination by Pitch Publishing

Printed and bound in Great Britain by TJ Books, Padstow

Contents

Preface 9

1. 'What Do You Think You're F****** Doing Woman?'. . . . 15
2. Times They Are a-Changin', But Not
   in the Horseracing World 22
3. Riding Against Harvey Smith and David Broome 31
4. Ladies-Only Races Were Fine for Some, But Not for Me. . 38
5. America Trip Convinces Me I Can Be a Jockey 49
6. I Had to Get This Job – But Only on My Own Terms . . . 52
7. My New Guv'nor – a Japanese Prisoner of War
   Camp Survivor. 60
8. 'Have You Ever Seen a Jockey with an Arse that Size?' . . . 69
9. I Discover a New Scent: *Eau de Muck*. 79
10. I Have to Keep Convincing Myself this is all Worthwhile. . 86
11. Confronted with the Perils of Life in a 1970s Racing Stables . 94
12. I Had to Ask Myself: 'What's More Important: Racing
    or Staying Alive?'. 101
13. Head Lad Tells Me: 'You're Brave and Determined – I'll
    Make a Jockey of You Yet.' 106
14. My Mother is Shocked by the Sight of my Bruised and
    Skeletal Body. 115
15. Bill's Instruction was Clear: 'Don't Let Them Know
    You're a Girl' 126
16. A Romantic Entanglement 139
17. A Marriage Proposal out of the Blue. 146
18. My Week of Wasting Hell 148
19. The Most Embarrassing Moment of My Life 161
20. A Confrontation with the Guv'nor as I Threaten to Quit . 172
21. I'm In Despair – I Need to Ride Better Horses 179
22. Head Lad Tells Me: 'Win it for Me – You've Got to Prove
    a Lot of People Wrong'. 191
23. Victory! I Thought: 'Now I'll Probably be Quite Famous...' 200
24. A Piece of Sporting History that No One Wanted to
    Talk About. 204

25. I Heard a Voice Say: 'Don't Move Her – She Must Have Broken Her Neck'	210
26. A Decision to Make: Marriage or my Career?	220
27. Encouraging Words for the Girls from the 'Kentucky Kid' Steve Cauthen	231
28. Riding at the Home of the Derby	240
29. Facing up to the Continued Prejudice of Owners and Trainers	250
30. Some California Dreamin' Before I Wake up to Reality	254
31. An Emotional Return to Ower Farm	265
32. More than 40 Years on from my Historic Win, there's Been Insufficient Progress for Women Jockeys	272
Bibliography	281
About the Authors	283

Dedication

This book is dedicated to my daughter Lara, my father Ronald, and to the memory of Bill Wightman, the man who offered me a career in the 1970s when, there is little doubt, no other trainer would have. Bill was in many respects 'before his time' just as I was, as a woman professional jockey.

I wish to pay tribute to the selfless support of my devoted mother Eileen which made my life as a jockey far easier and the envy of my colleagues.

This is also dedicated to all women riders. Although we pioneers were confronted by the most daunting challenges, more than four decades later women professional jockeys on the Flat are facing, from certain quarters, the same discrimination as me. That is why I will continue to campaign for an improvement in female jockeys' opportunities.

I am also indebted to the assistance of Richard Newman, a fellow apprentice at Bill Wightman's yard. His recollection of events and his reminiscences were crucial to the writing of this book.

Preface

KAREN WILTSHIRE first came to my attention in 2010 when I was commissioned by the *Racing Post* to write a series on pioneering women jockeys. It immediately became apparent to me that Karen's little-known story was a remarkable one and deserved a wider audience, revealing, as it does, how, despite all the odds against her, she fought tenaciously for the right not just to compete on the racecourse but to be offered opportunities on horses with winning chances. This was the late 1970s, and 'sexual equality' had not only just become lawh, but also the battle cry of the chattering classes. Yet, it was also a time when everyone was advising this young woman to maintain a respectful distance from an acknowledged male domain, heavily fortressed by prejudice. The professional racing saddle was 'no place for a girl', was the constant refrain.

Yet, partly out of sheer bloody-mindedness, partly out of what she concedes was naivety, Karen refused to accept such counsel. She regarded such warnings as discrimination on account of her gender – pure and simple. And, for her, discrimination had to be overcome. In years to come, the successful women riders of today will, no doubt, pen their own stories. But Karen's will remain as important as any. In times when men dominated a sport founded on tradition and an anachronistic belief system, she steadfastly refused to be ground down by prevailing attitudes that extended from trainers to owners and jockeys, and to some (though not all) of the predominantly male staff in the stables where she worked.

Her one stroke of fortune was the support of an old-school, but in terms of his acceptance of what *some* women jockeys had to offer, remarkable sexagenarian trainer named Bill Wightman. He played a crucial part in her story.

As a sports journalist and author, this issue has long fascinated me – my interest first being provoked in the early 1990s when I interviewed the US phenomenon Julie Krone for the *Daily Mail*, for whom I then worked as a sports feature writer. Within any book on this subject, the inspirational name of this astonishing woman must be included. Krone was 4ft 10in and barely 7st when she entered the frequently merciless world of American racing. But, as I wrote then, Julie Krone was no Julie Andrews.

This feisty individual, inspired – as coincidentally Karen had been – by the 'Kentucky Kid', Steve Cauthen, once punched a fellow jockey on the nose after he had slashed her face with a whip during a race. He retaliated by throwing her into a swimming pool, but she crowned him with a deckchair. 'You can't let yourself be a victim out on the track.' Or off it. That was her dictum. She broke her back in one fall, and was nearly left without her left arm in another.

Yet, still she was patronised. 'Yeah, she's the best girl around – but playing at a man's game.' That was the oft-quoted observation of her before she became the first (and still only) woman jockey to win a Triple Crown race, the Belmont Stakes on Colonial Affair, and later the first female to secure a Breeders' Cup event when she rode Halfbridled to victory in the 2003 Breeders' Cup Juvenile

Fillies at Santa Anita, and retired (only because of serious injury) with 3,704 victories.

Her affinity with horses was remarkable – the ability to conjure hitherto unrealised resources from her steed. Krone talked to them as friends, not as creatures to engage in battle. 'I've dedicated my life to horse psychology, to understanding their mentality,' she told me. 'I'm not one to brag but I guess I've learned a little by now.'

I would later report on women's excellence in many other sports worldwide for the *Mail*, the *Independent on Sunday* and the *Sunday Times*. But always it was women succeeding against members of their own gender, in teams or as individuals.

Race-riding was different: this was one physical sport in which women compete in the same arena as men and on equal terms.

Perhaps for that reason, that interview with Julie Krone somehow stayed with me, and does to this day; not least because her achievements made it all the more extraordinary to me: why had there been such a marked lack of success by women riders in Britain, even into the new century?

Too many talented riders have fallen by the wayside. They have conceded defeat, unable to forge a career, or opted to work abroad.

The truth is that progress here has been agonisingly slow – for all the achievements of the remarkable Hayley Turner, now in her 24th season, and more recently the phenomenal Hollie Doyle, Saffie Osborne and others.

Pleasingly, I have discovered, over the years, that other writers share my views. Notably, they include Steve Dennis, the columnist who wrote in the *Racing Post* in 2014: 'Female jockeys have won Group 1/Grade 1 races all over the world, have won Classics, have won at the Breeders' Cup, have won on the big days at the Spring Carnival in Australia. Surely, only those whose mindset has not moved on from the entrenched prejudices of the 1970s could consider female jockeys to be inferior to male jockeys.'

The following year, referring to my interview with Karen in the *Racing Post*, Dennis wrote of her: 'It's only right to chisel her name on the walls of the pantheon as the first female professional to ride a winner on the Flat. Female jockeys do not need weight allowances [Dennis alluded to these being introduced in France], they do not need allowances made for them. What they need is a sea change in perception, a move away from the antiquated view that a woman can't do the job as well as a man can, which is why opportunities for female jockeys have been shamefully so infrequent.

'Progress is being made, but it is still a very long time since Wiltshire started the ball rolling.'

True. And as will swiftly become apparent, Karen started the ball rolling on a very uneven playing field, ridged with some brutally unacceptable obstacles …

Nick Townsend
Oxfordshire, August 2024

The following is a true story, but some names and details have been changed.

Chapter 1

'What Do You Think You're F****** Doing Woman?'

Warwick racecourse. Early spring, 1979

CREAM CAKES. Huge, sickly cream cakes. The thought of demolishing just one had preoccupied me all the way to the course. That's what a near-starvation diet does to you. Normally I didn't even care for the things.

But as a young woman with one obsession in life I was not living a normal existence.

Shedding pounds dominated most of my waking hours. The most spartan of Weight Watchers regimes had nothing on my schedule. 'Wasting' had become a way of life. It had to be if I was to continue to satisfy an even more voracious hunger: for a successful career as one of the country's few female professional jockeys; a number so few, I was only aware of one other at that time.

I had arrived here to ride in the 4.45, the Haseley Handicap, for which my mount, a four-year-old filly named Ardtully Lass, was set to carry 7st 13lb. Handicaps are races that tend to attract large fields because all horses participating carry weights relating to their current form – the best carry the biggest burdens – and on paper that means many have some sort of a chance.

Another 7lb was deducted because I was an apprentice, and that meant taking my riding gear and saddle into account, I'd had to get down to barely over 7st. My natural weight was around 8st 7lb. I had got that down to 7st 7lb with an, at times, tortutous 'wasting' regime over the previous two years, a period in which I had spent far too long in a battle with the scales. I could get my weight even lower, with some notice.

A lengthy sauna session the night before and fasting over the previous 24 hours had dominated my preparatory schedule. I was not alone in adopting such a lifestyle. There were some diminutive male jockeys who could do light weights, but there were those of a larger frame who struggled to make the weights demanded. The legendary Lester Piggott, at 5ft 7in, was said to exist on coffee, cigars and dry toast.

As I quietly cantered my horse to the start, the dank chill cut through to the flesh beneath my lightweight racing silks and breeches. I shivered, from hunger as much as cold. But not from nerves. A feeling of exhilaration outweighed any discomfort I felt. I sensed my filly was not without a chance in an open race.

I glanced at the opposition. The race had attracted a large field: 23 other horses, partnered by 23 men. Some of the jockeys stared at me. Perhaps glared may be a better description in the case of a few. No words were exchanged, but I knew that many felt I shouldn't be there.

These men were quite content for females to ride – as long as they knew their place. And that place was in their own company in amateur events. This world was their domain, those expressions said, and was no place for a woman. I felt their stance was: 'You shouldn't even be *trying* to be as good as us.' Some of these characters were journeymen; hardened to life in the saddle, leathery featured, vastly experienced. Others, though, were in the infancy of their careers.

How contrasting their fates would be. Among the riders at the start that day, John Reid would develop into a Classic-winning jockey. The 1992 Derby victor Dr Devious would be among his tally of nearly 2,000 winners. Another of my rivals that day was Joe Blanks, an apprentice I had often ridden against. Two years later, he would be killed when a fall at Brighton led to him being trampled by a number of following horses. Throughout its long, rich existence, this has been a sport fraught with danger.

As for me, I knew not what the future held, but I lacked neither desire nor confidence. One momentous day the previous September, when I had become the first female professional jockey to win a race, had settled any doubts on that score.

Not that my historic feat had received anything like the attention it would today, for reasons I will detail later. Indeed, most racegoers on this day at Warwick would have assumed my mount was partnered by a man. Why would they have known any better?

Today a jockey's first and last names are spelled out on race cards and in the national media alongside their mount. Back then, just a first initial and surname sufficed: L preceding Piggott. W before Carson. P before Eddery. And, in my case, K before Wiltshire.

As far as spectators were concerned, it could have been Kevin Wiltshire. Indeed, at the command of the veteran Hampshire-based trainer, Bill Wightman, to whom I had been apprenticed, I went to extreme lengths to conceal my gender.

The starting stalls clanged open, and immediately a rhythmic thud of hooves on turf competed with a cacophony of curses being hurled by my rival jockeys. Some were exchanged between themselves, but I was the target of many. I remember them to this day. 'Get out of the f****** way,' someone cussed me. 'You c***,' was how another voice assailed my ears. 'What do you think you're f****** doing woman,' someone warned me when I attempted to push my way through a gap.

A few years previously, my convent-educated self would have been utterly shocked, not just by the language, but by the fact that much of it was directed at me. I had long before become accustomed to it. I was damned if I'd allow such abuse to cow me. I was familiar with such hostility by now and had largely become hardened to it. On the contrary, it made me all the more determined. It made me aggressively competitive and I took more risks than I probably should have done.

A characteristic of Warwick, a left-handed course, is an exceptionally sharp turn before the home straight. That means jockeys invariably head for the advantage of a place on the inside rail. The number of runners this day – a sizeable field on any racecourse – all seeking the best position inevitably produced frantic scrimmaging. By any judgement, it was a rough passage.

I had expected the congestion to produce some bumping and barging and, just for an instant, my filly was knocked off balance by a rival, virtually going down on her knees, but we somehow managed to continue. Yet, if I had anticipated the verbal abuse and the hurly-burly at the start of the race, I was utterly unprepared for what happened next. It wasn't just the stinging pain that made me seethe as a rival jockey's whip caught me hard across my unprotected backside. It was the humiliation.

I knew it was no accident. I was furious, but I couldn't dwell on it. I knew I had to concentrate on getting the best placing for my horse. Ardtully Lass finished in mid-field. Given the skirmishing early on, it was a decent result on the filly's seasonal debut on the Flat. I also felt she would have benefitted from a longer distance.

But the indignity I experienced during the whip incident was not over yet. After dismounting, as I made my way back to the weighing room, I became aware of a trainer staring at me in a rather strange way. Perhaps he wished to offer me a ride on one of his horses? Optimistically, I pondered the thought.

I strolled past him, but the trainer approached me from behind and tapped me on the shoulder. 'Er, Miss,' he muttered politely, before rather hesitatingly adding: 'Did you know your breeches are split?' He should have stopped there. Instead, he offered a well-intentioned but rather clumsy explanation: 'Those breeches weren't made for women's backsides ...'

Still simmering from the treatment meted out to me, I was horrified by what he had told me. To do the low weight allotted to my mount in this race, every ounce had been crucial and even my underwear had to be minimal. Bear in mind, this was a male sanctuary. A large number of trainers and jockeys were milling around, and all were men. Fortunately, another trainer spared me further embarrassment by offering to walk close behind me, gallantly averting his gaze while protecting me from that of the public's, to the privacy – as I thought – of the lady jockeys' 'changing room'.

The racecourse had thoughtfully created a partitioned-off area of the men's changing room – although on this day I was the sole occupant. Before then, at other tracks, I had changed with the men – without anyone being aware I was a woman. Bill would register me as K. Wiltshire for races and no one was ever the wiser about my gender.

I slumped down, exhausted and dejected in my bra and pants. My ordeal was by no means over, though. One of the well-known jockeys from my race jumped over the partition.

'Hey, get out. This is the women's changing room,' I yelled, grabbing a towel to protect my modesty.

'Don't worry, love. I've seen it all before,' he replied with a shrug, continuing as though his presence was the most natural thing in the world.

'How did you do in the race? Any spare soap? Don't worry about me. It won't take long. It's a fight to get near the wash basin in our room. It must be lovely being a girl and having your own room.'

He then attempted to grab and kiss me. I screamed and fought him off and he jumped back over the partition when he heard someone coming to my rescue. I dressed slowly, ate the last cream cake in the cafeteria, and stopped for fish and chips on the way home …

Weeks later, at a racecourse on the other side of the country, Steve Woolley, another apprentice jockey at my stables, was asked about the girl jockey who had showed her backside to all and sundry. Yes, he told them, he knew her well …

This was my life as a pioneering professional female jockey in the so-called progressive 1970s. The nation may have been about to elect Britain's first female prime minister, but horseracing wasn't so accommodating to the distaff side.

Today, such a sequence of events would be unthinkable. It would be inconceivable that the now-retired Irish horsewoman Nina Carberry, over jumps, say, or the prejudice-defying Hayley Turner in her pomp on the Flat, would suffer such treatment. But it has to be placed in context. It had only been four years earlier, in 1975, that women had been allowed to gain a firm foothold in the stirrup and compete as professional Flat jockeys on racetracks. The principal concern, apparently, was safety. Patronisingly, race-riding was considered a highly dangerous sport for women. Men, apparently, had to accept the perils as an occupational hazard, as a means of earning their families a living. Then, in the mid-1970s, legislation brought in meant women had every right to take their chance in one of the few major professional sports in which men and women compete against each other on equal terms.

Despite that, many professional male jockeys didn't feel comfortable about a woman in their midst. And certainly, as far as I was aware, few trainers had shown immediate inclination to take advantage of the supposed new equality of opportunity and recruit female apprentices. I only achieved that distinction because my employer, Bill Wightman, in many other respects a traditionalist, was a rarity among racehorse trainers at that time in being an enthusiastic advocate of women riders and prepared to take on a female apprentice with a view to turning her into a jockey. It was a significant staging post in the progress of women jockeys.

Emphatically what Bill didn't want, however, was for me to become a *cause célèbre*. The Jockey Club, which ran racing then, wouldn't like it, I was told.

The cumulative result was that I had arrived on the scene in the late 1970s in what could be described as a blaze of anonymity. That suited me just fine. I was determined to concentrate minds on my riding talent, not the fact that I was a woman trying to cut it in what was regarded then as an exclusive boys' club.

But what I hadn't appreciated when I first approached Bill – more than a little naively, I concede – and asked him to take me on, were the agonies, physical and mental, I would have to overcome in order to reach my goal.

Chapter 2

Times They Are a-Changin', But Not in the Horseracing World

LOOKING BACK, it was absurd. To even consider the concept of me, a young woman, becoming a jockey *as a career* in the 1970s, when it was not just the exclusive domain of men, but with legislation at that time providing no access to their world. It was sheer fantasy.

True, the 1970s was a supposedly socially progressive period when, as historian Dominic Sandbrook put it, 'the cultural texture of British life probably changed more quickly than during any other post-war decade'. It was a decade, remember, that started with the publication of Germaine Greer's *The Female Eunuch* (her view was that the traditional suburban, consumerist, nuclear family represses women sexually, and that this devitalises them, rendering them eunuchs), which polarised dinner party debate. If that wasn't thought-provoking enough, the decade would end with Britain electing its first woman prime minister.

Times, they were certainly a-changin', as one of my teenage idols, Bob Dylan, wrote and sang. But not the attitudes within horseracing. The social revolution was slow to embrace a sport run by the ultra-traditional, aristocracy-dominated Jockey Club, which had by then administered it for over 220 years. Formed by a group of gentlemen with a shared passion for horseracing, it was a self-electing oligarchy and it was not until 1977 that women were even allowed to be its members (the one exception was the Queen, though she was an honorary member).

It was as much a 'closed shop', in its own way, as some trade union operations. It didn't just establish the rules and adjudicate upon transgressions, but set the tone of racing. And that included a reluctance to accept female participants.

The prevailing attitude towards women in racing somehow reminded me of Harry Enfield's cringe-making pastiche on those grainy, black and white post-Second World War public service information films. In Enfield's celebrated skit on his BBC TV show, a dinner party is brought to an embarrassed silence by a woman switching from being an empty-headed giggling young thing to inexcusably expressing 'an opinion' that horrifies the men present. The sketch concludes with the authoritarian male voice-over: 'Women ... know your limits.'

Knowing our limits had been the attitude in so many areas of working life, but, it was true, particularly on the turf, within 'the sport of kings', as it is often known. It was an impenetrable fortress to women – except those who were engaged in relatively mundane activities.

Even female trainers could only despatch their charges to the racecourse *under their own names* after 1966 – and that followed a long campaign by the redoubtable Florence Nagle, 'the Mrs Pankhurst of British racing'. She had trained her first winner in 1920, but the Jockey Club refused to acknowledge women trainers, so (like other women) she had to train under the name of her head lad. When she was granted a judicial review, the Court of Appeal declared that the Jockey Club 'was entirely out of touch with the present state of society in Great Britain'. The Jockey Club backed down before the action could be heard, and began granting training licences to any 'suitable woman'.

It was not only a victory against prejudice, but illuminated a misguided concern for the welfare of women. A steward of the Jockey Club had told Florence Nagle, somewhat bizarrely, that they couldn't risk women falling into the hands of 'bad men'.

It appears inconceivable now but it needs emphasising that, from the First World War years, women were only allowed to ride competitively in point-to-points (a version of horseracing over fences for hunting horses and amateur riders), albeit rarely and in separate races. It was not until the 1950s that they rode against men at these meetings, and they could do no more than ride work at racing stables. They could not race on British racecourses.

Typically, and somewhat ironically, the way that women were restricted by their supposed 'limitations', as defined by the Jockey Club, was exemplified by Iris Rickaby, mother of Lester Piggott, the 11-times Flat racing champion jockey, a nine-time winner of the Derby, and a man recognised as one of the finest jockeys of all time. Reputedly an excellent rider, Iris rode out at a number of Newmarket yards, but the only race she was allowed to compete in was the Newmarket Town Plate, instituted by King Charles in 1666. It is a 4½-mile event that Iris won twice, but as it has never been run under Jockey Club rules, it isn't an official race.

Perhaps thankfully, I was oblivious of such an insurmountable barrier to women in my formative years. Certainly not at the age of only three, when I had been sitting with my grandmother in her living room one warm summer afternoon when we heard some intriguing noises outside. In the garden, my Uncle John was sitting astride a beautiful horse. He lifted me gently into the saddle, and

I pulled eagerly at the reins. The docile animal didn't bolt, but stood quietly while my father took the first photo for what would become a packed album of my association with horses. I suppose my obsession began at that moment.

Three years later, my parents Ronald and Eileen allowed me to have riding lessons at stables behind our home at Down End, outside Fareham.

'We'll start with "Going Round the World",' exclaimed my enthusiastic but very strict instructor, Ruth Bennett; she was referring to a circular tour of the saddle, pivoting on my bottom and flinging my legs over. I can still hear her beautifully intoned barrage of instructions: 'Left leg up, balance child, balance.' The next stage was learning to rise to the trot followed by a canter while being led by the mounted Miss Bennett. By the end, my legs were trembling from the strain and I stumbled home, but feeling as though I'd achieved the first step.

A few years later, Miss Bennett decided to sell the business and I dashed home with the exciting news that the pony I'd been riding and looking after was available for purchase.

'Daddy, Rocket is for sale. Isn't that wonderful? He's a super pony, and if we don't buy him, someone else will. He's just the right size for my age, and I'll be able to go to gymkhanas and Pony Club.'

I will have been one of many young girls to beseech their parents: 'Please can I have a horse, a pony? I'll take care of him. Please. Please …'

And probably, like many parents, my father didn't appear exactly enthralled by the prospect. He knew next to nothing about horses, or their keep. I persuaded him to visit the stables and take a closer look at Rocket, a Welsh cob at 13.2 hands. (A pony is 14.2

hands or under. A horse is 14.3 hands or over. A 'hand' is a unit of measurement equal to 4in, and is used to measure the height of a horse at the highest point of the withers – the ridge between the shoulder blades. The number of whole hands is measured, then the remaining height is added in inches. Thus Rocket's 13.2 means he measured 52 + 2 inches at the withers.)

'A superb mount for Karen,' cooed the riding school owner. 'An ideal child's pony.' He bit my hand as I tried to pat him, one of his less-endearing habits. That provided a more accurate test of his temperament and his suitability for me.

In fact, he was hard to handle, belligerent and downright dangerous. But I didn't care. I made allowances for him, and looking back, he provided me with a superb, if unorthodox, education. He wasn't easy to load into the horse trailer. It could take four people to persuade him. But once we arrived at gymkhana and Pony Club meetings we'd usually win.

Not that it was a simple matter to reload him afterwards. I recall my father leading him on a rope towards the trailer, but as soon as his hooves felt the matting on the ramp, he turned and galloped crazily around the field, which wouldn't have been that great a problem except that my father had the rope entwined around his arm and, in a desperate attempt to control him, was galloping round with Rocket – to cheers from the crowd. The pony finally came to a halt, but the legacy of that incident was a massive rope burn down my father's forearm.

My parents didn't just succumb to my insistence when Rocket was purchased, but to my great fortune and delight, they moved home, near to the village of Hambledon in Hampshire so that I could indulge my love of all things equine. If that name sounds familiar, it's because it has long been associated with the thwack of willow on leather. Its cricket club, founded in 1750, was once the most powerful in the country and is regarded as the 'cradle of cricket'.

Hunting is also a tradition in the area. Encouraged by my friend Clare, an amateur hunt whipper-in (their primary role is to keep the pack together and round up missing hounds) – a role she still undertook until recently – I attended a local hunt on Rocket. That meant open countryside, albeit with some obstructions. How he relished that freedom. When the hunt moved off, Rocket took off, bolting with me, as he careered though everything he encountered. Busy country lanes, hawthorn hedges, low-flung branches, we somehow negotiated them all unscathed as I, aged only 11 and with my small, 5½st frame lacking strength, tried unsuccessfully to control him.

I screamed, shouted and pulled on my reins with all my strength, to no avail. Never mind the majestic hunters, who dwarfed him. Rocket was determined to be the leader. And that even meant racing past the Master of the Hunt, which, under hunting convention, simply isn't done. By that time, I was a sobbing, snivelling heap, clinging on for dear life. It's probably fortunate that I didn't hear the irate shouts from the Master as we finally came to a halt. I cried my eyes out, feeling totally disgraced. Looking at it more positively, you have to deal with every kind of situation in the hunting field. So, it did me no harm to undergo that experience.

For all the implicit dangers of any form of horse riding – hunting, showjumping and later riding in races – the closest I came to significant injury was when, aged ten, I was run over by a car. My mother had pulled me across the road in which there was a traffic jam and hadn't noticed an overtaking car speeding past. I felt the full impact of a vehicle travelling at 40mph and apparently at that speed you have only a ten per cent chance of survival. I had concussion for ages before eventually coming around. I escaped that near-death experience with a broken kneecap. My mother suffered broken ribs – as well as guilt.

After that incident, whenever it was a dark night with torrential rain, similar to the night I was run over, I felt anxious about crossing the road. The fear of being concussed again and engulfed by the blackness never left me, but it didn't deter me from a career in which concussion is an occupational hazard you have to accept.

After years of taking part in gymkhanas on Rocket, when I began competing at showjumping events and hunter trials at the age of 12, it was on Wandering Minstrel, a friend's pony. He was bigger than Rocket, but this was more of an equal relationship. Competition was important to me. I loved the excitement of it; not just the taking part, but ideally the prospect of winning. It also taught me to handle defeat.

The eventer Lucy McCarthy once expressed the value that riding gives a child. Apart from the confidence it instils, the health benefits and the basis for new friendships, she is quoted in a *Horse & Hound* article as saying: 'Riding offers great lessons in life. The value of perseverance and dogged determination, hard work, the rewards of empathy, how to deal with disappointment and losing while also tasting the sweet taste of success are all aspects that come into play.'

I lived and breathed horses. Couldn't get enough of them. Out of the saddle, I read the *Jill* books. Long forgotten now, they were written by Ruby Ferguson between 1949 and 1962. She wrote a series of nine children's novels about young equestrienne Jill Crewe and her adventures with her two ponies, Black Boy and Rapide. The first was *Jill's Gymkhana*.

But it was a trip to Newbury races with a friend, Anne Lambert, and her older sister Jane, on their weekend break from boarding school, that convinced me of my destiny. I was only about 12 at the time, and a young-looking one at that, yet somehow managed to have a bet on the Tote – successfully winning £10 for an outlay of £1.

Yet, something else about that day stayed with me. Inevitably, the noisy ritual of punters, bookies, tic-tac men, and the cacophony of the crowd, the spectacle of punters acclaiming a winner or tearing up their betting tickets struck me. But more crucially, it was the vibrancy, the kaleidoscope of colour, and, yes, naked aggression on display as the jockeys galvanised their mounts near the finish line. These tough little men hurtling past me at what appeared to be incredible speeds, gaunt features intense and pitted with concentration, entranced me as I pressed my face close to the fence.

I imagined myself in their place … with the awesome power of a half-ton racehorse beneath me, summoning all my vigour and skill to steer my mount home by a nose. As my fantasy continued, around me the defeated jockeys drooped their heads in despair. As the crowd acclaimed me, I was greeted by owner and trainer bearing the broadest of smiles before I returned to the winner's enclosure on my sweating, hard-blowing charge whom I'd persuaded to give his all. It was my kind of paradise.

I was bewitched. I scrutinised the jockeys as they emerged from the weighing room to walk to the paddock for their next race and thought: 'Are they nervous?' Their faces certainly didn't betray any emotion as they touched their caps before addressing the trainer and owners. Once mounted, they handled their charges in a businesslike manner. Both human and animal were highly trained, they were here to do a job. No standing on ceremony.

The more I watched, the more I wanted to be one of them. I knew I could do it, if I had the chance. The problem was that everyone told me there was none. This was no place for a girl, I was swiftly admonished. Not in practice. Not traditionally. Not legally.

Utter madness, I was told; my aspirations swiftly and brutally placed in context. These men whose skills had so entranced me may have appeared slender and small, but they were heavily muscled – a factor that a woman simply could not match. Apart from any other consideration, it was highly dangerous – and that fact would be confirmed to me many times in the coming years – which made it, supposedly, a totally unsuitable job for a woman.

Yet, I thought of little else from that day. It would be no passing phase. I had developed an almost obsessional desire to become a jockey: paid and respected, just like the diminutive, lithe men I had watched. Even as the years passed, I never contemplated what could be considered a 'normal' career, certainly not a sedentary one. My view then, and now, was that if you don't try to achieve the seemingly impossible in life you're never going to be truly happy.

I was determined to make it happen. What I was determined not to be was 'a housewife', a life that satisfied my mother but I knew would never be right for me.

Chapter 3
Riding Against Harvey Smith and David Broome

IN MOST respects, I had a traditional 1960s upbringing. My mother Eileen looked after the home, my father Ronald, and me. My father hailed from a naval family in Portsmouth – his own father regularly spent two years at sea while his mother, a businesswoman who owned a shop, also brought up eight children – and he worked initially as a building and public health inspector for Portsmouth City Council. However, he then became a successful property developer and was very much the kind of hard-working, self-made man who would have been admired by Mrs Thatcher when she came to power in 1979. He epitomised the Conservative ideal.

My mother's side were very much Labour supporters, with the exception of my Uncle John, my mother's brother, who first put me up on a horse as a small child. John Harris, who was in the meat trade, had a large house with a pool, and around 50 acres. He was also something of a TV personality, originally appearing with Jack Hargreaves on the Southern TV programme *Out of Town*. He later had his own TV programme *Country Boy*, which focused on country pursuits, including fishing and shooting.

A first cousin of my mother's was John Stonehouse, the former Labour minister of aviation and the last postmaster general, who made an ultimately unsuccessful attempt to fake his own death in 1974. John Stonehouse was very close to my mother and her brother and he would often visit Uncle John. I got to know him well. Later, Uncle John would be a witness at his wedding to his former secretary Sheila Buckley, whom I still see often.

I recall a conversation I had with John Stonehouse at an 80th party for my great aunt (his mother). It was late 1974 and, at the time, he had been tipped to become the next prime minister. However, he confided in me that he couldn't be a Labour prime minister. He was opposed to the then trade union-dominated leftward trajectory of the party. It was heading in a similar direction to the one it would go under Jeremy Corbyn. He told me: 'I've realised I'm not Labour anymore.' I asked him why he couldn't just change parties, but in those days that was not such a common event as it has become in recent years. I've never seen a man so despondent.

Not long after, it was reported that he'd drowned off the coast of Miami. In fact, he'd fled to Australia, where he only came to the attention of police because his 'aristocratic' good looks meant that he was mistaken, initially, for Lord Lucan. It was a huge shock to the whole family that newspaper headlines, referring to sightings of Lord Lucan, transpired to be sightings of our uncle, John Stonehouse! He eventually returned to the UK and was jailed for seven years for fraud, though he was released early after suffering three heart attacks.

In the 1980s, he joined the Social Democratic Party, which would amalgamate with the Liberal Party to become the Liberal Democrats. Intriguingly, John, who became a novelist, offered to collaborate with me on a book when the idea of my story being published was first mooted in the 1980s, but he died of a heart attack, aged 62, in 1988 just as we started work on it.

My mother is a Catholic but that wasn't the reason I was sent to the private Convent of the Cross School in Hampshire after being at a Catholic prep school called Seafield. The explanation was that it was the only private school with extensive grounds that would satisfy my hunger for sport. I loved playing hockey, although I was often criticised for being aggressively competitive. I also enjoyed tennis, hurdling, running and judo. The school was very strict; the kind of institution where you incurred the wrath of the sisters if your skirt was above your knees. And we had no association with boys. There was a school dance in conjunction with St John's in Portsmouth, the boys' equivalent, but no physical contact was allowed.

I was easily bored and, in class, used to draw horses as I contemplated my future. The punishment was being made to stand in the corner, or the cane. Yet, as will become apparent, adherence to strictness and a very disciplined life did me no harm at all when I began my racing life.

For my riding education, at 14 I spent a couple of weeks with my friend Anne Lambert at Stocklands Equestrian Centre – sadly now closed down – at Liphook, Hampshire, taking lessons in showjumping, dressage and cross country. My instructors were well qualified and gave me the confidence to pursue a future in that sport.

They advised me to learn from the best and to watch the top showjumpers like Harvey Smith, and my childhood heroine Marion Mould.

I left school at 16 with six O levels and my father, perhaps understandably, wanted me to concentrate on my education. So, as a compromise, we agreed I would do my A levels in the evenings at college instead of at school and have more free time to compete in novice showjumping events all over the country. I also had a part-time job as a veterinary nurse in Petersfield.

By now, my parents had decided I deserved a better mount than the capricious, temperamental Rocket, and bought me the Ambassador of Blashford. He was 15.2 hands and was half thoroughbred, his grandsire being the 1939 Derby winner Blue Peter. Though the Ambassador of Blashford was only a BSJA (British Showjumping Association) registered grade C horse, I thought perhaps that owners of grade B, and hopefully even grade A, horses may want me to ride for them. I also hoped I could persuade my father to buy me an even better horse. He didn't – this would have involved serious money!

Competing at county shows and at Stocklands indoor school during the winter months gave me the opportunity to ride against top showjumpers bringing on their young novice horses in the *Daily Express* Foxhunter Grade C competitions and other BSJA Grade C events.

In time, I'd ride in the same programme as top professional showjumpers but at a lower level. They included Harvey Smith, David Broome, Marion Mould, Caroline Bradley, Fred Walsh and also my neighbour Bill Smith, the jump jockey who rode for the Queen Mother. Princess Anne also competed at Stocklands. They would all ride in my grade C events, on their less experienced horses.

Harvey Smith – the Yorkshireman who had become a public and media favourite following the famous V-sign after winning his second successive Hickstead Derby in 1971 – was a particularly important influence on me. He was utterly single-minded. Whatever event he was in, even if in the same lesser event as me, he would put everything into it.

Those experiences saw me grow as a character, and for that I'll always be grateful. I had always been very shy and reserved at school, but once on horseback I developed a different personality. I remember six-time champion jockey Kieren Fallon saying something similar. Naturally, he was always shy but once Kieren got on a horse, he was a man transformed. This was a world in which he felt at ease. He came into himself. That's how I felt. As soon as I climbed into the saddle of a horse, confidence surged through me. Riding against the likes of Harvey and David Broome was a thrilling experience. And if I could compete against the leading men in showjumping, why shouldn't I do the same on the racecourse against male jockeys? That was the logic that fed my addiction.

Much as I loved showjumping, whatever your talent you can only rise as far as the horse under you will allow. My whole aim had been to emulate people like Harvey Smith. Given the horse, I believe I would have attained a high level. But I didn't have the horse – and there was never any likelihood I would.

Horseracing, though, was a different matter. You were partnering other people's horses. If you possessed sufficient aptitude, they'd want you to ride for them. That was the theory, anyway. I had already announced to my parents that I intended to be a jockey – a proper jockey such as men like Lester Piggott, Willie Carson and Pat Eddery, all Flat-racing champions in the 1970s, and figures still revered today by racing aficionados. I'd first been fixated by watching them on TV.

Sometimes I would shorten my stirrups, jockey-style, and race the Ambassador of Blashford – nicknamed simply as Umphy – against my friend Jilly's horse Flavia in fields near my home. We would pretend to be Flat jockeys. Yet for me, it was more than just pretend. It was preparation for what I had planned.

When I was around 11, I took part in a Pony Club race in a field near us. I didn't win, but it was the thrill of actually racing that stirred me. I thought, 'This is what I really want to do.' Pony racing has long been a big feature in Ireland – it's where many jockeys start their careers. They're beginning to organise more in the UK – and I think that's an excellent idea. It's ideal for riders before starting their apprenticeship.

I had been intoxicated by the experience, returned home thoroughly animated and informed my parents what I had in mind. I can still hear my mother trying to reason with me: 'Oh, don't be so stupid, Karen,' she'd say. 'It's like me saying I wanted to be a film star, or a singer. I had ambitions of being a singer, but knew it would never become reality. You're being ridiculous.' I thought that attitude was completely unreasonable, and ignored it.

Though most of my social life involved attending equine events, I should stress I wasn't besotted with riding to the total exclusion of other interests. Encouraged by my friend Jilly, at 13 I had joined the local Young Farmers' Club. We all met in a pub in Hambledon, and did quizzes and socialised. Discos and balls were organised. It was at one of those discos that I recognised a member named Grahame Cox who was helping a local farmer at weekends and was soon to join the Royal Marines. He had chased me for a kiss outside the hall and being only in my early teens and extremely shy it was an embarrassing experience.

However, Grahame came over to help muck out my stables and put up jumps in the field for me to practise over. I think he felt that I would change and we would become more seriously involved as I grew older.

After he joined the Royal Marines, he sent me a love letter when he was stationed in Belfast in 1973. A few days after I received it, he was killed, shot by a sniper. When someone who has declared their love for you dies in such circumstances, it has a long-lasting devastating effect – made more traumatic by the shock of learning of his death on TV news. All I had left was memories, and his huge record collection of artists including Jimi Hendrix and Simon & Garfunkel. He had left them at my home before his last fateful trip to Northern Ireland.

As a teenager I was a big fan of David Bowie, and, at 17, saw him in concert in Southampton. I also saw Yes, The Strawbs and Wishbone Ash in Portsmouth. Jilly and I were mad fans – and we'd try to get up on the stage and dance with the band until we were pulled down by security staff. In that sense, I was a typical teenager.

We both attended formal, strict schools and the concerts, discos and Hunt Balls provided opportunities to let our hair down and push barriers. Yet, the pursuit of my one true ambition, becoming a jockey, was rarely out of my thoughts. And there it may have remained, but fortuitously, in my teens, fate and social progress intervened.

Chapter 4

Ladies-Only Races Were Fine for Some, But Not for Me

I FIRST heard the news on the radio: the Sex Discrimination Act was about to become law. I was already acutely aware of its implications. I told myself: 'This is going to change my life. This is *my* opportunity. Now there's no reason why I shouldn't race with the men.'

Five years after my first day at the races, the new law was passed by the Labour government, during Harold Wilson's second term. It was December 1975 and this was a hugely significant, if belated, piece of legislation, which followed the Equal Pay Act of 1970. It gave women the right to equal pay and status in the workplace and in society.

Sex discrimination by employers, unless they employed five or fewer people, was now illegal. The Equal Opportunities Commission was also set up and, under the Act, it had a duty to promote equality of the sexes.

Three years earlier, the Jockey Club, presumably acutely aware that legislation was on its way down the line, had responded to the clamour for equality. It had finally acquiesced to the demand for women to race officially, under Jockey Club rules, by introducing a series of 12 races for lady amateur riders in 1972. It was launched as 'a new era for British racing'. The first race, named the Goya Stakes, was at Kempton Park. It was sponsored by the cosmetics firm whose most popular product was Goya Black Rose. The connection between a perfume and a ladies' race was an obvious one, though it was perhaps just as significant that Christopher Collins, managing director of Goya at that time, was a racing enthusiast who would later become a steward of the Jockey Club.

A press release from the Racing Information Bureau (RIB) that accompanied this event noted that 'although women already ride with marked success in showjumping competitions and three-day events … racing at 30mph in a tight bunch of horses, when striking into the heels of horses ahead can cause a serious accident, has its own problems and demands its own skills.'

That was why, 'in this experimental year, the women's races are all for three-year-olds or older horses, and over middle distances of from 1m to 1m 4f [1-mile 4-furlongs], which gives more time for sorting things out than a sprint, and does not require the same stamina as a long distance race.'

Obviously, there were no female changing facilities at Kempton so 'a large coach, used by theatrical companies, together with a shower unit' was hired for them to change in.

Many ladies 'scented' success in this historic event. There was enormous interest in the 1-mile 1-furlong race, and 81 original entries were whittled down to a maximum field of 21.

One remarkable woman was ruled out by the Jockey Club's medical advisers. Louie Dingwall, who had been a driver for the Canadian Army in the lead-up to the First World War, became one of the first English female racehorse trainers. She trained her horses on the beach at Sandbanks, in Dorset, though the licence then had to be in her husband's name. The dauntless 'Mrs D' was determined to take part in the Goya Stakes and threatened 'to ride the pants off the girls'. She was then 79. Probably wisely, the Jockey Club refused to permit her participation!

However, in truth the initiative did not have the intended result. Deborah Butler, an academic, who worked as a stable 'lad' herself, described this series of races (in her 2018 book *Women, Horseracing and Gender: Becoming One of the Lads*) as, 'being "hijacked" by women with economic and social capital'.

She wrote: 'Unfortunately many of the women who rode in the series were those who had the economic, social and cultural capital to do so, thereby negating the original thinking behind this series of races.'

Of amateurs, she wrote: 'The implication is the individual has the time and financial resources to indulge in such practices, doing it for the love of the sport, their own well-being, and because they can.'

So, who were these women, who, predictably, became known as 'jockettes', determined to take their place in turf history? Participants in the Goya Stakes included such top equestrians as Sue Aston, the champion point-to-point rider, and Mary Gordon-Watson, who the same year secured a team gold in eventing at the Munich Olympics.

Also, according to the RIB press release, there were 'a number of trainers' wives and daughters who, in addition to riding in point-to-points ride regular work for their stables'. They included Jeni Barons (wife of trainer David Barons) and a top point-to-point rider, and Diana Nicholson (wife of trainer David Nicholson).

The release added: 'Lady riders are about to take their place on British turf, and these races will add colour and interest to the Flat-racing season.'

The whole concept irritated me. Yes, it was progress, of sorts. It actually allowed women to compete on the racecourse. But I knew I'd never take part in something similar. Ladies-only races were anathema to me. I regarded the concept as sexist, patronising and condescending; that women were effectively being patted on their little heads and expected to race on their own, and banished like second-class citizens.

Of course, I was aware of that first event, and of Meriel Tufnell, who won on a 50-1 outsider, was also successful in her second race at Folkestone, and proceeded to become Britain's first woman champion jockey with three winners from seven rides in the 12-race series. She was also the founder of the Lady Jockeys' Association (LJA) of Great Britain that was formed the same year.

The series was described in some quarters as 'a blow for sexual equality'. 'Why?' I thought. It was women competing against women. I couldn't understand the need for these races. I never wanted to race *just* with women. I'd long ago decided that I only wanted to race against men, and in professional races.

According to reports, Tufnell had emerged from the field, riding her mother's horse Scorched Earth. 'I had orders to get her out fast,' she recalled, according to reports. 'So I pushed her on, and suddenly found myself in the lead and then, to my immense surprise, was first past the post.'

Scorched Earth had never run in a Flat race before, while Meriel herself had never ridden in a race of any sort. Hitherto her interest had been confined to showjumping on her successful pony Higham Mignonette, and to the hunting field.

Inevitably, Tufnell's surprise victory was the subject of much patronising ribaldry from the male racing establishment. At 5ft 8in she had been the tallest jockey in the field and, although she had shed a stone in weight before the race, she was the only rider to declare any overweight. One professional jockey remarked, 'Those are the nicest couple of pounds of overweight I ever saw.' Today, such a sexist comment would be regarded as completely unacceptable. But those were very different times – in many respects.

My comments may be viewed as harsh, uncharitable even. But there was no disguising the fact that – at the time – ladies' races assumed second-rate jockeyship. To my mind, this wasn't real progress. It was little more than tokenism and was against all my principles.

I wasn't born into a racing background – far from it – but I would soon discover that lady riders then were ridiculed by professional jockeys and stable lads. Their style of riding was wrong, they had long stirrups and their hands were sometimes bad. They couldn't ride a finish. They weren't fit enough.

Do I feel that situation has changed for the better since then? Today, some trainers' daughters who are too heavy to ride as professionals on the Flat are very good jockeys. But generally, women amateurs haven't improved on the Flat (it's not the case for women jump jockeys, which I discuss later). They're still not fit enough, have a bad style, with no idea of riding a finish, and can rarely ride a tactical race. Curiously, the best amateur lady riders in the past, Emma Spencer and Clare Balding, have become TV personalities, but they are among very few. Princess Anne was also a very good amateur jockey.

Returning to the 1970s, essentially this was a pastime, a fun pursuit, enjoyed by those who loved their sport and the fellowship, and no one could dispute that the new opportunities offered to lady amateurs were very popular with the participants.

The Lady Jockeys' Association newsletters of that era are illuminating. Apart from recording its members' achievements on the racecourse, including abroad, they reveal that there were dinners, dances and even cruises organised.

It would be another two years after the 1972 Goya Stakes before women could ride against men and, even then, only in certain amateur events. Linda Goodwill, daughter of Newmarket trainer Arthur Goodwill and 1973 champion lady rider, seized her opportunity and won the first 'mixed' race under Jockey Club rules in 1974, but as an amateur.

By the 1975 Flat season, the LJA reported that there had been 34 ladies' races and a further 24 mixed amateur races, of which 11 had been won by lady riders. No fewer than 644 horses ridden by lady riders had gone to post. By now 258 ladies had ridden under Jockey Club rules.

Finally, the 1975 Sex Discrimination Act was passed and in the same year women were allowed to ride professionally on the Flat. That meant women could now be paid and apprenticed to trainers – just as men had been for years. Though there were courses at racing schools, to which some apprentices were sent, their 'education' – as I would discover – tended to be on the job.

Talented apprentices were, and are, always keenly sought because, to compensate for their relative lack of experience, they were given a weight allowance. That meant their mounts could carry anything up to 7lb less than their allotted weight – a valuable incentive to trainers to put up what are known as 'claimers'.

However, it also meant that apprentices had to be both light and strong – not necessarily an ideal combination. I should explain that the minimum weight that could be allocated in a handicap at that time was 7st. In addition, apprentices could claim a maximum

7lb allowance to compensate for their lack of experience. It meant they could be asked to ride at 6st 7lb, although rarely.

Weight allowances for apprentices were first introduced in the last century. During the Second World War, the Jockey Club, conscious there could be a shortage of jockeys post-war, brought in a sliding scale of allowances – 7lb until six winners, 5lb until 20, 3lb until 40, or until the apprentice had reached the age of 21. Today, an apprentice jockey can claim a weight allowance of 7lb until they have 20 wins, 5lb until 50 wins, and 3lb until 95 wins, until the age of 26.

The ability 'to do' a light weight is a crucial factor in Flat racing – and has been since the earliest years of the sport when 'gentlemen' competed against each other.

The emergence of lightweight jockeys is thought to be due to the prevalence of gambling owners seeking to gain an advantage, and also believing that lower-weighted riders would be less likely to cause a valuable horse to break down. It is difficult to visualise now, but in the mid-19th century jockeys weighed 4st. Four stone, for heaven's sake! In 1875, the minimum went up to 5st 7lb, and after the First World War it was raised to 7st. Inevitably, jockeys' minimum weights have increased over the years as the human frame has become larger because of improved health and diets. This century, the minimum weight was initially raised from 7st 10lb to 7st 12lb, and in 2013 increased to 8st and in January 2022 to 8st 2lb.

Stories are legion about what punishing regimes jockeys have put themselves through to 'do a weight'. Edward Hide, one of the talented lightweights against whom I would ride, kept a diary in which he detailed that he sweated off a total of 18st in the course of a season.

At around 8st 7lb, I assumed I could relatively comfortably lose the necessary pounds if required. How misguided I was …

Returning to 1975, Jane McDonald, a 21-year-old apprentice with Stanley 'Snowy' Wainwright at Malton, East Yorkshire became the first woman to compete as 'a professional', though against other male apprentices. It was the first day of the Flat season, and Jane was racing on a horse named Royal Cadet in round one of the Crown Plus Two Apprentice Championship Handicap Stakes. She finished 11th in the 17-horse field.

Jane was one of an exceedingly rare breed. According to the LJA newsletter to members in 1975, she was one of a mere five lady riders who had taken out licences in that first year, 'and while acquitting themselves safely and competently against the men, are not finding it all that easy to get rides'.

Apart from Jane McDonald and Linda Goodwill, only Mavis Yeoman (wife of a York trainer), Shiralee Hall (apprentice with Denys Smith) and Sandra Crick (with Scobie Breasley) had turned professional. Though the LJA sent 'all good wishes to these pioneers', progress was desperately slow.

Goodwill, the 1973 champion lady rider-turned-pro, had had 24 rides and finished second twice. Yeoman had a dozen rides, but no win. McDonald had three rides, and was in the frame once, before suffering a back injury that put her out of action for the rest of the season.

It was all too apparent that the majority of girls employed in racing in the 1970s had scant hope of becoming apprentices.

According to an upbeat feature story released by the Racecourse Association ahead of the series of ladies' races in 1975, 'Stable girls will be delighted that they can ride in new ladies' races during the coming Flat race season … they thoroughly deserve the encouragement this new opportunity gives them.' The release added that: 'Between 100 and 200 girls [were] employed as stable hands at this time, although fillies are almost always allocated to the girls, leaving the lads to handle the more obstreperous colts.'

It was noted that the Wiltshire trainer Richmond Sturdy said that he found girls quieter with the horses and more conscientious. 'They handle the horses better,' he said.

Noting that 'the number fluctuates with the season and because some girls stay in racing stables for a comparatively short time', the Racecourse Association release added the following: 'Undoubtedly, many stable girls have reached already the high standard [to take part in ladies' races] necessary. They ride in fast work and put their charges through starting stalls.'

Here, I must add a comment on the jumps code, or as it is more formally known, National Hunt racing. (Races are run over hurdles or, in the case of steeplechases, fences are negotiated.) The minimum weight for jump jockeys was 10st (raised to 10st 2lbs in 2022). A 'conditional rider' (the jump code's equivalent of a Flat apprentice) could claim up to a maximum of 7lb. It meant that a number of Flat apprentices whose growth spurts weren't compatible with their aspirations turned to the jumps game.

Jump racing differed greatly to the Flat in that under National Hunt rules you could start out and race as an amateur, and ride against professionals. In 1946, for instance, the first post-war Grand National was won by an amateur – Captain Bobby Petrie, formerly of the Scots Guards. He was successful on Lovely Cottage at 25-1. Rather more recently, the 1990 renewal of the Aintree spectacular was won by Mr Frisk, partnered by Marcus Armytage, who has been for many years racing correspondent of *The Telegraph*.

Jump racing had long been considered too dangerous for women. The belief then was that, in public perception, it wouldn't look good for the 'weaker' sex to finish races battered, bloodied and bruised, or worse. Even more so than on the Flat, this was quite definitely regarded as no world for a woman.

It wouldn't be until the 1976/77 season that women were allowed to ride in jump races under 'Rules'. Diana Thorne was the first to win over obstacles, winning a chase at Stratford on 7 February 1976 – coincidentally beating her own father, John, by a neck.

It would be fair to say that National Hunt trainers weren't all enamoured with this development, or what was perceived as women's riding prowess. In her book *They're Off! The Story of the First Girl Jump Jockeys*, Anne Alcock quotes Josh Gifford, four-time champion jump jockey and trainer of the 1981 Grand National winner Aldaniti. He had one word for the prospect of women racing: 'ridiculous'.

One of Gifford's counterparts, David Nicholson, the successful jump jockey who would become champion trainer twice in the 1990s, added that a woman did not have the physique to hold her own against the top professionals, but conceded that they could be capable of becoming 'reasonably competent' in the hurdling field.

He criticised the eventing style, or 'fanny crouch: legs back, bottoms up, all bust and backside' of the women riders at that time, adding: 'There will be an uproar when a lady-ridden horse comes to the last at the Cheltenham Festival, and both are laid out cold. I hate the idea of a woman being smashed up.'

Leading jump jockey Jeff King commented: 'Women'll never make jockeys, but so long as they keep out of my way, let them enjoy themselves.'

In fairness, not all trainers held that view, and those that did were primarily referring to amateurs. The belief then was that there would be few women professional jump jockeys who would get the chance to ride in public. In the event, Lorna Vincent became the first woman to win a National Hunt race as a professional. By the end of 1978, she boasted ten wins, six second places, eight thirds, and two fourths from only 39 rides.

However, few could have foreseen the day when women secured well-fancied Grand National mounts and rode Cheltenham Festival winners. More than four decades on, that gifted jump jockey Bryony Frost, and women including Nina Carberry, Katie Walsh, Rachael Blackmore, Lucy Alexander, Lizzie Kelly and others have demonstrated that those initial fears (mostly of men) were nonsense. Rachael became the first female jockey to win the Grand National when partnering Minella Times to victory. Her other victories have included the 2024 Queen Mother Champion Chase at Cheltenham on Captain Guinness.

But that is an aside. Flat racing was always my code, not jump racing, which may be spectacular at times but is much slower than the Flat. From the moment I had watched those jockeys at Newbury, I had craved speed.

Chapter 5

America Trip Convinces Me I Can Be a Jockey

THE YEAR after the passing of the Sex Discrimination Act, my eyes were opened further to what was possible while visiting relations in California. There I discovered that women were racing professionally without any kind of furore. Young women, just like me, were contesting races at Bay Meadows. They were jockeys who could do a job. Simple as that.

Indeed, in the decade that followed, the formidable Julie Krone would burst upon the scene – a veritable shooting star. Just 4ft 10in, Julie was a woman who refused to capitulate in a sometimes highly physical battle with the men and won 3,704 races, and was the first to win a Triple Crown race (the equivalent of our Classics), the Belmont Stakes, and followed that up with her triumph in a Breeders' Cup event.

It was true, however, that in the United States, not all women jockeys had initially been welcomed. Penny Ann Early's bid to ride against the male jockeys at Churchill Downs, home of the Kentucky Derby, in the late 1960s reportedly resulted in boycotts and name-calling. After four months, she quit, and instead played basketball for the Kentucky Colonels. However, she did later obtain a jockey's licence to ride in California, a much more progressive state. Others fared better, though. There's the story of Mary Bacon, a former Oklahoma cowgirl, whose working life began – almost unbelievably, but apparently true – with her jumping out of cakes topless. Then she began exercising horses and eventually riding. She obtained her jockey's licence to ride at Finger Lakes Racetrack in Upstate New York in 1969. By the age of 25 she had become one of the top female jockeys in the US.

Possibly, the most romantic story was that of Robyn Smith. According to the *Los Angeles Times*, in 1968, she was broke and knocking on barn doors at Santa Anita Park in Arcadia, asking for a chance to exercise horses in the male preserve of horseracing. Four years later, she made the cover of *Sports Illustrated* as the first great female jockey in a difficult, dangerous profession.

Some faulted her for muscling her way through with 'blinders' (blinkers) on. She was described as obsessive about her work, often tactless and strung so tightly that the least irritation would set her crying. She often preferred the company of horses to people.

Robyn, who was 5ft 7in, but weighed just over 7st, made such an impact that she was asked to film an advert for a soft drink company. However, she quit racing shortly after marrying, of all people, Fred Astaire. He was concerned for her safety. Astaire would die in her arms in 1987.

I must stress that racing in the US generally was not like racing in Britain. Here the idiosyncratic courses make it far more of a challenge. In the US, the courses all look similar, are left-handed, and are mostly dirt tracks, and about 1 mile 4 furlongs round. The horses are led to the stalls by mounted stable lads and, unlike on our turf courses, once racing there is no concern about gradients or whether the going is heavy or firm. The clock is more important there and the riding style is what's called 'Acey-Deucy', with the rider using a long stirrup on the left or inside leg, which means they travel round bends rather like motorcyclists.

It could become monotonous, I'd imagine. Indeed, many American jockeys have come to Britain because they enjoy the quality of racing and the diverse conditions. Notable among these riders was Steve Cauthen, against whom I would ride, and Bill Shoemaker.

These American visitors had a great deal of influence on our sport. They brought with them a much more streamlined style. However, the crucial part of that America trip was that it finally convinced me that I could be a jockey. Not *hoped* to be. *Could* be.

Chapter 6

I Had to Get This Job – But Only on My Own Terms

THE YEAR 1976 will undoubtedly be remembered by those of a certain age for a heatwave so pronounced and lengthy that a Minister for Drought was appointed by the government. For me, it would be a defining period in my life.

That autumn I wrote to the racehorse trainer who appeared to be the nearest to my home. Bill Wightman trained around 55 Flat horses, I was to discover, at Ower Farm, Upham, around a 20-minute drive away.

I had long recognised it had to be a Flat yard I should approach. I needed to concentrate on the code that offered me opportunities to race. Despite everything I've said, I wasn't deluded by my obsession.

I was acutely aware that, to take on a girl in the first place at that time, there had to be some advantage to the trainer – some value.

I would have to persuade a trainer to employ me as a lightweight work-rider, and their numbers were limited. If I could prove myself in that capacity, then I could push to ride on the racecourse. But would Mr Wightman be willing to employ me, not just as a stable girl but with aspirations of being a professional jockey?

If that 1975 legislation was extraordinarily timely, providence aided me once more when I applied for a job at his stables. In my letter, I provided generous details of my background, my abilities, my enthusiasm, my ambition, my age, my weight – oh, and my gender. Did he, I asked, have a vacancy for an apprentice jockey?

I didn't expect a reply, except possibly a rejection. Still, nothing ventured, as they say ...

The response was the following letter, dated 9 October 1976:

Dear Miss Wiltshire,
Thank you for your letter. I think it would be a good plan for you to come and see me and talk it over. I have a vacancy.
Yours sincerely,
W.G.R. Wightman

He had a vacancy! *He actually had a vacancy!* I was shocked. I read those words over and over again. But they never changed.

I must stress that for him to even consider me was an epoch-making moment. At that time, it simply didn't happen. Trainers and owners, with rare exceptions, didn't want women partnering their horses. They were not considered to have the strength of men. Indeed, looking back, I don't think there was any other successful trainer at the time who would have given me a chance. I was to discover that Bill genuinely admired women riders – and, in that, he was a man ahead of his time.

A fortnight later, I drove up the long tree-lined drive to Bill's imposing mock Tudor house, hidden in the most glorious setting in the South Downs. I had left behind a mother gravely concerned that, if I was accepted, her daughter could end up being badly injured or worse.

In the vale below was his stable yard from where I could hear the commotion of horses neighing, whinnying and clip-clopping, and instructions being issued. I felt both intimidated and excited.

I was greeted by a tall, grey-haired man in his 60s. Bill had a charismatic presence about him and he somehow reminded me of Roger Moore in his later years. He possessed old-world charm and it would become clear later that as well as an astute eye for horseflesh he had a ready eye for the ladies. And they for him.

But I digress. In a kind yet authoritative tone, he invited me through to his study. On the way, we passed Diana Roth, who I discovered was very much his right-hand woman. She had joined Bill as secretary in 1968, had ridden out, organised the office, driven to race meetings, and liaised between lads. She knew breeding horses inside out.

Bill eyed me up and down. I had received that look before from men, but mostly considerably younger ones, and at parties and discos. I smiled back. In other circumstances, it may have been considered faintly embarrassing to have a man old enough to be my grandfather scrutinising me. But I assumed, correctly, that he was assessing me for the job.

'You're a bit on the heavy side,' he declared firmly, before continuing swiftly: 'There'll be some very hard grafting with Head Lad, and he'll soon have that off.' He paused before adding: 'Also, you're tall.' I immediately dropped 4in by kicking off my – at the time highly fashionable – platform shoes. He was relieved. 'That's more like it. You are more or less jockey-sized after all.'

'Phew!' I thought.

As for my weight, at around 8½ stone I would have been regarded as a decent healthy stature for my height of 5ft 1in in normal life. But, as I was to discover, in terms of a racing stables in the 1970s, I was borderline obese! In part, I am jesting – but only in part. My weight, and how much I could shed, was utterly crucial to what I had to offer Bill.

He told me he needed me to be able to do 7st. That weight included the saddle, so in reality I needed to be able to get down to 6st 10lb. When I said I could do it, I honestly didn't really know if it was possible. I'd never been anything like that weight, even as a teenager. However, my overriding mission was that *I had to get this job*. But only on my terms.

I was quite forthright. I emphasised I only wanted to race, and to do so professionally. It was a repetition of what I'd said in my letter to Bill, in which I had stressed that I wanted to compete against men. And now at my interview, I told him as firmly as I could muster in the circumstances: 'Don't *ever* try to put me in a ladies' race.'

I've often reflected about this stance I took. Was I purely doing this for myself? Or was it to advance the cause of equality? The latter definitely played a part. I simply felt opportunities to race professionally should be open to everyone. The legislation of the previous year was one thing. I wanted it to happen in reality. In that sense, I was a feminist, and still am. It explains why I would never race just against women.

I realised later that not many people spoke to Bill like that. It would have made life a lot easier for him if I'd simply accepted that I would ride in whatever type of race he decreed, amateur or professional. But my philosophy has always been the same and later would apply to relationships, too. If I'm not satisfied with a particular situation I'm in or about to embark on, I walk. I don't accept second best.

I wondered for a second if Bill would politely ask me to leave. I realised later that he wasn't used to ultimatums from anyone, let alone a member of staff who hadn't even started work. Yet, he smiled benignly. In a way, I think my insistence that I would not ride in a ladies' race was what made him want to give me a chance.

That moment confirmed that I was deadly serious about making it as a proper jockey. He said solemnly: 'I promise you – you will get on the racecourse.' He came across as a man of his word. That's what kept me going through some daunting times.

We chatted briefly about cars. I had a Triumph Spitfire, a 17th birthday present from my father. Bill had a navy blue Jaguar XJS – and he joked about the perils of having to push speeding restrictions to the limit in an effort to get to the racecourses throughout the country on time.

Then came the crucial part as he proceeded to discuss my employment as an apprentice jockey. God was smiling on me. Could this be happening? 'If you survive the winter, you'll stick it out for years,' he declared. 'But those yearlings will really test your skill in riding.'

Yearlings are precocious young horses who would not be racing until the following year as two-year-olds at the earliest, but were prepared for their careers over the autumn and winter.

Bill paused before adding, measuring his words carefully: 'And you'll be working with all men and boys. You'll find in this business, they're not always the easiest to deal with …' That last phrase would echo through my mind many times in the coming months.

Bill emphasised that he'd have to treat me like a man, adding that there was no way he could give me preferential treatment. He didn't want to upset the boys. He needed to maintain harmony in the yard; he wanted team spirit.

I understood that. He couldn't show any favouritism, or allow me to get away with not doing anything expected of the lads. He told me, 'If you want the same thing, have the same ambitions, then you've got to expect to do the same work and ride anything.'

Bill broached the question of an apprentice contract. In the 1970s, apprentice jockeys signed a three-year contract that was virtually impossible to break, but at least an improvement from 20 years previously when contracts had lasted five years. Your trainer practically owned you. Back then, he was not only an employer responsible for feeding but also for housing his lads, though, as I lived locally, I didn't require accommodation.

This annual renewable contract meant that you couldn't ride as an apprentice beyond the age of 24. Once you signed on the dotted line, the trainer became your legal guardian. You even had to put your fingerprint and a thumbprint on it. These absurdly anachronistic Indentures of Apprenticeship included such demands as: 'The apprentice shall faithfully serve the Master, keep his secrets and obey his lawful commands ... will not contract matrimony or play at cards or dice tables or any other unlawful game ... and shall not frequent taverns.'

You even had to ask him (normally it was him then) if you wanted to take a driving test. Work-wise, he could ask you to do anything and work any hours, and – as it would transpire – ride any horse, even if you thought it was too dangerous. Health and safety concerns didn't figure highly then. It was almost Victorian in the approach to employment rights.

The terms were onerous and demanding. The ban on nights out at the local pub was not just because of the alcohol intake and the effect that could have, but more about the fact that lads' lips, loosened by drink, could impart tips of his horses' chances to all and sundry.

Bill added: 'If you make it to next March, then you can decide whether or not you'll want to sign on.' Make it until next March? That was four months away.

If I made it? That sounded quite ominous, but I realised later that he wanted to ensure that I'd stick at it through the depths of winter when I'd have to deal with the yearlings, while simultaneously losing weight and building up my muscles.

Frankly, even three years sounded like signing my life away, but I decided not to debate the issue at that particular moment. Just in case I hadn't made it clear in my letter, I reminded Bill of my showjumping experience, having competed in many Grade C events. If he was impressed, he didn't betray it. He still hadn't committed himself to actually offering me the job. I felt nervous. Perhaps he'd had second thoughts. I glanced down. My shoes were still lying in a heap. Not a good look. I surreptitiously slipped them back on before sitting upright and beaming at him. My full charm offensive.

Finally, he asked: 'Would you be able to start tomorrow?' Well, in truth, I *was* doing something tomorrow, I was planning to go away at the weekend, but the words came out instinctively. 'Why, yes, of course,' I burbled.

He told me to report at 6.30am, work through until 12.30, break for lunch until 4, then back for evening stables until 6pm. Wages: £35 a week. As we parted, he added: 'Report to Head Lad. I'll tell him you're coming.'

I departed, but didn't need to drive home. I was flying, way up in the clouds. This is what I had planned since that first day at the races. I was to be an apprentice jockey. I couldn't have been more content. Little could I have envisaged what the stark reality would bring.

Chapter 7

My New Guv'nor – a Japanese Prisoner of War Camp Survivor

I'M NOT certain how I discovered Bill Wightman's stables. It may even have been in the *Yellow Pages*! Yet, in a strange conjunction of circumstances, I'd somehow chanced upon one of the country's most able and certainly most experienced trainers and one who, whilst regarded as 'old-school' in many respects, was also a forward thinker.

Today, you'd do an instant Google search, or scrutinise the *Racing Post* website, to discover all you needed to know. But this was years before the internet dominated our lives. (Steve Jobs and Steve Wozniak may have just created Apple, with the plan to develop small, easy-to-use computers, but that concept was many years from fruition.) Telephone and letters, newspapers and terrestrial TV, were the means of communication and information.

Only as I started work at Ower Farm, Upham, did I begin to piece together the career and life of this illustrious individual whose stable I joined when he was entering the veteran stage of his career – although his demeanour was such that you'd be hard-pressed to believe that description.

Bill was insistent that this was a highly ambitious yard and, despite his successes, he still yearned to improve. In attitude, it was like dealing with a 30-year-old. He was actually 62 then and had already been in the industry for four decades, although with an 'interruption', to which I'll return.

Over time, I discovered he had been born William Gilbert Rowell Wightman in Streatham, London, just days before the start of the First World War. He was the son of an insurance inspector, and was educated at Dulwich College in London. Bill was Scottish by parentage. (His parents were from Edinburgh and the Shetlands.) Divorced from his wife Antoinette, known as Toni, in 1964, he had one daughter, Dulcie.

I learned later that two old Etonians were instrumental in his establishment as a trainer. The most significant was Evelyn Baring of the merchant banking family. However, a chance encounter at a cricket match with Geoffrey Gilbey, racing correspondent of the *Daily Express*, and scion of the gin family, would also play a part. Through Gilbey, Bill, just 18, started working for trainer Laing Ward just outside Winchester and two years later began training Gilbey's ponies at a yard at nearby Worthy Down. But when Baring became Bill's patron and set him up at stables on his estate at Ower Farm in Upham, he could have had no idea that the horseracing institution he had helped to create would last nearly six decades.

Bill voraciously seized his opportunity at this idyllic location, swiftly proving himself to be as adept with National Hunt horses as on the Flat, after being granted a training licence in 1937, aged just 22. Bill's training career was soon interrupted, when he was 25, by Second World War service, though the word 'interrupt' scarcely does his experiences justice.

When, in August 1939, Bill legged up jockey Bill Rickaby – Lester Piggott's cousin and a great friend – at Salisbury, he cannot have imagined that this would be his last runner for seven years. Nor the horrors he would experience in the intervening period when he survived the most terrible deprivations as a Japanese prisoner of war.

A gunnery officer in the Royal Artillery, Bill was captured by the Japanese when Singapore surrendered and spent three and a half years as a prisoner of war in Sarawak. In his biography (*Months of Misery, Moments of Bliss* – a phrase Bill often used about his subsequent training career) he revealed how prisoners wore what were little more than G-strings and simple shoes on their feet – made by themselves. If the Japanese had problems feeding their prisoners, they simply moved them elsewhere. Many died on the way on these so-called 'Death Marches'. The prisoners' diet was 'weevily' rice, a teaspoonful of sugar, a few veg and just enough pork to flavour it. Dysentery, fever and worms were rampant. By the end, they were burying 15 men a week.

Bill never doubted he would survive. 'Human animals are most extraordinarily tough and resilient,' he told Alan Yuill Walker, author of his biography. 'There are two outstanding things about life. One is procreation – the other is survival. It's built in. I had one tremendous asset because I had no dependents, no encumbrances, if you like. Men with wives and children did nothing but worry and there were more deaths as each successive Christmas passed.'

He added: 'The atom bomb was the only thing that saved us, that's for sure. If they had not dropped the bomb, thousands more British prisoners would have died.'

Starved and emaciated, he was released in the summer of 1945 after the atom bombs were dropped on Hiroshima and Nagasaki.

Bill returned to Britain in November that year. At least 6ft, he weighed a skeletal 7st 12lb … and who knows how much he had been scarred mentally by what he'd witnessed.

As far as I am aware, there was no counselling then. Men who had served in the forces were simply expected to return to normal life, even those like Bill who had experienced far worse than many of his generation. This was before PTSD became a familiar acronym. Mental problems as a result of wartime experiences were then talked about using the all-embracing term 'shell shock'. Luckily, Bill recuperated well and within a year had saddled his first post-war winner.

'I was one of the lucky ones,' he told his biographer. He had not only survived but returned to renew the career he loved, 'because of the support of Evelyn Baring and my other owners, who stood by me, although I had been reported missing for 18 months.'

I have no doubt that those experiences shaped Bill's attitude to life, and his training career. They had moulded the character of the man he was when I first encountered him, and, as I will discuss later, had a significant bearing on his attitude towards all those he employed.

I soon learned he ran a highly disciplined regime – almost on army lines. He was so acknowledged in the racing industry as being ultra-strict that Bill was sent one rider, a talented but wild young Irishman. His previous trainer simply couldn't control him. Bill managed to extract the best from him.

Many of Bill's early winners, in the 1930s and 40s, were owned by his patron Evelyn Baring and the intriguingly named Contessa di Sant'Elia. She was the daughter of the owner of a Liverpool shipping line who had married an Italian count and who once held the title 'Dame of Sardinia to Queen Elena of Italy'.

Fortune would bless Bill when Captain Dick Smalley, later the Jockey Club's senior starter, came to him with a little hunter called Halloween, with whom he had won two point-to-points. In 1951 Bill trained Halloween to secure five hunter chases in five attempts, including the Foxhunter Chase at Cheltenham, all ridden by his owner. Smalley then sold the horse to the Contessa di Sant'Elia and the vacant saddle became occupied by Fred Winter who, in a majestic career, would become champion jockey four times and, later, champion trainer eight times.

Winter rode Halloween in 17 races and only once were they out of the first three. The victories included the King George VI Chase – the Boxing Day crowd-puller at Kempton – in 1952 and 1954, and they were second in the Cheltenham Gold Cups of 1953 and 1955 and third in 1956. Bill described him as having, 'the heart of a lion but he was also a natural jumper and a complete athlete'.

The name Halloween would always be inextricably linked with Bill – a testimony to his aptitude as a trainer. He represented such a proud badge of honour to him. However, by the time I arrived in late October 1976, Bill was concentrating on the Flat, where prize money and, for many potential owners, prestige, was higher.

The stable's first high-class Flat horse was Kingsfold, runner-up to the Aga Khan III-owned Tulyar in the 1952 St Leger. It would be the only occasion Bill had a horse placed in a Classic. The following season Bill's colt broke a leg three days before he was due to run in the Ascot Gold Cup, a race that many believed he'd win. He had to be euthanised. Bill never trained as talented a horse again.

One prolific, classy performer was the sprinter Pneumatic, originally owned by Bill's wife, Antoinette. Between the ages of two and ten, he won 17 races and was placed 33 times from 78 runs in the 1950s and early 60s.

In the decade I arrived at his yard, Bill was acknowledged by the media as being a 'handicap specialist'. Most horses must run three times on the Flat in order to qualify for a handicap rating. They then move up and down the handicap, depending on their form, and weights they carry are allotted accordingly. Only the elite horses contest Listed and Group races – the latter include the Classics.

Bill was regarded as a character who would always target a significant prize at some future date, rather than aim for a run-of-the-mill race. The fact was that Bill loved a coup. Many owners do too, and a decent-sized bet on a winner can be worth far more than the prize money won.

All successful trainers place horses to their best advantage and few were better than him at 'laying out' a horse for a big race. Bill had no qualms about it. 'We were busy trying to outwit the handicapper – you had to try and get on a handicap mark where you could win,' he told his biographer, adding: 'I have never been averse to telling an owner that didn't bet to have a little on, when everything was in the horse's favour.'

That all said, Bill did not regard himself as a gambling trainer. 'The fact I have won money over the years is not the point,' he once said. He regarded it as a minor point of racing, and fortunately never got carried away with it.

And this must be stressed, too ... Bill was never found guilty of contravening racing's Rule 151, concerned with running horses on their merits. The first responsibility of a trainer to his owner is to win, at whatever level, and Bill trained the winner of just about every major handicap. Those triumphs would not have gone unbacked. They included the likes of Import, who won the prestigious sprints, the Stewards' Cup at Goodwood and the Wokingham Stakes at Royal Ascot, and Air Trooper, his Magnet Cup victor at York.

Import was usually ridden by Taffy Thomas and Wightman always referred to the Welsh lightweight as 'my secret weapon'. He would later play a significant role in my story.

Myrddin 'Taffy' Thomas, born in Caernarfon in 1945, was apprenticed to Newmarket trainer Geoff Barling, who trained the best horse of Taffy's career, Tower Walk, winner of the Group events, the Flying Childers Stakes and Greenham Stakes in 1968/69, and second to Right Tack in the 2,000 Guineas. Taffy later rode for Ryan Jarvis, who trained his second-best mount, the 1978 Haydock Sprint Cup winner Absalom, but he was eventually 'jocked off' both Tower Walk and Absalom in favour of Lester Piggott. Taffy would not be alone in such an experience.

Bill never benefitted from the patronage of racing's really big hitters. He largely trained for friends and small owners and that meant cheaply-bought horses or home-bred ones. He lived in hope of finding something rare and precious. However, this was a man with important connections in racing and beyond, whom he cultivated. His sense of humour and self-deprecation made him popular in racing circles. The status of owners he attracted and who would frequently visit the yard to discuss and watch their horses at work on the gallops, opened my eyes to his renown as a trainer and the company he kept.

Glance through his winners at that time, and you'll find a good sprinkling of politics and old money. His owners included William Douglas-Home, the dramatist, politician, and a younger brother of Sir Alec Douglas-Home, prime minister from 1963 to 1964. He lived quite near Upham at Drayton House, East Meon.

Another significant titled owner of Bill's was Lord Leverhulme, grandson of William Lever, 1st Viscount Leverhulme, whose firm manufactured such brands as Lifebuoy, Lux and Sunlight soap, and whose name is still known today through the multinational Unilever. Philip Lever, the third and last Viscount Leverhulme, was a highly significant name in the racing establishment, rising from deputy senior steward in the Jockey Club to senior steward in 1973–76, during which time he helped settle the 1975 'stablemen's strike', industrial action taken by stable lads who were TGWU members in pursuit of a wage increase. He was a good friend of Bill's and would often visit the yard and took a great interest in my career.

One of his three daughters was the Hon. Susan Elizabeth Moon Lever, who through her marriage to Michael Pakenham became Lady Pakenham. She was also an owner whose horse The Goldstone would be such a crucial component of my story.

Other patrons of Bill included Simon Wingfield-Digby, the former MP for West Dorset, and a prominent racehorse breeder, Sir Derek Vestey who made his fortune from the wholesale meat business and the Dewhurst butcher chain, and Lieutenant-Colonel Martin Gilliat, the Queen Mother's long-serving private secretary.

The footballing aristocracy were also regular visitors to the yard. Bill's owners included England footballers Mick Channon, Kevin Keegan and Alan Ball. Mick's colt, Man On The Run, jointly owned with Keegan, was the first foal of his first horse Cathy Jane, who had been trained by Bill to win the 1973 Brown Jack Stakes (a prestigious event named after a great stayer of the 1920s and 30s) at Ascot. Mick, who was to become a formidable trainer in his own right and was a sound judge, believed that Bill was the shrewdest placer of horses.

One of my earliest experiences was observing the then huge class divide between wealthy, often aristocratic, owners and the lads and even successful professional Flat jockeys who tended to originate from poor backgrounds. There would always be a master and servant element. When eventually I got to the racecourse, I had to remind myself to touch my cap to owners in the paddock, and address them as 'sir' and 'ma'am'.

Though Bill was first and foremost a businessman, it soon became clear that he enjoyed mixing in such rarefied company. In terms of class, he was acutely aware of a person's station in life. He felt that, because of my background, I'd be socially acceptable to his owners and may have believed that, by meeting them, it would help me getting rides. Later, he would introduce me, with some pride, to his visitors and mention that I was from private school, although, from their expressions, I could see them wondering how I would survive the culture shock of working long, arduous hours in what was perceived to be a male, working-class domain. Clearly, they were surprised how I could cope.

Not long after I started, I would be asking the same question myself.

Chapter 8
'Have You Ever Seen a Jockey with an Arse that Size?'

THE MORNING after my interview, I duly presented myself to Head Lad, Bill Nash at the attractive brick and flint main stables. Originally from Brentford in London, he had 'served his time' – as a racing apprenticeship is known – with Percy Carter at Chantilly. He had ridden winners at Saint Cloud and Maisons-Laffitte. The sight of him was warning enough of the hazardous world into which I was stepping.

Bill Nash bore the wounds of battle; one a scar below the eye, where he had once been kicked; the other a limp and a plate in the knee from another argument with a horse. I learned he had been clipping it when the animal turned around and cow-kicked him, smashing his knee. That was the end of his racing career, although it didn't prevent him from riding work on the gallops for many years.

'Lad' was hardly an apt description of him. Bill Nash, like the guv'nor, was in his 60s and had been at the stables for the best part of 50 years. He lived in a splendid cottage that overlooked the main yard.

In the 1950s, he had partnered Halloween and Bill's greatly talented but ill-fated colt Kingsfold in most of their serious work.

Bill Nash was a steadfast and thoroughly loyal character. I swiftly came to realise two things about him: he doted on the guv'nor and would do absolutely anything for him. If Bill Wightman directed me to do anything, Bill Nash ensured I carried it out. Also, having been injured badly himself, he was anxious about my welfare.

Like Bill Wightman the previous day, Bill Nash similarly regarded me with a seasoned eye. I was certainly fit enough from riding my own horse in showjumping events and, though I never dieted, I wasn't flabby in any way. But his immediate assessment was that, as things stood, I was too frail to work in a racing yard. I could see that his concern was not borne out of any male chauvinism, simply all those years' experience.

'Don't carry anything that's too heavy. Break yourself in gradually,' he warned, evidently somewhat apprehensive at having a girl apprentice in the stable. 'We've got to build up those muscles slowly.' Then he took me to meet my working 'companions'.

First the most important ones: over 50 horses. They ranged from precocious, nervous yearlings who would race as two-year-olds the following year, to the experienced handicappers like Air Trooper and Bell-Tent, and William Douglas-Home's Goblin, of whom much was expected the following season. The equine contingent definitely took priority. I learned quickly that people came second.

Horses could be worth many thousands and they brought in training fees and a percentage of any prize money. Stable lads were the deficit on Bill's balance sheet, albeit at not much more than £35 a week (around £15,000 p.a. today), and if one quit or was injured, they were easily replaced.

Bill's equine charges had to be handled with great care – and their owners with great diplomacy. The latter can be demanding individuals, which is probably why Bill Wightman was once heard to have reflected wryly that the best patrons were 'those that lived abroad and corresponded by cheque'.

All owners exist on belief. It is the lifeblood of the industry. Especially in the early stages and before the reality becomes all too apparent on the racecourse, all harbour belief that their horse is the most handsome, the most powerful, and undoubtedly a star in the making. You couldn't blame them. Why would they get involved otherwise? Ownership is like belonging to a cult. You have to be a follower. The majority of horses are no more than moderate, of course. Though under Bill, that didn't mean they couldn't be winners.

Finally, I was introduced to 'the lads' – a combination of full-time staff and those who came in on an occasional basis. My welcome was at best begrudging, you could say unnerving from some, as around 25 pairs of eyes sized me up. By now I was getting used to this male appraisal of my physique.

'We've all got to be on our best behaviour now, lads – guv'nor says,' piped up one voice, laden with sarcasm. 'Look at her arse,' he added to a chorus of sniggering. 'Have you ever seen a jockey with an arse that size?'

Jack, who considered himself something of a joker and prankster, had been an apprentice jockey but had failed to progress and race-ride. He was to become the bane of my life. He was not untypical of lads who had entered the game full of expectation. The book *Under Starter's Orders*, published in the mid-1970s, stated that becoming a fully-fledged jockey with reasonable success 'is achieved by about one in 2,000 of the young hopefuls who originally sign on. The rest stay in the game as stable lads or just drift out of racing altogether.'

That book made it quite apparent that the French were far advanced in the education they offered would-be riders – the same was said of the United States. My introduction to the lads, and their response, set the tone for the remainder of my years at Ower Farm and immediately brought to mind my father's view on industries, like his own, which tended then to employ all-male workforces. He had never wanted me to go into the property business – he simply didn't think I'd be able to cope with the builders' crude language and sexual innuendo.

Here I was in exactly the same position in a racing yard. Frankly, at that moment I did feel somewhat isolated. But I knew I had to hold my own here, somehow. I glared back at them, determined not to rise to the lads' attempt at ridicule as Bill Wightman's words of the previous day came immediately to mind. What was his warning? Oh, yes. 'Not the easiest of men to work with ...' I decided my policy should be friendly, not hostile, but to keep my distance and not antagonise them.

On reflection, I possibly hadn't helped myself by wearing jodhpurs – the normal wear for showjumping, hunting and riding my own horse – only to swiftly discover they were definitely not the preferred stable lads' garb in the 1970s. The two Bills wore jodhpurs. For the lads, jeans were more in vogue. The fact that I had also driven to the yard in my bright orange sports car, and had parked it in full view of everyone, next to the stable lads' accommodation, confirmed the suspicion that I was middle class, 'stuck up' and quite definitely 'a snob'.

As I had swiftly discovered, my arrival had provoked streaks of bitterness at the spectacle of a new face coming into the yard with a plan to be a jockey – feelings that were multiplied by the fact that I was a woman.

It was clear that some men then believed that females shouldn't be in racing at all.

I must stress that Bill Wightman ran a highly professional yard, and did his best for all his staff. It was simply that this was regarded as a workplace for working-class males. Most were from poor backgrounds, some from Ireland. Bill had a contact there to encourage suitable young men to come over and work for him.

Not all the lads were hostile to my arrival. Richard Newman was one fellow apprentice who became a friend and remains one today. Later, he'd be competing with me for mounts, but was always supportive. He recalled, many years later, that the hostility towards me was fuelled by 'pure jealousy'. The feeling among some was, 'we're not having her coming in, and getting rides' and that typical of the comments made behind my back was: 'Here comes the little rich bitch.'

He added, 'They didn't mind girls working in the yard – there were other women that helped with the mucking out. But they weren't at all happy about having women jockeys, or even work-riders. They never thought they had the strength or the skill.'

There was also another commonly held belief. 'Oh, we can't have women around the colts,' it was said. 'It'll excite them.' As it was, I was told not to wear perfume around them. I wasn't even allowed to wear sunscreen on my face because of the possible effect of the smell on the colts. It did concern me that could mean I'd suffer from premature skin ageing. I normally wore sunscreen from March until November when I was riding my own horse. It occurred to me, no wonder jockeys' faces aged so quickly with no sunscreen and having to dehydrate!

There is no place for vanity in racing. Most jockeys didn't have their own teeth, having had them knocked out in riding accidents.

My mother had always said the best thing about my looks was my teeth and the lads couldn't wait to tell me I wouldn't have my own for very long.

I soon realised that some of the lads could be violent, some were bullies, and they didn't restrict that inclination to me. They quickly detected any weakness and preyed on it. Richard, with whom I gelled, didn't have an easy life. He was quiet, shy, and looked young, about 12. They used to pick on him, too, seizing on his perceived vulnerability, and giving him a hard time, just as they did me. He handled it, but has told me since, 'I don't know how you coped with it all.'

I knew my first task was to survive. I tried to brush it off. I blocked out the comments and hostility. I suppose eventually I became immune to them. From those first few moments, my mind had been made up – I was going to have to show the lads, or at least my principal detractors, that I was as tough as they were. They'd already decided I'd never make it as a jockey and I had to prove them wrong.

I realised later I had been more than a little naïve. I couldn't say that people hadn't warned me. I was well aware that a racing yard was regarded as an alien workplace for a girl – at least one intent on become a professional jockey. They clearly believed that if they made life hard enough, I'd quit. I decided there and then: they had another think coming.

I knew I just couldn't allow them to get to me. When I realised what a number of the men were like, it made me more determined to stand firm and not yield an inch. I was regarded as something of an innocent, which to a large extent was correct. They relished trying to make me blush. As a former convent girl, with all that implies, I had lived a relatively sheltered life and had never had what you'd call a serious relationship when I first started working for Bill Wightman.

These lads had yet to see me ride so – as bullies will do – they picked on the obvious: comments about my female physique and sexual innuendo were to become common in the coming months. There was constant use of the f- or c-word, particularly in my vicinity, in an attempt to embarrass me. While those words are commonly used in stable life and other industries today, and I don't want to portray myself as resembling some Victorian matron suffering from the vapours, they were not then in constant use. My parents, who had brought me up quite strictly, would have been horrified if they'd known what was said in my earshot. They never swore, at any time. And certainly, if I'd used those words at school, I'd have been expelled.

Working with the lads rubbed off on me, and over time, swearing became part of my language. I've never seen my father more annoyed than if he heard me utter the f-word. 'I don't want to hear that word in my house,' he'd bark. Bill Wightman didn't approve either. One of his sayings was: 'Too much blaspheming means a lack of vocabulary.' But that didn't indicate he was averse to the occasional profanity himself.

To some, using such language in my presence was mere entertainment; a welcome distraction during what could be an onerous working day.

Others, as I have said, clearly didn't like the idea that I may get to race-ride – and that antipathy never abated. I was encroaching on their domain, their territory, and they were determined to deny me my chance. They did everything to try and intimidate me, clearly believing if they made life unpleasant enough, I'd burst into tears and quit.

I wouldn't like my daughter Lara to have gone through what I did. I can't pretend it was a pleasant experience. I just had to try to blend in as best I could – and look after myself. The reality was that it hardened me up to handle events in the rest of my life. I would certainly need that once I reached the racecourse.

Perhaps underscoring the lads' opposition was a traditional attitude to the roles of men and women. There remained a residual belief among them that they, the men, were the wage-earners, or at least the potential ones. I would eventually get married, they assumed, I would be supported, probably by a rich husband – given that I was regarded as 'posh'. I didn't need the income. That perception was entirely wrong, certainly in my case. As I've said previously, I'd never considered being a housewife as my idea of a perfect destiny. My belief was simple when I arrived: why shouldn't I have the same as you? Why shouldn't I have an equal opportunity? This is the life I want, too.

I must explain a little of the hierarchy at Ower Farm. While the majority of the lads had arrived at the stables in the hope of becoming a jockey, unfortunately many either became too heavy as the years passed, or just didn't get sufficient races to make a living, but continued working at the yard as stable staff. That created, within certain individuals, residual resentment at my presence.

These lads may also have cantered and exercised the horses but they weren't involved in the serious business of 'riding work' on the gallops. The work-riders did that, and hopefully I would soon join them, as well as race.

On 'work' days, usually Wednesdays and Saturdays, senior jockeys would also come in to gallop the horses. These notably included the aforementioned lightweight Taffy Thomas, who could ride at 7st 7lb, and whom Bill Wightman regarded as an excellent judge of pace. Others were Geoff Baxter, Richard Fox, Claude Francois and Frank Morby, as well as, on occasions, major names such as Pat Eddery, Willie Carson and Greville Starkey.

Gradually, I realised their participation was as much a valuable exercise to the jockeys as to the guv'nor. They'd be looking out for which of the mounts they'd want to ride in a race, and then ask Bill.

The work-riding contingent also included retired jockeys like TV racing presenter Brough Scott, a close friend of Bill's who had ridden 100 winners over jumps as an amateur and professional before retiring in 1971, and Robin Gray, an amateur in the 1960s and 70s, who was a journalist and commentator.

A racing stable employs a large complement of people with different skills. Among other staff was a travelling head lad, Geoff, who'd attend race meetings with the yard's charges in Bill Wightman's absence. You'd also see the farrier, the horsebox driver and the gallops manager. Even a stables of around 50 equine charges – not enormous in racing terms – required a large number of staff. Under the command of the two Bills, Wightman and Nash, all staff worked exceptionally hard. Anyone not prepared to do so wouldn't have stayed long.

The great majority of horses at Ower Farm were never going to be anything special, but the lads took as much care and trouble with a no-hoper as a top-class horse.

Bill's selection criteria for apprentice jockeys was that they had to be small and capable of getting down to under 7st. Though it sounds strange to say, no riding experience was required. I was unusual in arriving with an equestrian background. My friend Richard Newman, for example, had joined Bill at 15, straight from school, but had never been near a saddle. He was sent to racing school at Goodwood for six weeks, and would progress to work-ride and race, including for other trainers.

In contrast, I was expected to pick up race-riding expertise on the job. I regarded that as a compliment.

Chapter 9

I Discover a New Scent: *Eau de Muck*

THE IMAGE of a racing stables may bring to mind the key ingredients of a Jilly Cooper novel: a touch of glamour, of glory, of joy, often of despair – and, of course, high-spirited stable lads and raunchy adventures in the hayloft. Leaving the raunchy behaviour until later, I found the reality rather different when, the following day, I took a first step in my new career.

I was acutely aware I had twin targets: to muscle up and lose weight before I could begin to think about racing, or even riding work. But what I'd walked into was the antithesis of a life of glamour. A complete shock to the system. I was instructed to start mucking out the stables. Of course, I knew what this involved, having done it at home, with my horse and pony. But here it meant mucking out several horses, and there were no mod cons. Bill, definitely one of the old-school regime, refused to allow the use of wheelbarrows. Instead, I encountered the dreaded muck sack.

At a run, which soon became a jog, and by the end a walk, I had to fetch a sack, run back to the stable, throw it to the ground, pitchfork as much manure as I could carry into the middle of it, pull the four corners together and fling the entire revolting bundle over my shoulders. Bent double beneath the weight, I had to stagger across the yard up to the muck heap and tip it all out. It took three or four such trips to clear each stable.

Of course, someone has to do this work. And, indeed, some may consider this not *that* onerous a task compared with many occupations. However, I should explain that manure is not dry – it is decidedly fluid, and on my first morning I discovered that sacking is far from waterproof. The revolting liquid muck seeped through my anorak, then through my jumper to my skin. It oozed down the back of my neck and soaked my hair.

As I drove home that first lunchtime, I was shivering with exhaustion, my hands so cramped with carrying the sacks I could hardly grip the steering wheel. And I stank to high heaven. Arriving home, I leaned, in a state of collapse, against the front door. If I had expected warmth, comfort, or just a hint of sympathy from my mother, the reality was that she recoiled from the noxious stench. She refused to let me through the door until I stripped off down to my underwear – there and then in the garden and no matter that there was a distinct chill in the air – and went straight to the shower.

'I've never smelled anything like it,' she said as I struggled out of my wet jacket, jumper and trousers.

'Thanks, mum,' I thought, before the sweet smell of soap overcame the stench of *eau de muck*, and relaxed my muscles.

That routine was something with which I became quickly familiar as I discovered that my early days of becoming a jockey entailed mucking out, driving home for lunch, stripping off on the doorstep – even in the most extreme weather – shower, collapse, back to work, evening muck out, groom and feed the horses, then back home to clean up for a second time, before bed, utterly exhausted.

I'd also visit the gym and sauna at the Meon Valley Golf and Country Club near Southampton on my way back to the stables after lunch, but wasn't aware of any of the other jockeys doing so. I kept my gym sessions a secret from the lads and felt they gave me an advantage and the confidence that I could compete with an equally physically fit body. Even when I wasn't working, I went jogging in waterproofs to lose weight – that was a priority.

At least on my first Friday, I could look forward to a lie-in at the weekend – as I mentioned to one of the lads. I eulogised about the prospect, saying I was going to stay in bed all morning. He looked blank for a second, and then let out a great guffaw. You'd have thought I was the stable stand-up comedian issuing a great one-liner. But as I soon discovered, I was the butt of it.

'Listen to this,' he told anyone within earshot. 'Miss Posh from Hambledon thinks we have weekends off. You know, mummy bringing us breakfast in bed on a tray. She lives in another world. Tell her, someone.' They were all beside themselves laughing.

Being tired and irritable, I was close to tears, but I refused to betray that fact. 'I've worked all week – I must have some time off,' I tried to reason with them. This observation provoked yet more hysterical laughter before the first lad spelt out the awful truth to me, one word at a time: 'We. Don't. Get. Time. Off ...'

That declaration was followed by paroxysms of joy from the assembled group. I went cold. No one had mentioned this. I sought out Bill Nash. Was this unpalatable fact actually true, I demanded to know, asking how I would be able to meet up with friends if I was working seven days a week, from seven in the morning to six in the evening?

He appeared surprised. 'What do you want a social life for?' he retorted, before adding: 'It's up to you. If you really want to be a jockey, you need complete dedication. Without it, you'll never succeed.

'Horses need care every day. You can't leave them at weekends while you go off and meet your friends. Who else do you think will look after them?'

I should have realised, of course. There was considerably less racing then – no Sunday meetings (that didn't start until 1992), no all-weather tracks (started in 1989) and no evening floodlit meetings (started in 1993) – but the horses still needed looking after. Also, Saturday was the busiest race-day in the Flat season. Weekends were compulsory overtime, although rarely, I was told, I *may* get a whole Sunday off.

It was a blow, but Bill Nash was right. A choice had to be made: accept the hours and rigours involved in striving to become a professional jockey or continue doing the social round. I'd already made that decision. It was just that I hadn't appreciated all the implications. It didn't end there. Before too long, I would be forced to make further choices.

Some may have questioned the wisdom of my continuing at that precise moment. Not only would I have to spend many working hours a day in this hostile environment, there'd be scarcely any escape from it. This was about as far removed from my – perhaps over-romanticised – perception of what lay ahead as I could have imagined. But to quit now would have been playing their game and surrendering. For so many years, my whole aim, my whole being, had been directed at getting on the racecourse. That desire to achieve something that only a very small number of female professionals in Britain had done, to compete against experienced male jockeys, dominated my emotions. When you harbour such ambitions, you put up with just about any outrageous words or deeds.

Those of us clearly perceived as the most vulnerable were constantly teased by the lads, and sent on 'fool's errands'. One apprentice was told to fetch some striped paint. I was told to go and ask Bill for a bucket of steam. Richard Newman was asked to find a left-handed hammer. If you refused, they'd carry you and put your head in the dung heap. Yet, on more than one occasion, it got beyond stable yard 'pranks' and verbal abuse. The lads tended to be testosterone-fuelled and – for the most part – gauche young men. A few of them tried to corner and grope me, sexually. Fortunately, I had come well prepared.

At the Convent of the Cross we'd had judo lessons, and I knew the moves to deal with them, and, if necessary, how to throw them. I think the shock that I could do that deterred them to some extent! Sister Ruth Mary used to say to us: 'Girls, you've got to learn how to protect yourselves from men!' It amused us at the time. It was as if men were some kind of enemy. Yet, I could not have known how useful that instruction was.

Why didn't I report this to either the guv'nor or Head Lad, it might be asked. Indeed, Bill Wightman had told me at the start, 'if you have a problem, come up and tell me'. I didn't. But why would I? That would mean him reprimanding them, or worse. I was acutely aware that, if the lads knew I'd complained about them, it would just have made an unpleasant situation worse and they'd gang up on me even more. I simply had to tough this one out.

I did attract one admirer – one I didn't need: an exceedingly shy 16-year-old apprentice who was my only companion in the morning during mucking out. During my early days, the other lads were out walking and riding the horses. Fresh from school, he was innocent and naive. Whenever he overheard comments about sex, invariably in the crudest language, his features turned crimson. He swiftly became known as 'Pinky'.

If he was present, the talk became ever more uninhibited as the lads baited him. I sympathised with him, and tried to be friendly. He became infatuated with me, but his idea of an amorous advance was to chase me round the stable yard with drowned mice that he found in water buckets! Flinging down my pitchfork, I would yell at him and run away until Bill Nash intervened. Pinky was given a stern lecture, but it didn't deter him. The attention I gave him afterwards, explaining to him that he really should grow up and not be so childish, meant more to him than making his peace with Bill Nash. At one stage I had recurring nightmares about being chased by a frightening character with dead mice. Fortunately, in time, he at least changed his blandishments to chocolates.

Of course, if Bill Nash saw or heard anything untoward from any of the lads, he wouldn't tolerate such behaviour. He'd deal with it straight away. But inevitably, it was never done in the open.

Bill Wightman wasn't oblivious to the perils of employing one girl apprentice in an otherwise male yard at that time, and always had his concerns. A few months after I joined the yard, Bill actually took on another girl, named Kerry. His thinking was clearly that it would be a sensible idea for me to have another female around. But she also came from a 'privileged' background. Kerry found it more difficult than me to come to terms with being shouted and sworn at. I reassured her it would become easier. Nevertheless, I don't think she ever fully accepted it and didn't stay as long as me.

I've no doubt the lads were surprised that I hadn't reacted similarly – they clearly fully expected that the 'posh bird' from Hambledon would clamber back into her sports car, chastened by the experience, return to her mother, and never be seen again. That was what the bullying was intended to do. Some of the barbs were crude, and to say sexist scarcely does them justice. They clearly believed that if they pushed me hard enough, I'd crack. They misread me totally. Yes, I got depressed on occasions, and very downhearted, though other factors were also responsible for that, but I refused to be their victim. I went out of my way to demonstrate that it didn't actually bother me that much – even though that probably encouraged them to intensify their efforts.

Bill Wightman had warned me at my interview that I'd be treated like a man, and, as far as I could, I played along with things. I even agreed to try boxing. Stable staff boxing was a tradition in racing, and exceedingly popular at the yard – before it was stopped in the industry generally at the turn of the century.

Well before my time, one of Bill's lads, Brian Lawrence, from near Southampton, and the younger brother of ABA champion Ken Lawrence, became the stable lads' 6st 7lb open boxing champion. Like many of Bill's recruits, Brian had never ridden a horse when he joined the yard in 1950, aged 15, but became a very decent jump jockey: the pinnacle of his career being victory on Bill's Oscar Wilde in the 1958 Welsh Grand National at Chepstow.

Returning to my 'bout', the lads at Ower Farm told me I'd have to do everything they did. 'You're one of the lads now,' I was told and directed towards the tack room. 'You've got to get in there and fight.' So, I gave it a go. I said I'd take on one of the lads in the yard, and I did, just to prove to them that I was no different. Fortunately, my fight was against Pinky and it was stopped before either of us was injured. Neither of us wanted to hurt the other.

Chapter 10

I Have to Keep Convincing Myself this is all Worthwhile

CHRISTMAS WAS approaching, and I had now got into a routine of mucking out at speed, though on a bitter winter morning, with the yard frozen, that meant slipping and slithering and falling on my backside, and having to shovel my load of muck back into the sack.

To complete all my tasks on time was exhausting, but at least it meant I was strengthening up satisfactorily. No longer could I be considered 'frail'. To increase that muscling-up process, I took my turn on the chaff cutter. This was a simple but ingenious device for cutting hay into small pieces ready to be mixed together with other forage and then fed to the horses. Apart from being more economical than previous methods of feeding, this aided the animals' digestion and prevented them from rejecting any part of their food.

The machine had a large cutting wheel where one person fed in thick bundles of hay and another turned the handle – an act that aided muscle strengthening in the arms and shoulders. It could be a three-quarter-hour stint and as I turned the handle with numbed fingers crabbed like claws, I found that, even on the coldest day, sweat poured off me. It was painful, but – I kept reminding myself – it was beneficial.

One mid-morning, when all I wanted to do was have a hot shower and sleep in front of a roaring fire, I climbed up into the hayloft to fetch a bale of hay. I couldn't see a thing. Suddenly, out of the gloom, a great whooping figure swooped towards me. Terrified, I screamed, rushed for the door, slipped and went flying, twisting my wrist. It was Jack who, knowing that I would be in the hayloft, had lain in wait for me. As I scrambled to my feet, a picture of abject despair, Jack nonchalantly kicked me in the shins. What a laugh it gave the lads. But for the first time, my tears flowed; a mixture of self-pity and just sheer misery. I had known I was in for a tough time. I hadn't known how tough.

Always there would be someone watching my every move and I knew that if I gave the slightest indication of weakness, Jack and his pals would take advantage and revel in my discomfort. I told myself: 'You must display no vulnerability whatever the physical pain, personal humiliation, depression or fear.'

Pondering how much more I could take, I took stock. In late October, I had arrived at Ower Farm nervously expectant, burning with ambition, hungry for success. A few weeks later, I considered my progress and realised I was little more than a stable navvy, helping to keep the place spotless. My stimulus to keep going was the belief that my time would come. The sweating and the daily grind at least had two positive effects, and they kept me going through periods when it would have been all too easy to have conceded defeat. Now I was under 8st — although still too heavy to be a lightweight jockey. I was also developing powerful muscles in my arms, shoulders, stomach and back.

Muscles are heavy and so increase your weight, making it more difficult to lose pounds quickly, but I had an advantage over most men jockeys as I didn't drink alcohol (except at the social occasions

I rarely attended), which can increase your weight drastically. Too many jockeys of my generation chose alcohol over food and ended up with drink problems.

I knew that weight reduction was absolutely crucial if I was to fulfil my ambition to become a jockey, and win races. Whether I liked that conditioning, I wasn't sure. My hands were becoming hard and ugly, with ingrained dirt. In the cold weather, the skin at my fingertips cracked and became so painful I could hardly withstand it. When I regarded myself in the bathroom mirror, I realised my whole physique, and my looks, were changing. It was as though I was slowing transforming myself into a man. But I knew that was the way it had to be. Jockeys – professional jockeys – could remain feminine and still have bulging muscle; I told myself something to that effect as I worked on the chaff machine one day, so cold my breath was visible.

'What say?' mumbled the lad feeding in the hay. 'Oh, nothing,' I grunted. 'I'm just trying to convince myself this is all worthwhile.' I received no sympathy. 'Can't you turn any faster?' he complained. I eased my hands from the handle. I couldn't feel them, but they shook, as did my entire body. My teeth chattered like castanets, I was cramped, covered in icy sweat and muck. I ached from head to foot.

Bill Nash appeared. 'Looks like the cold has set in for some time,' he remarked. 'You two had better get some muck down before the morning exercise.' My chaff machine companion swore vehemently. I suspected I would not enjoy this any more than my present task.

When the ground became frozen, horses did not go out on the roads. Instead they were exercised in the paddocks. However, they were still liable to slip outside the loose boxes and on the paths to the paddocks. A cheap and simple remedy to try and prevent this was to spread muck on these areas. What joy! Having spent weeks making a significant contribution to the muckheap, I now had to labour just as hard undertaking the same process in reverse – collecting it and spreading it. By now, there had been a chemical reaction within the hillock of muck, which accentuated the pungent odour of horse manure. It made me want to throw up.

'Hurry up girl, hurry up,' Bill's tones echoed across the yard as I undertook the task. I cursed to myself. I was not only beginning to resemble the lads in physique, I was swearing like them.

One morning, as I was conducting this muck-spreading chore, Bill asked me to spread the manure from the stable I was cleaning around the roses in the garden of his cottage. He loaded a very heavy sack on my back. I staggered across the yard before slipping on a patch of ice on his garden path and went straight down on my backside. The contents of the muck sack were propelled all over my head and shoulders.

It would have been hilarious for anyone watching and I found the Bills, Wightman and Nash, were doubled up in laughter as I cleared the foul stuff out of my eyes, nose and mouth. It must have been like that scene from the Bridget Jones film, *The Edge of Reason*, when Bridget lands in a sty of pigs! Bill Wightman did at least help me up, and together with Bill Nash, refilled my sack for me and returned it to my back. As I picked my way cautiously across the garden, trying to regain my dignity, I questioned, for the umpteenth time, whether such humiliation would ever actually lead to me riding a racehorse.

It wouldn't be until the end of December that I was actually allowed to partner yearlings. But this still seemed far from riding a horse at speeds of up to 40mph at the racecourse.

When I had joined Bill's yard in late October, it was the end of the Flat season and the new intake of yearlings were just starting to be 'broken in', in readiness to run as two-year-olds in the following year. Within a few weeks, these nervous youngsters, purchased at sales or sent to Bill by home-breeders, would be transformed from untamed beasts to horses you could ride, control and persuade to do your bidding (well, to various extents initially). It was difficult to imagine that these precocious animals, with high hindquarters, low withers, long gangling legs and shaggy coats would, in time, become the graceful, powerful horses seen on racetracks. For any yard, it is an exciting period of discovery; a time to consider what rich potential they may possess. Would there be a cheaply purchased star-in-the making among them? However, it was also one that can produce many perils for the lads and work-riders. The process is an intriguing battle of wills.

Racehorses have one role in life – well, two if you include breeding, in the case of the best colts and many mares – but all as youngsters, when confronted with the idea of a human mounting him or her, would react by saying: 'No thanks. I'll just kick my hooves in the field and feast on grass at my leisure.' That's their natural instinct, even if the trainer and his staff have other ideas. As I would discover, young equines, like some young humans, would go to extreme measures not to comply with the discipline demanded of them.

The yearlings start off being lunged. This involves driving them gently in a circle on a long rope or rein using just voice and body language. At first, yearlings have light weights – maybe just light sacking – placed on their backs before eventually a rider is able to sit on them. It is a long, protracted process requiring much patience. It cannot be rushed.

Finally, the yearlings would be ridden in the schooling circuit, known appropriately as the 'bull ring'. This was a circuit composed of 5ft-high straw bales, laid with peat and wood shavings. Riders were left to fend for themselves. At times, it would resemble a mini-version of a rodeo. If riders were thrown, they just hoped they weren't kicked. Once there, the yearlings sensed they had a bit of freedom. Some were as good as gold. Some were not and were decidedly quirky.

From the bull ring, the yearlings progressed into the field behind Bill's house and also did some road work. Finally, in January they started their training on the gallops, at first just cantering.

Because Bill Nash was overprotective in my early weeks and didn't want to take the risk of me being injured, I didn't ride the yearlings in the early stages of breaking them in or in the bull ring. He was right, of course. Racing was Bill Nash's life and he was extraordinarily knowledgeable. He knew and had experienced the hazards. He was a kind, avuncular character, but as firm with me as he was with the lads. He was always concerned I'd get badly hurt and was always determined to look after me – but couldn't be seen to be like that.

Of course, this distancing of me from the yearlings in my early days meant I received a lot of ridicule from the lads, who maintained that I was too scared. It wasn't true. I'd have been quite happy to be involved.

For now, I had to continue with mundane stable work, which was varied twice a week when the horses were fed hot bran mash, consisting of bran, water and linseed. These ingredients were boiled together in a vast copper cauldron suspended a few feet above the ground. The problematic part was, when tipping the cauldron to fill an apprentice's bucket, to avoid the scalding liquid slopping over hands and arms. This was one occasion when there was never any horseplay. The dangers of it were exemplified when, one morning, an apprentice was badly burned when some of the mix splashed over his outstretched arm. Despite his arm being covered in blisters, and in considerable pain, he was out riding the next day. He nearly fainted when he dismounted, but didn't miss a day's riding. It was a demonstration of the commitment all of us had to get in the saddle.

Twice a week, after the hot bran mash feed, the mangers had to be cleaned thoroughly. Often, I had to break the ice on the water buckets before I could even start scrubbing. One day, after cleaning mangers in a temperature five degrees below freezing, I was huddled near tears with intense pain in my hands and feet when Bill Wightman walked into the stall I was working in. I was at just about my lowest ebb, and I told Bill I'd like a word with him before I went home. I confronted him and released all my pent-up frustration. It was like a volcano of indignation erupting.

I had no social life, I complained. I was losing friends because I had to miss weddings, and 18th and 21st birthdays. If I did socialise, I was out on my feet and no fun. I was desperately tired and the hours were too long. I couldn't carry on. But most crucially, I told him, I *wasn't riding*, and didn't feel like I was an apprentice jockey.

'What had been the point of it all?' I thought. I considered myself a highly capable rider after all those years in showjumping. I had assumed I'd just join the yard and immediately start riding out.

Bill listened with admirable patience to my lament, and heard me out. Then he regarded me and responded firmly: 'I know you want to be a jockey, Karen. But it isn't easy. You have to be totally dedicated to get anywhere in life. Other professional people like dancers, athletes and pianists have to give up everything to achieve greatness. Their ambition is their life.'

I took his point, but also came to realise that Bill's reluctance to get me started in the saddle was about far more than convincing him of my dedication. I realised later that he just wanted to keep me safe at what was the most dangerous time of the year at any racing stables. Perhaps understandably, he was wary of allowing me on these often headstrong, unruly yearlings, the equine equivalent of fractious children, until I was strong enough.

His words made sense and, to a degree, quelled my sense of irritation. I felt he was on my side. However, I pleaded with him: 'If only you would allow me to ride the yearlings. At least then I'd feel a step nearer to my goal.' He paused for a second or two, no doubt understanding my sense of grievance, before replying: 'Head Lad is worried that you aren't strong enough yet, but as you are so determined, I'll let you ride the yearlings. And I promise you rides in public next year.'

I drove home feeling euphoric.

Nothing would stop me now ...

Chapter 11

Confronted with the Perils of Life in a 1970s Racing Stables

IN MY early weeks, during rare breaks from mucking out several boxes a day, trying to run with muck sacks, carrying bales of hay and feed bags with my legs close to collapse, while being harried by Bill Nash, I had watched the lads break in the yearlings, and then start to do road work before cantering them.

I had been consumed with envy.

For so long, witnessing the other apprentices had been the nearest I would get. It was intensely frustrating not to be immediately allowed in the saddle of these capricious creatures.

I fully understood why Bill Nash, concerned about my lack of strength in those early weeks, deliberately didn't involve me at first. He preferred me to wait until the yearlings were partially broken in, being gravely concerned I hadn't had enough experience of the breaking process and could easily injure myself. In hindsight, it was probably for the best. Bill Nash also believed that a continuation of my manual work, which I'd describe as more like hard labour, would make me strong enough to cope with them.

Witnessing what I had of the early breaking-in process, during which the precocious youngster is ridden into the bull ring – as potentially dangerous for lads as the real thing is for matadors –

would have been enough to deter most people. But I was so single-minded. I thought, 'Why not me?' I soon realised there were many opportunities for a yearling to part company with his rider. Indeed, early on at Ower Farm, I had experienced my first loose horse after his rider had been unshipped. It provoked the equine equivalent of a prison break-out as everyone stopped what they were doing on hearing loud blasts on the horn of Bill Wightman's Land Rover and rushed towards the sound.

'What's happening?' I asked.

'Loose horse,' replied Bill Nash nonchalantly. 'Is that all?' I said, not understanding the commotion. 'You wait until you're out there yourself,' retorted Bill.

Normally, the horse was simply cornered, but each occasion required much time and manpower. They could leap fences, even barbed wire ones. Rarely, in a frenzy, they could tear themselves to ribbons. The lads, attempting to avoid flying hooves and the wire, had to free an entangled horse as quickly and gently as possible so that it didn't injure itself. Fortunately, horses are herd animals and rarely go far from the string of horses being exercised.

If possible, a string of horses would be ridden at a walk around a loose horse, and often he would re-join the circle. There was one problem with this. Young colts are often sexually excited, particularly in the vicinity of a filly, and it wasn't unknown for such a horse to try and mount another. Conversely, if he came into the circle head-on to the other wild-eyed colts there could be a fight for hierarchy. Either way, it was not ideal for the rider, for whom it could be a perilous position to be caught in.

The dangers were perennial; the consequences serious injury, as I would discover, or worse. A woman who I admired greatly would be killed in such a freak accident. I will return to that incident.

You quickly realise you have to live, or die, with that possibility. You've got to be quite analytical about everything. You tell yourself: 'I'm making this choice and, yes, it does mean so much to me. It's more important than not going through with it.'

So far, the closest I'd got to the yearlings was grooming them. It required two of us 'lads' working in tandem. We had to be quiet, soothing and calm. One of us would hold the horse while the other gently brushed him with a dandy brush (which has long stiff bristles used for removing dry surface dirt out of the coat, usually used on the less sensitive parts of the horse's body), followed by the body brush (a linen or cloth towel used to give a final polish to a horse's coat). Even standing on terra firma, both lads had to be wary the whole time. The slightest noise, a loud voice, or the touching of a horse's ticklish spot, could have your charge jump and kick out.

Picking out the hooves required even more caution and patience. As I raised each leg up in turn, in an attempt to remove mud and stones from the hoof, I knew I was just one muscle contraction away from being kicked in the face. That's why it took 20 minutes to clean all four hooves, and I frequently ended up with bruises and backache. It would be easy to lose your temper with such an unpredictable, recalcitrant customer, but you had to remain calm and firm. Let the horse know who was boss.

It had been a long frustrating winter, but finally, following Bill Wightman's promise the previous day, I had the chance to ride a yearling: venturing out, first on the roads, then cantering on the gallops. After a night in which I'd struggled to sleep because of my state of anticipation, I arrived at the yard and rushed to look at the list pinned to the tack room door, stating which riders were allocated which horses. It was 7am and pitch black.

The first horse I was allotted was named Smarten Up, a lovely chestnut filly, a daughter of Sharpen Up. After her racing career, she would be the dam of the top-class sprinter and stallion Cadeaux Genereux.

Bill Nash helped me to tack her up in the loose box. He introduced me to breaking tack, which I'd never seen before. It was a crucial part of the equipment. The draw reins, which run from the girth through the bit rings and back to form a second pair of reins were new to me.

Draw reins prevent a young, wilful horse from thrusting its head down between its legs, which, at any speed, can mean the jockey is unceremoniously thrown forward. Conversely, they also prevent the horse throwing its head up suddenly and striking the rider in the jaw.

At first, with my fingers already frozen, I threaded the draw reins through the wrong rings. Bill Nash offered to give me a hand, talking to the horse to keep her calm as he said, 'Always make sure you tack up correctly and check it thoroughly, even though you may be pushed for time. *Don't put your life at risk.*'

That last phrase was to stay with me throughout my career. Bill Nash carefully gave me a leg up. I was acutely aware the filly was still not fully broken.

'Sit quietly, remember the horse is young and nervous, and she needs you to give her confidence,' he advised me. 'Take it easy. You'll be fine.' With Bill's aid, I mounted the filly with utmost care. No fast movements. I took up both pairs of reins, trying not to let them dangle against the horse's neck and tickle or irritate her.

Bill muttered: 'Hold your reins correctly. You're not riding a hack now.' (A hack is an experienced horse, sometimes the mount of trainers on the gallops.) I looked at him in disbelief. After all my years' showjumping, I did at least know how to hold my reins! But racehorses were different, as Bill demonstrated. 'When you ride a racehorse, you always hold your reins with either a double or a single bridge.'

Finally, he nodded approval, and stood back in order to allow me to move off. I should have felt a surge of anticipation, but I felt the filly's back tense and stiffen. The feeling was more one of apprehension. Bill Nash told me: 'Don't worry. She's got a cold back and is a bit fresh. She'll relax soon. Away you go then.'

He still sounded slightly uneasy. For an instant, it crossed my mind that, perhaps unfairly, he was more worried about the horse than me. Knowing priorities in the stable, quite possibly it was true ...

We walked gently, quietly, out of the loose box, in the direction of the road, only for Smarten Up to give an almighty buck and shoot me off her back. I flew through the air as if I had been fired from a cannon and landed head first in a pile of frozen manure. I struggled to my feet as Smarten Up happily danced around, relishing her freedom until cornered by some of the lads. My embarrassment turned to irritation when I heard the giggling of the lads who, as always, had watched my every move, constantly scrutinising me for signs of weakness.

'Look at Rudolph,' someone hooted. 'What will mummy say about her darling's little nose?' It had taken the full force, and was red, raw, grazed and bleeding.

Unabashed and unfazed, I made a second attempt, this time successfully, and we walked warily across the stable yard and met up with all the others waiting patiently in the road. I'd cracked it. Yes, I'd been thrown, but I'd remounted and conquered any residual fears, and my horse had learned who was boss.

The trouble was that horses are creatures of habit. They have good memories. No matter what I tried, Smarten Up had me off at that gate every morning. I soon had a nose that resembled a strawberry. And my name became Rudolph. I couldn't even switch horses and let someone else try – not that I'd asked to do so – because an apprentice wasn't allowed to give up on a horse. You had to stick with them. You stayed on that horse – until you stayed on. Not just for the horse's benefit, but for the rider's. You had to master the horse and that could be a painful experience. I had learned that by watching the lads during my weeks of muscle-building in the stable yard.

Yearlings have soft mouths and overuse of the bit during their infancy would make them sore and hard – and hence less responsive during their racing careers. So, we relied on the neck strap, which as the name suggests is a leather 'collar' round the neck. It was on to this device that I clung desperately as Smarten Up and other yearlings reared, bucked, jumped, kicked and squealed their way through exercise periods.

'Hang on to your neck strap or you'll pull her over,' shouted Bill Nash repeatedly.

At the time, I felt, and indeed was, brave when riding them – but that, as I mentioned previously, was because I was relatively ignorant of the possible consequences. I had yet to witness a yearling do a backwards flip, but had been told by one of the lads that it was a dreadful spectacle, to see a horse laying on its crushed rider.

As I wrote earlier, at times it would resemble a scene from a rodeo show, with these frisky young horses careering around, with no sense of direction, and riders able to do little more than hang on. We weren't tough cowboys displaying our bravado in front of a cheering crowd, but a group of slight apprentices determined to make our way in racing.

The colts were worse than the fillies. They all saw themselves as leader of the pack and were constantly challenging each other, colliding and raising up on their hind legs, and kicking out, quite often somersaulting because their hind legs were still relatively weak and couldn't support their weight. We had to ensure we got control of the horse or, if the worst happened, roll away. This was no place for those of a faint constitution and less than 100 per cent determination. It sounds like chaos, but there was a method to the apparent madness. This was what the Bills, Wightman and Nash, had overseen for decades.

I had to repeat this procedure on three different mounts each morning, and one of the most anxious moments was arriving at the stables at 6.30 to discover the names of the horses to which you'd been paired. Some struck fear into the hearts of apprentices. They were mad, bad and dangerous to know – at first, anyway, as I will detail later – and the consequences could be exacerbated during winter in icy conditions. I would later appreciate that you were far safer when you were racing – and that is dangerous enough.

As is frequently pointed out, in what other occupation do ambulances follow participants around their workplace, which is the case at all racecourses, whether a Flat or jump meeting?

Chapter 12

I Had to Ask Myself: 'What's More Important: Racing or Staying Alive?'

NO MATTER how talented a rider you were, it was really just luck whether your mount would rear up or not during exercise. One of Richard Newman's sisters, Lynn, was crushed and cracked her pelvis in that way and never got on the racecourse. Grant Eden, an apprentice, broke a leg on the Yew Hedge gallops where the yearlings worked before they transferred to the main gallops later on. But in my early weeks of riding yearlings, I tried not to dwell on such thoughts. My focus was purely on my daily routine, which was as follows:

Arrive 6.30am and discover on the tack room list which horses I'd been allotted.

Fight for a pitchfork and dry muck sack.

Muck out my first stall in a maximum of ten minutes, no matter how many trips to the muck heap.

Fight for a brush, clean out the stall, clear round the drains. Put down clean straw so that the horse wouldn't slip. Remove his night rug, dandy brush and body brush him down. Replace his rug. Pick out his hooves.

This all had to be done by 7.20am.

Still running, fetch tack from the tack room. With arms laden with heavy equipment, run back and tack up my first horse. Ride out to join the others by 7.30. There was no waiting for latecomers.

We'd congregate in one of several country lanes around the stables and make our way to the Downs. Once there, the young horses would canter in a group – though some individuals were still incapable of maintaining a neat line. Our charges would be endlessly urged on by the increasingly exhausted riders who, apart from anything else, were engaged in keeping their mounts' heads up to forestall any bucking-off attempts and to persuade them to canter along the gallop behind the lead horse.

We would canter 3 furlongs before taking the horses back to road work. That meant steering well clear of any passing vehicles, including near-silent milk floats, which would have had our youngsters bucking and rearing. Even cyclists could spook them. I once saw an elderly lady quietly pedalling towards us on an ancient cycle when one of the yearlings kicked out at her bike. I've never seen anyone move so fast – she shot up a steep bank into the hedge. Meanwhile, the horse kicked her bicycle for good measure.

We walked and trotted the horses on the roads for a few miles every day, always alert for animals scuttling in the hedgerow or birds preparing for flight, which was sufficient to startle them. I learned to anticipate anything, however slight, that may alarm my horse.

Spring's approach brought a change to the Downs, with green buds appearing in hedgerows and on branches of trees. Like children suddenly spying their favourites in a sweet shop, our horses could decide to grab a mouthful of these without warning. Our mounts could also suddenly decide they'd appreciate a mouthful of fresh grass, and we riders found ourselves perched precariously as our mounts munched away.

If something startled them, you had no chance of staying on. Indeed, it became so second nature to be alert that my senses were sharpened for the sight and sound of fluttering wings and flapping pieces of paper, even when I wasn't riding.

That may sound bizarre, but the possible implications of a horse being spooked became all too real later in my time with Bill Wightman when I was partnering my mount along the lanes one morning behind Grant Eden, a work-rider. Suddenly his mount was spooked by a sound and reared up. The horse somersaulted. Grant, who had courageously stayed in the saddle hoping to recover the situation, fell beneath him. Grant lay in the road motionless, blood drained from his features. I was certain he had been killed. Fortunately, he had just been winded and suffered a broken leg. I say *just* – because it could have been so much worse.

Robert Baker, an always thoughtful and considerate apprentice, rode alongside me after the incident. 'Now, Karen,' he said, 'do you realise the dangers of the game?'

Thankfully, Grant was soon back in the stables, mucking out and cleaning up with his leg in plaster and armed with crutches – until the plaster was removed and he was fit enough to return to the saddle. Our dedication ran deep.

This was the first serious incident I would witness and, although we all carried on in a professional manner afterwards, almost as though nothing had happened, it was a sharp warning jab in the ribs. It made me fully aware of what could befall me.

It was nothing like showjumping or the relatively docile horses that I was used to riding. As majestic as these beasts were, they could be unpredictable, nervous creatures. A number had behavioural problems, some of which were inherited and, to an extent, we could predict them if we knew their dam. They were also powerful athletes whose natural instinct was to expend their energy. A downright danger, if the fates conspired against you.

They say that the young believe that nothing can ever happen to them; that they're indestructible. But I never thought that. I was only too conscious of my vulnerability. On many days, I would remind myself as I'd drive to work, 'Right, Karen. You're making this choice. You could die today. You could kill yourself.'

I tried to rationalise things, and said to myself: 'What's more important: racing or staying alive?' By dedicating myself to the former, I knew that every day I was placing my health, even my life, in jeopardy. It must have been how racing drivers contemplated life back in the same era. Eight drivers died in Grand Prix races, practice and qualifying in the 1970s.

Yet, it did not deter me for an instant. I'd do anything, even risk my life, just to get on the racecourse in the coming season.

The demands placed on me before that day arrived had been unrelenting. Christmas had meant an extra day off, and another on Boxing Day, but other than that we still worked all the days through a decidedly un-festive season. No parties, dancing, discos, family get-togethers. I now had fewer problems with my weight, but because of the riding and stable work I still had to watch my diet and abstain from alcohol.

After being kept away from breaking yearlings when I first began working at the yard, the fact that I was now riding these young horses meant that, as the New Year dawned, I was relatively content. The first of January is an important date in the racing calendar. It's the day when all racehorses age by one year regardless of when they are born. Our yearlings had become two-year-olds, or juveniles as they are sometimes known. However, it didn't mean that magically they all matured overnight. Far from it. By now, I had come to fully appreciate their strength in comparison to my showjumper, and why I'd had to build up so much muscle in my arms and shoulders.

Apprentices fell and remounted. The luckless amongst the group were hurt. We all wore protective skull caps – all stable staff had to wear them. Back then, there were no body protectors, which all work-riders and jockeys must wear today.

Neither was there too much protection from the elements. Despite being clad in multi-layers of clothing, in those early months of the New Year we'd return to the yard frozen, or soaked, or both. We received no sympathy. The horses came first.

Chapter 13

Head Lad Tells Me: 'You're Brave and Determined – I'll Make a Jockey of You Yet.'

THROUGH JANUARY and February, the youngsters continued their journey towards their first date at the racecourse: a process that had begun with schooling and slowly making them less resistant to having a human on their backs, then moved on to road work and canters. By the end of February, with spring soon to offer its welcoming arms, the 'early' two-year-olds (those expected to race early on, based on breeding and physical maturity) were doing fast canters or half speeds (a gallop at a controlled pace).

Finally, it was my first day to ride work: the serious business of getting a horse fit on the wide-open spaces of Bill's gallops. Stephen's Castle Down was the name of the main gallops and, on this downland, real jockey skills were required to cope with the youngsters. This magnificent area of turf had been left undisturbed for centuries, and only grazed upon by sheep, rabbits and hares. It produced good ground throughout the year. In total, it was a horseshoe-shaped two miles.

What Bill Wightman liked about this terrain was that its undulations provided far more of a searching test than, say, the mainly level open spaces of Newmarket Heath. He considered it ideal for long, steady canters, but would add, 'It's the hills that get them fit.'

As I mentioned earlier, I learned on the job – a highly unusual procedure, even then. Work-riding and race-riding require a great deal of technical ability, but I received no instruction. I was predominantly self-taught. Today, that would be unthinkable. It is mandatory to complete a Level 2 Diploma course – also called a pre-apprenticeship – with either the British Racing School or the Northern Racing College. These courses are normally fully residential and can take up to one year. Completion of the course is followed by the 'real apprenticeship'. That takes up to 18 months, and two weeks of full jockey training afterwards. Only once that's done will apprentices be able to apply for a licence and ride against professional jockeys.

Even in my time, young apprentices would attend racing school, as most of my stable colleagues did, including my friend Richard Newman. When he told me he had spent six weeks at a training school at Goodwood, he was astonished that I hadn't attended something similar. Looking back, it was strange that I wasn't given the same opportunity as Richard and the other lads. It did cross my mind that perhaps colleges weren't taking girls. However, I later discovered that there was a course at the National Equestrian Centre at Stoneleigh, in Warwickshire, for girls wishing to become 'jockettes'. However, I think it's more likely that Bill Wightman was aware I was an experienced horsewoman and had a natural rapport with horses. He was confident enough in my abilities to let me pick up the technique of riding racehorses as I went along.

Effectively, Bill was saying: 'I know you're a decent horsewoman, Karen. That's why I took you on. Race-riding will come. All you need to show me is that you can do the weights I need, and make yourself as strong as the boys.'

I watched and listened, and asked those around me – particularly Bill Nash, whose responsibilities included bringing on the apprentices. It would become clear that Head Lad was determined I would succeed. Other than occasional comments, Bill Wightman never spoke to me directly about my riding – all his observations came via Bill Nash. My discussions with Bill Wightman only concerned the individual I'd been riding in work. His prime interest was feedback from me on the horse. Understandably, his principal concern was his horses and evaluating how they were working on the gallops.

Bill would direct work-riders to work over different distances and afterwards he wanted to know from you how much your horse was pulling – how much did he have left in the tank? Or were they weakening? It would be like a top football team assessing the fitness and attitude of their key players.

Bill was never a trainer who'd bring through and develop jockeys. In that respect, he was very different to trainers through history who achieved renown for being superb educators of young riders. One man so lauded was 'Frenchie' Nicholson, whose small stable was known as the 'riders' academy'. His protégés included Pat Eddery, Tony Murray and Paul Cook. Bill Wightman's absolute priority was his horses.

The way it worked was that Bill Nash would offer words of advice when I got back from work-riding. He thought I was a natural, had good hands, and that horses went well for me. Under his guidance, my riding was improving day by day. I recall one morning I was using all my energy to keep my horse upsides of the lead horse. Clearly, my riding must have impressed Bill Nash, who was overseeing the work. 'I'll make a jockey of you yet,' he remarked jovially afterwards. 'You're brave and determined – just what's needed in an apprentice.' It was music to my ears, a rare moment of approval. Bill Nash had given my ego, deflated by the sarcasm and ridicule of my fellow apprentices and lads, a much-needed boost, particularly as he rarely gave praise to the lads. I will always be grateful that Head Lad was in my corner. He was a great supporter. He'd try to offer encouragement quietly, though there were always those who thought I was receiving favouritism or having allowances made because I was a girl.

Bill Nash also helped me with my understanding of thoroughbreds and their temperaments and idiosyncrasies. The youngsters were so highly strung it was almost impossible to anticipate their behaviour. Some were nervous and quick-tempered. Others were quiet, more biddable and, dare I say it, loveable.

I would also scrutinise experienced jockeys closely when they came to the yard to work-ride. These included men I'd been watching on TV from the age of six. On my first day on the gallops, Bill told me that Brough Scott would look after me. I rode upsides him and was highly appreciative of his advice. Brough always had a calming influence on me. He was such a gentleman, so polite and caring – in contrast to some of the lads and jockeys. Brough, who had won the 1968 Imperial Cup on Persian Empire and the Mandarin Chase on The Otter the following year, had suffered his share of injuries, including a broken back, broken neck and a punctured lung. However, he was perhaps better known to the wider public as horseracing's anchorman at ITV and then Channel 4 for many decades. He returned to ITV Racing in 2017 and, in addition, he is a distinguished sports journalist.

I was already aware that to race, in contrast to showjumping or eventing, required me to adopt a completely new style. In Flat racing, the jockey's backside is raised out of the saddle so that his or her weight is placed where it can most easily be carried by the horse – that is, in a position where the rider's and the horse's centres of gravity are aligned. At the start, I appreciated that a rider must mould their style according to their build and, if necessary, adjust it to allow for the size and substance of their mount. It should enable them to combine the scientific distribution of their weight with security and efficiency.

Once we were riding out on the gallops, I'd put my stirrups up and ride as short as I could and quickly learned how to streamline my body. Bill Nash was particularly hot on style, and took great interest in honing mine. He would be watching me all the time. I'd ask his advice and, in time, offer ideas. Later, these would include adopting the American Steve Cauthen's more streamlined style, designed to cut down wind resistance. Any small advantage could be vital.

Coincidentally, in the same year as this, 1977, the wonder 'Kid' from Kentucky, aged just 16, weighing naturally under 7st – how I envied him! – and standing only just over 5ft, was starting his first full season. He would be a positive influence on me – though never could I have forecast that in two years' time I would ride against him. But that's getting ahead of myself.

Developing style was all-important. I had to demonstrate that I was not just some enthusiastic lady amateur who had accidentally found herself in a stable full of would-be professional riders.

There were many who would have been delighted had I failed. One was Frank, one of the arch-chauvinists at the yard, and one of those who did his best to shock me with his constant sexist expletives. Today, in any working environment, he probably wouldn't last a day. But four decades ago, he got away with it. Like the previously mentioned Jack, he had set out to be an apprentice jockey, but with age, piled on the pounds. He would constantly try to belittle me and put me down.

'Karen, you look the same as the other girls riding in ladies' races and they all look like sacks of potatoes on horses,' he would comment. 'Women can't help looking that way. They're just not physically built to be jockeys.' How I had wearied at hearing that observation.

Part of the problem, as I alluded to previously and will do so again, was the reputation acquired by lady jockeys that preceded my arrival. As much as you could admire the enthusiasm of those early lady pioneers, they did nothing for the perception of female riders planning to become professionals.

Frank's disdain for me was probably born of his own disillusionment. This was one of the many who had failed to make it himself, but who had stayed in the business because it was all he knew. For him to now witness a young woman who could do low weights, and who clearly possessed ambition and ability, arrive at the yard and be in contention for races, riled him intensely. Such characters ended up begrudging anyone else's success.

Part of me could understand that. They had to watch big-name jockeys like Eddery and Carson as well as journeymen like Baxter and Thomas, people who *had* made it, ride out at the yard.

Yet, despite being infuriated by Frank's attitude, I quietly vowed that, one day, I would prove him, and others, wrong.

In early 1977, a two-year-old I helped to break in and partnered on the gallops was the previously mentioned Man On The Run, the Mick Channon-owned horse. Thankfully, he was a quiet ride!

It was always fun to have Mick around. A brilliant, effusive character, he was then at the end of his first, 12-year, spell at

Southampton before joining Manchester City. He was a racing enthusiast and, on frequent visits to Ower Farm, was always keen to discuss horses, including Man On The Run, who had been the first foal out of Cathy Jane, the foundation mare of Mick's stud. Mick and his team-mate Brian O'Neill had paid £400 between them for a yearling filly. They named her Cathy Jane after their wives – mainly, Channon has mischievously suggested, to stop them complaining if their ownership venture depleted the housekeeping money!

The story goes that on the night of his greatest triumph as a footballer, Southampton's 1976 FA Cup Final victory over Manchester United, he excused himself from the post-match banquet and went to see his first foal being born.

Early in the season, two-year-olds run in the minimum distance 5-furlong races, and later 6 furlongs. Only towards the end of the season do some have the strength and stamina for further.

Man On The Run lacked the pace of the more precocious horses bred for shorter distances. Initially, he didn't display much on the track. Some well-known owners could have found it embarrassing, particularly if attending the races with friends, but typically Mick and Kevin Keegan (the horse's co-owner) turned it around and found humour in the situation, turning up at races with T-shirts bearing the legend 'Man On The Walk'. The fact was that Man On The Run was a stayer and once entered over longer distances his stamina came into play. He proved himself by winning three races on the Flat and three over jumps.

There were still moments when I wondered whether I was a stayer, and if my own race would end in triumph. Sometimes there were still occasional twinges of doubt about whether it would ever happen – that I still wouldn't be allowed to race because of perceived lack of strength. I knew I was capable and possessed an iron will to succeed – but would others recognise that and, most significantly, would Bill Wightman and his owners?

But those concerns were allayed when, one crisp early March morning, as I was walking across the stable yard with a feedbag for Man On The Run, Bill Wightman approached me.

'Now, Karen,' he said. 'Have you made your decision? Do you wish to sign today? Your apprenticeship papers are in my office.' There was no hesitation on my part. I'd been waiting for this moment. In fact, both Richard Newman and myself were among the last to sign three-year indentured apprenticeships. Soon afterwards, these three-year antediluvian contracts were abolished and were replaced by an annual agreement – with fewer strict clauses. That didn't come a moment too soon. A red seal indicated the formality and legal recognition of the three-year version. They had been so binding that there were stories of boys being dragged back to their stables by police after running away. Fortunately, that did not apply to Bill's stables!

Bill Wightman and Diana Roth talked through it with me. In terms of getting racecourse rides, Bill said he'd do everything he could for me. He respected people with ambition, but I felt he was surprised by how hard I'd worked and what I'd put myself through. Perhaps he'd never quite believed that I'd stick it out through that exacting winter.

Immediately, I banished the thought of five months of a punishing regime and the damp and cold to the back of my mind and thought only of my future opportunities. In a few weeks, I would receive my apprentice licence to race.

Inevitably, though, my sense of elation and pride was soon diminished by the reaction of the lads. Word quickly spread round the stables, and it wasn't long before I became aware of the lads' traditional 'initiation ceremony' for anyone signing their apprenticeship indentures. It involved stripping the unfortunate victim and coating their genitals with hoof oil. As you can imagine, I wasn't having any of that, though they always threatened me with that ritual. One lad chased me round the yard with the grease pot, taunting me: 'If you don't believe in sex discrimination, then you should be treated in the same way as the boys.' The other lads joined in.

'You wouldn't dare,' I shouted, managing to dodge them. 'I'll tell the guv'nor. I'll fetch the police.' Eventually they gave up. They were probably more interested in frightening me than making me go through with it. Somehow it wasn't unexpected. But by now I'd become impervious to their treatment of me. I had more important matters on my mind.

By the start of the 1977 Flat season there had still not been a victory registered by a girl apprentice. Indeed, the 11 girls by then apprenticed *and* given races could muster only 62 rides between them.

'Their turn will come,' was the Lady Jockeys' Association's highly optimistic observation. 'But only when a stable puts its full weight behind a girl rider, as Seamus McGrath had done with the talented Welsh girl Joanna Morgan in Ireland.' (It was at Seamus McGrath's stable, near Leopardstown, incidentally, where Pat Eddery began riding out at the age of eight and began his formal apprenticeship at the age of 14.)

Joanna Morgan had won five races in 1975, including her first against senior jockeys on Muscari at The Curragh in Ireland on 12 November that year. But I was all too aware that no one had emulated her feat in the UK.

Chapter 14

My Mother is Shocked by the Sight of my Bruised and Skeletal Body

THE DATE was 24 March 1977, and, after all the hard work, breaking in the yearlings and beginning their education in the cold and rain, there was a feeling of intense anticipation within the yard as the Flat season began.

For my own part, I had signed on officially as an apprentice jockey. I derived a sense of enormous achievement at having made it this far, having braved the physical demands, the scorn of some of my stable companions, the scepticism of friends, and my own occasional doubts and apprehension. But the thought persisted: when would I get my first ride in public?

As mentioned previously, with another season under way, there were two 'work' mornings a week – Wednesday and Saturday. These were occasions when all the horses galloped, bar those injured. Bill Wightman required many to be partnered by lightweight jockeys, and these gave me plenty of opportunities to improve my riding talents. He would scrutinise the horses as they were walked around in a circle on the gallops, then would call the name of a horse and that of a rider.

'Please don't give me a mad one,' I'd silently plead.

Some mornings, I'd be allocated eight horses and eight gallops, and it was exhausting. Each gallop was different, with new orders, distance and pace for each individual. It was an electrifying experience to have a keen, muscled horse beneath me: a creature who wanted to break into a full gallop. My task was to ensure he remained under my control, but this isn't easy when your charge is fighting you, as his instinct is to seek top gear. Horses become overexcited at the thought of galloping and when they gallop closely upsides another horse their innate competitiveness fuels further excitement. Horses naturally love racing one another and sharing that experience with them is one of the thrills of being a jockey.

Now, with my weight reduced to 7½st, having sweated and dieted steadily over the winter, controlling the horses was no easy feat. Even with, by now, powerful arms and wrists, it required all my strength to contain a young horse determined to run free. I can say definitively that there's no better way to gain fitness – this contest of wills: the horse's energy and fitness pitted against the rider's strength and skill. It requires the use of muscles in so many parts of the rider's body.

When it comes to skill, a crucial part of riding is a jockey's sensitivity with his or her hands on the reins. This is what is meant by a rider having 'good hands', which I knew Bill Nash believed I possessed. The worst criticism you can have is other apprentices and your trainer comparing your hands with 'bloody shovels'.

The best riders feel an affinity with their mount. There is a co-ordination of minds and the horse can detect its jockey's confidence, determination, patience – and courage.

How the exercising took its toll on my appearance, though. Jeans, wellingtons, and thick socks didn't provide enough protection. I was developing large ugly bruises all the way up the insides of my calves. My knees were raw and the insides of my ankles were cut and bleeding. The sight shocked and upset my mother as she helped to ease my boots off one day.

'Karen, you shouldn't have legs looking like this. You're a young lady,' she chided me.

It would be fair to say I wouldn't have looked great in a swimsuit, and I would have been reluctant to wear skirts in public. As well as destroying my social life, my new career had changed the shape of my body.

I surveyed myself in the mirror. Beforehand I had never been overweight. I'd have described myself as petite and toned. I'd looked after my appearance. My showjumping had kept me fit and healthy enough. But as for racing fit? That was another matter entirely. The conditioning you require – then and now – to be a jockey would astonish most people. They don't always realise how riding, possibly, several horses a day, you've got to be absolutely ultra-fit. And that can make significant changes to your body – as I could testify. As fat had disappeared, so had my hips and bust. All my ribs and hip bones were protruding. In many areas, I was close to skeletal. My shoulders had broadened and my arms and legs were thick with muscle; at least my new body shape would allow me to look the part in a racecourse weighing room – when I got there. Perhaps it was a good job I wasn't vain …

Like it or not, this was the physique I needed to work horses daily, and later to make it on to the racecourse. I looked around the stable yard. Other than a slightly larger posterior, in terms of shape you could barely tell me apart from the lads!

I would learn that there are a multitude of considerations involved in race-riding. You have to ensure the horse doesn't run his race too early, particularly if he's a hard-puller. You have to think about your position, and what is going on around you at 30mph and more. And all the while, you have to remember your orders and react tactically to positions you find yourself in. There's shouting, some of it intimidating and crude, some of it a genuine warning that you're in danger of colliding with another runner. You have to have all your wits about you and have extremely quick reactions. It's physically and mentally exhausting.

You also have to ride a good finish – an art in itself, requiring strength and rhythm and adoption of correct use of the whip. By now, I had learned the appropriate use of what is an essential piece of equipment in *steering the horse*. I emphasise that phrase deliberately.

The former jockey Bill Anderson (another Bill who worked at the yard – it could be confusing!) was a decent, helpful character. He had fantastic hands and could adeptly handle any horse, even tricky ones. He demonstrated to me how to use the whip and pull it through from one hand to the other. We would stand outside the stables or in the feed store practising. If you are drifting towards another horse and impede him, you must be able to correct that with the whip, or there is a danger of a collision, being disqualified and, worst of all, an accident. Poor use of the whip would show you up. Today, it's not so problematic because you're not allowed to use it overhand. But it's a question of keeping it straight when you bring it through.

The whip, and its use, is a controversial issue, but you would find very few horsemen wanting to ban it completely. To a large extent it's used to coax the horse, to encourage him. I would never have hit one hard. I used to practise on my horse 'Umphy' at home, but without actually using it on him, of course.

All the while, I'd be constantly looking at and listening to the other apprentices. They'd talk about 'changing hands'. This is when the rider shortens his reins, which the horse interprets as an instruction to go faster, rather like changing up gears in a car. It needs skill and balance, and many novice riders struggle with the technique at first. When I asked Bill Nash about this, he said he hadn't mentioned it as I was already changing hands naturally while riding work.

Another of our responsibilities was to teach the two-year-olds to enter the old rattling starting stalls that were positioned on Bill Wightman's gallops, in order to prepare them for the racecourse. Not all horses do so without some encouragement. Again it could be a thoroughly dangerous part of the job. When you first attempted it, some would rear up and try to go over the top or dive underneath. To illustrate the potential hazards, three years later Lester Piggott had his right ear partially severed when his mount ducked under the staring stalls at Epsom when it tried to duck under the gates of the starting stalls.

Perils lurked everywhere. This world was not one for the faint of heart. But you had to experience all aspects of it. There was no way you could avoid any part of the process and get a ride on the racecourse.

The only criticism I received from Bill Nash was for forgetting my goggles. Another aspect people don't appreciate about riding work and race-riding is how, on soft conditions, mud and stones splatter across your face. You also have to remember to keep your mouth closed. I would often spit out lumps of mud. Goggles ensure your vision is relatively clear, although they can steam up on the inside or become covered with mud on the outside. But without goggles, you are close to riding blind.

On the gallops, horses work best in pairs, 'upsides' as it is known, and one morning Bill Wightman called me over and said: 'Go and do a half speed with Charlie.' My heart sank. Not Charlie Swift! He was one of the older lads, and an ex-jockey. He'd be bound to mess things up somehow, I thought. And he did.

I was paired with Charlotte's Choice, an attractive bay colt sired by the 1969 Derby winner Blakeney. As a yearling, he had been one of the mad individuals, and would throw me. We had, as they say, history. But he was clearly talented – as I was in a prime position to recognise. I frequently rode Charlotte's Choice in his work.

On the gallops, as we worked, Charlotte's Choice appeared mesmerised by Charlie's mount and drew closer. In reality, his horse was drawing closer to mine. By now, the two horses were practically clamped together. Charlie let go of his rein and, with one hand, embraced me. This was highly dangerous.

'Get away,' I shouted desperately. My cries had no effect. Charlie just grinned, and shouted back: 'I love it, I love it. What a way to ride.'

After what seemed an eternity, we came to a rise where we could be seen by Bill Wightman. Charlie reluctantly released me. I had no strength to hold my horse together, and he galloped on too fast for Bill's liking. I didn't want to get Charlie in trouble, so took it on the chin when Bill chastised me for a poor ride, while, out of his eyeline, Charlie waved cheerfully.

In an earlier chapter, I recalled my horrific experience of witnessing a work-rider, Grant Eden, being crushed by his horse when it had somersaulted backwards after being spooked, breaking Grant's leg in the process. It just shows how perilous this career could be – and why Charlie's behaviour towards me, though a prank, was unacceptable. No doubt he regarded it as quite literally horseplay. And I accepted it as that. Yet, it was far from the only occasion other riders tried to grab me on the gallops and even drag me off. I put it down to fear of the unknown – the lone female in their midst. They'd only seen women race over jumps and as amateurs on the Flat. Such experiences were character-building and I learned to live with them, but one incident on the gallops appalled the other riders, even those not enamoured by my presence.

Richard Newman recalls to this day how four or five of us were riding up the main gallop.

'All of a sudden, another of Bill's apprentices went upsides Karen, and smacked her hard across the backside with a whip. And those whips, particularly in those days, smarted. I remember thinking to myself, "Really?" He'd done it for a laugh. He thought everyone would find that comical. But they didn't. It was unacceptable. Everyone thought it was well out of order.'

Richard once expressed his surprise to me that I apparently took that kind of punishment in my stride. But I rolled with the punches, as boxers say. From what Richard says, such treatment was meted out much more than I now recall. Maybe I became immune to it, or erased it from my brain. He was just amazed how I coped with it.

'You just didn't respond,' he'd say, admitting that I'd have been quite justified in reacting. But I knew that if I did, if I remonstrated with them, or retaliated, or got upset, it would merely make them redouble their efforts. It was all part of my determination to blend in, assimilate myself. I knew I just had to survive.

Apart from anything else, I didn't want Bill Wightman to think there was a problem. He'd warned me at my interview that he wanted everything to run smoothly – and to my mind, that meant no dramas, even if they weren't of my making.

As I suggested earlier, Richard believed that such behaviour was primarily fuelled by resentment: a concern that, in time, I may take their rides. They were trying to intimidate me to the extent that I'd quit. I was aware that the atmosphere was highly competitive among apprentice jockeys and that made an already dangerous job even more hazardous.

One apprentice I was certainly in competition with for rides was Steve Woolley, although our rivalry was always conducted in the right spirit. He apparently struggled with weight and later I would 'jock him off' twice and take his mount in races. He had arrived at the yard about the same time as me and he hated the thought of me getting rides ahead of him. He was not alone. Those that did race didn't give up the opportunity lightly. Some individuals were constantly scrutinising me for evidence of poor horsemanship. I'm pleased to say I gave them precious few opportunities.

In fairness, it wasn't just me who became a target for the back-biters. As Richard Newman told me later: 'If someone made a mistake, or didn't look right on a horse, you were slammed. There was no holding back at all.'

But they reserved their worst for me. 'You'd hear lads who were grooming particular colts or fillies make remarks like, "I don't want her on my horse" and "Why's she riding that?"' Richard recalled. Apparently, these comments were commonplace behind my back. And worse.

Soon, the most precocious of the two-year-olds began to be given trials. They would be ridden 'with hands and heels', no whips used. It was designed to give an insight into how they would perform once they reached the racecourse.

Judgement of pace was vital, and Bill Wightman, who used to wave a little white handkerchief to indicate the point at which he wanted us to quicken up on the gallops, would exhort me furiously, bellowing 'Come on, come on!' if he felt I wasn't pushing my mount strongly enough.

One training routine was to do a fast canter in groups of around ten beside the main gallops. The idea was to encourage some of the horses to gallop in close proximity to the hind quarters of the two horses in front, then force a gap and ride between them and ease into the lead. This is as important a part of the training regime as achieving fitness.

Two-year-olds are unfamiliar with being urged past other horses while tightly grouped, and it doesn't come naturally. It takes the jockey's urgings and confidence they instil in their mount to achieve it.

The first time I did this successfully, it only increased my yearning to do it on the racecourse.

Some horses went particularly well for me. They included Charlotte's Choice, mentioned earlier in this chapter. Bill Nash said to me one day: 'You really did ride that work well – you're just made for each other.' I'd have really loved to have been given the opportunity to extend that relationship to the racecourse, and really did push for the chance later on. But to no avail. I'm not certain, but maybe Bill Wightman couldn't get the owner's permission.

As a four-year-old, Charlotte's Choice would win the prestigious staying handicap, the Chester Cup, under Willie Carson, defeating the mighty dual-purpose horse Sea Pigeon. I felt good, knowing at least that I had played my part in that and other triumphs. You get to know the mentality of a horse, and in the case of Charlotte's Choice, he was so competitive. He just loved racing, and to force his nose in front of the others.

Even when our horses' work was over, our labours weren't. I had to clean my horse's eyes and nose, then sponge his mouth, also sponge the saddle and girth marks away, otherwise when they dried the perspiration would set hard. If that happened it would require half an hour with a dandy brush to remove it, and also cause the horse pain.

We all put a lot of effort into our grooming. All stables place a great premium on their runners arriving at the racecourse at least looking the part. The most impressive at the racecourse are adjudged as 'the best-turned out' before each race and their grooms receive an award. It may not mean too much to the racegoers, but it does to the grooms. We were all determined that the horses we were responsible for were impeccably turned out. We took great pride in ours really gleaming in the spring sun.

Mind you, I still received the odd caustic comment from lads. 'Hey, come and look at my horse – you can see your ugly face in his coat,' someone shouted at me one morning. Sometimes you just had to laugh along.

With the Flat season becoming increasingly busy, horses, accompanied by their grooms, would be off to the races. All the lads were obsessed with *Raceform*, otherwise known as the Form Book. This publication, updated weekly, detailed the weights, betting and comments in running of every horse in each race, together with the name of the winning trainer, owner and breeder. The lads knew everything about any horse about to contest a race, as well as their own, and many bet accordingly. It would still be the case today, and goes with the territory if you're living and breathing a sport like racing. The belief that you possess knowledge that others don't is a crucial aspect of gambling.

Trainers have always disapproved, of course – particularly 'gambling' trainers like Bill. Indeed, it was part of the contract you signed not to pass on inside information. On a quiet midweek day, even a small amount of off-course money, or the lads spreading the news that a horse was expected to perform well, could affect the odds.

On big race days – usually Saturdays, apart from the Derby, which was then staged on a Wednesday – we were allowed to watch the TV races and gathered in the lads' hostel. Inevitably, plenty of money changed hands in bets between the lads or they'd visit the local betting shop at Bishop's Waltham at lunchtimes. I didn't – I've never been a gambler. The lads thought I was strange, although I think Bill Wightman regarded it as a positive!

I would, though, read *Raceform* carefully, but only when it concerned a horse I was riding in a race, and wanted to glean the form of its rivals.

And with my patience having been tested to the full, that momentous day finally arrived. Friday, 13 May didn't sound a particularly propitious date for a first racecourse ride – but it would be mine.

Chapter 15

Bill's Instruction was Clear: 'Don't Let Them Know You're a Girl'

I WAS ecstatic! My heart skipped a beat when I heard the news. And that was without knowing what I'd be riding or where. I had made it, at least into the weighing room – my reward for progressing through the yearling stage, as Bill Wightman had promised.

There was no major announcement by Bill. I was putting feed in a horse's box when Bill came in and almost casually mentioned to me: 'You're going to have a ride tomorrow.' That was always Bill's way – invariably understated. I'd have liked to have known sooner. I liked to be well prepared mentally as well as physically, but I wasn't about to complain.

Racing entries and declarations were different then and, with Bill, it was all very last minute, when it came to his runners, and who would be riding them. All the time, he'd be plotting and planning. He'd also have to take into account the jockeys who rode for him. Men like Geoff Baxter would always be on the phone to him, requesting rides. Today, you can't make late decisions like that. On the Flat, declarations, including the name of the jockey, must be made two days before a race.

Returning to my racecourse debut, I discovered I'd be contesting the 7-furlong London Apprentice Stakes (Handicap) at Newbury, a race worth £909.80 to the winning owner. It was to be ridden by apprentices for their own stables, and who had not partnered more than three winners.

If I still had doubts, there it was in the daily paper:

> **Mount:** Park Walk.
> **Owner:** Miss K Clarke.
> **Trainer:** W G R Wightman.
> **Jockey:** K Wiltshire.

When we arrived, Bill told me to walk the course. That was a ritual he demanded I must observe at every track I encountered. So, I trudged round the 1-mile 7-furlong left-handed track when all I wanted to do was conserve energy. This would be particularly the case later when making low weights and I was dieting and dehydrated. But Bill insisted. It was something he was very strict about. He felt it was really important to be aware of the contours and bends and, in particular, the going and discuss it with him or the travelling head lad. I could see the point when, later, I rode at Epsom, a very idiosyncratic course, but not Newbury, which was a slightly undulating, galloping track.

Physically preparing for a race didn't appear a concern then. No one seemed to think about you being in the best possible condition to ride. I certainly could have done without a morning's work in the stables and riding out before going racing, and then walking the course once I arrived there. But if you raised the question of your energy levels, Bill would remind you, by no means for the first or last time, that he had been a prisoner of war in Japan, and *he* had got through *that*. So, you should be able to deal with this challenge, with the demands on your body nothing like what he suffered. It was mind over matter, he'd declare.

Like many men of his generation, he didn't dwell on his wartime experiences, but sometimes he talked about them as a means of empathising with me when I was going through a tough patch. His and my experiences were hardly comparable, of course, but he'd say: 'I know you're starving yourself and you're having to do hard work. I know what it's like – having nothing to eat. I was starving in Japan, and I still had to do hard work. But it toughens you up.' It meant you couldn't complain or moan about anything. It wouldn't get you anywhere, and frankly there was no adequate riposte to Bill's argument.

Making the relatively short journey to the course with Bill, I didn't feel too many nerves. I had faith in my ability, I would be riding against other apprentices. The feeling was more a sense of intense relief that I'd made it on to the racecourse. I felt this was where I should be – a major racecourse that, coincidentally, was the very one where all those years before I had been enraptured by the spectacle of those top jockeys riding a finish.

Today I was joining that fraternity – if that was the correct word. In those more formal times, trainers' and jockeys' initials and surnames – and, in some cases, titles – were used on race cards and on racecourse wooden boards (this was long before giant TV screens bearing all relevant information became commonplace), rather than full names. So, it was trainer: W.G.R. Wightman, and jockey: K. Wiltshire. The assumption was that I was a boy, and that suited Bill.

As I have stressed in earlier chapters, in the late 1970s, just being a female rider gave me, and others starting out, a bad name. I cannot emphasise it enough: in racing yards, the riding style of amateur lady riders – or lack of it – was derided by the professionals. That was the view of both Bill Wightman and Bill Nash. And they were far from alone in that stance. Bill Wightman was adamant. 'Don't let them know you're a girl,' was his advice, or rather his instruction. He didn't want me to stand out from the male jockeys. He wanted me to avoid scrutiny and to stay out of the limelight.

I could understand his point.

Given what I'd gone through on the gallops – being whipped and riders holding on to me – I feared similar treatment on the racecourse. Camera patrols, enabling stewards to detect riding misconduct, had been introduced in 1960 (and video was used from 1966), but this assistance to officials was nowhere near as sophisticated as the technology used today.

At the course, I tried to maintain a low profile, and to blend in: to not appear as though I was there just to make some kind of feminist statement. Unlike some of today's reality TV celebrities I wasn't saying *look at me!* I went out of my way not to irritate anyone, or wind them up. I just wanted to be regarded as a talented jockey. Full stop. Not as a female jockey.

It was the same attitude that Hayley Turner, Hollie Doyle and their counterparts possess nowadays.

I was so determined not to look out of place once I made it to the racecourse that, over the preceding months, I'd made a conscious effort to 'de-feminise' myself. I was quite feminine naturally. If I went out socially, I wore dresses. But now I had altered my appearance to ensure I looked boyish and was inconspicuous among the other jockeys. I normally had quite long hair, but had cut it short; I also wore jeans and didn't use my usual face make-up or lipstick. I was like a skeleton with a bit of muscle in the right places.

My stable labours and work-riding had ensured that I now possessed the strength and stamina required to be able to ride a finish. The overall package contributed to what today would probably be described as a 'gender-neutral' look. Not, I must stress, that my transformation was quite as drastic as that of the Australian jockey Bill 'Girlie' Smith.

In Australia, women were not allowed to become licensed jockeys and race against men until 1979. Indeed, there had previously been much resistance. In 1971, a senior racing journalist had written that, 'Mixed races in which women compete against men are out.' Suggesting that he had no objection to women riding in races 'now and then', he added that, 'To begin with, such races ... should be placed last on the card so that those racegoers not interested can return home for tea and *The Magic Roundabout*.'

That didn't deter a woman from a small country town in far north Queensland, who, at an early age, decided she wasn't going to let gender impede her from following her passion. So, Bill – real name Wilhemena Smith – secretly lived her life as a man to pursue her dream. Astonishingly, she disguised her identity so well that no one knew she was a woman until she died in 1975. This was four years before women such as Pam O'Neill and Linda Jones went down in Australian history as the first registered female jockeys to ride against men.

Returning to my first racecourse ride, Bill accompanied me to the weighing room when I arrived at Newbury. This is the hub of a racecourse in which, as the name suggests, jockeys are weighed out before races and in again afterwards, together with their saddles. It leads through to the changing room.

My introduction to this inner sanctum was rather a shock, and for a second or two, all rather embarrassing. Bill just thrust me into the changing room full of men, pointed out a chap clad in an apron and said, 'There's your valet to dress you and look after you.'

Valets – said with a hard 't' – look after jockeys inside the weighing room, making sure they wear the right silks, weigh out correctly, have clean boots, breeches and goggles and generally ensure all the jockeys have to think about is riding. My valet was a man. Ridiculous really, but for some reason I had no idea I'd be in a changing room with all the men. I had assumed there'd be a women's changing area.

What it meant was that, suddenly, here I was, a young woman, in the company of some man I'd never even met before who was dressing me, even to the extent of helping me don my breeches and silks. It was also a hell of a job to get your tight, light boots on. I can't think of any other occupation where such a seemingly unacceptable situation would exist. Yet, I readily accepted it. I didn't actually want to appear any different, didn't – in Bill's words – want to let on I was a girl. I had to be inconspicuous in the weighing room. I tried my best not to look out of place, and to become one of them, just another apprentice jockey.

I endeavoured to ignore everything around me and concentrate on the race ahead. Fortunately, my presence didn't seem to faze my valet. He took it in his stride and was the complete professional. He did his best for me. He wanted me to feel at ease, and appreciated instinctively that I didn't want people to notice me. He really tried to make everything normal for me.

Fortunately, most of the male jockeys, possibly preoccupied with their own preparations, didn't appear to even realise there was a female in their midst. But then, with my figure all but disappeared, in many respects I would have resembled the boys. Even when I was in the paddock and had mounted my horse, few would have noticed I was a girl; not my fellow riders, nor the racegoers. So, when Bill Wightman gave me my first race, the majority present were oblivious to my gender before, during and after the race, and thought that 'K. Wiltshire' was a male jockey they'd never come across before. Among the few exceptions were my parents and Uncle John, always a supporter.

There's a photo of me striding out to the paddock for my first ride included in this book. I look like a boy, and my expression is one of deadly seriousness. I was determined to be just like the male jockeys and be businesslike – just like those riders I had watched all those years before on my day out with friends at Newbury. It was a novel, and not that pleasant, experience as I walked out to the paddock. My silks clung to my body, emaciated after sweating off pounds. I felt naked. There were no body protectors like today.

I conducted myself courteously as I was introduced by Bill Wightman to the owners in the paddock, told them what I knew about their horse and how he had worked. It was far more formal in those days than it is now. Bill was very hot on protocol.

But my preoccupation was ensuring I adhered to Bill's stable law; you must follow orders, whatever happens in the race. If you do that, you will get another ride. What Bill said, went; you followed his orders to the letter at the stables and the racecourse, or you got a major admonishment, or were out.

That was always in my mind. I was obsessive about it. From that day on, I lived in the constant fear that I wouldn't get another ride. Park Walk was a strong horse. I was aware that this four-year-old gelding was still a maiden (yet to win a race). His best runs had been third and fourth placings the previous season. This was his second run of this season and he still wasn't fully fit.

Bill was insistent that I shouldn't allow Park Walk to run away with me. The guv'nor told me, 'When he leaves the stalls, he's going to pull strongly. Hold him up and don't let him run free.'

Frankly, it was tough enough just getting my mount down to the stalls. It was an afternoon of torrential rain and wind and Park Walk had sweated up. I remember my reins felt as though they were slipping through my fingers on the way to the start.

I experienced such a myriad of feelings. I was so hyped up. That's what gets you addicted; why some jockeys, when they stop racing, can't cope with it. High-energy activity produces endorphins, which interact with the receptors in your brain that reduce your perception of pain and also trigger a positive feeling in the body, rather like a drug.

But what of the fear of being astride a half-ton mount moving at a breakneck (what an appropriate word!) speed in close company with several rivals? No, I never felt apprehension because I was used to it; first galloping my horse at home, and later work-riding. I loved speed. Was absolutely addicted to it. There would only be one occasion when I harboured some trepidation and that was riding Epsom and keeping a horse balanced around Tattenham Corner and into the cambered straight. But that is a subject to which I'll return later.

Of course, you're excited. But that exhilaration is tempered by being under pressure. Your reactions have to be so quick. In an instant the nature of the race can change. I'm convinced riders took more risks in my day because camera patrol scrutiny was then more limited.

Most crucially, you must keep your cool. You have the trainer there, watching you throughout and, if he's not there, the travelling head lad. But you can't let that take away the pleasure.

The only aspect that caused any stress, and would continue to do so, was remembering my orders. Orders. Orders. Must remember my orders. The phrase went over and over in my mind.

As for my debut, it was all over in an instant – or seemingly so. Somehow I managed to restrain Park Walk early on, but made some progress before fading late on to finish eighth of nine. He was not expected to be in the frame, and wasn't.

The comment in the *Sporting Life* newspaper was 'behind final 2 furlongs, tailed off'.

I never expected more. This was real life. Not fantasy.

Only afterwards did I realise what energy is required to partner a horse in a race. As I dismounted, I could hardly stand up. My limbs were like jelly. I spoke earlier about what was required to be racing fit. In truth, you don't get truly racing fit without racing. For that, you need rides. You need to be able to change hands, go up a gear and ride a finish, which doesn't happen on the gallops. There, the horses are not galloping at their optimum speed.

But I had done it. Bill had kept his word. I had given a defiant response to all the boys' scornful pronouncements of: 'Oh, you'll never get a ride.' And I hadn't revealed myself to anyone – apart from my valet and maybe rival jockeys – as a girl.

Bill congratulated me. Not profusely, but sufficient to reassure me. Thinking back, I believe that first race was a test by Bill. A test of my strength and my ability to restrain a strong-pulling horse, as well as my riding style and whether I'd ride to orders. Certainly, my performance was proficient enough for him to give me another ride around three weeks later.

When I was listed for my next race, the 1-mile Railway Apprentices' Handicap at Sandown, again as 'K. Wiltshire', I had to smile when I noticed that the tipping advice in *The Sun* pronounced that my mount, The Goldstone, 'likes this course and goes well for a boy'. I could live with it being assumed I was 'a boy' – for the moment.

The Goldstone was a grand servant to Bill. He was rightly described as 'genuine' by *Timeform* (the highly respected ratings and comment aid for punters on the running of horses, established by Phil Bull in 1948) and was a handsome, strong chestnut gelding, a very decent handicapper who had already enjoyed his fair share of victories. He was a miler or 7-furlong horse, and acted on any going.

He had first won in 1974 as a two-year-old and had subsequently succeeded under Edward Hide, Geoff Baxter and Pat Eddery. The Goldstone had also won a ladies' race – at Goodwood in 1976, partnered by the amateur Joy Penn. His owner was Sue Pakenham. As I mentioned early on, Sue was the daughter of Philip William Bryce Lever, 3rd Viscount Leverhulme.

The Queen's Silver Jubilee was celebrated that day (rather appropriately it was a year she also enjoyed great success as a racehorse owner – her filly Dunfermline, trained by Major Dick Hern, claiming a Classic double, the Oaks and St Leger) and, apart from more than one million people thronging the streets of London to view the royal family on their way to St Paul's at the start of the celebrations, many people stayed at home to watch the event on TV. However, thousands took the opportunity to pack the Surrey racecourse. The atmosphere made it a heady experience.

I remember Lester Piggott, observing me in my silks and breeches, commenting, 'I didn't know there was a ladies' race on the programme.' I replied, 'No, nor did I.' In the presence of one of racing's legends, such a smart comeback may have been rather impudent. But his attitude summed up the commonly held view at the time: women race-riding was a completely separate entity to the world of male professionals.

The Goldstone didn't go unbacked, starting 7-2 second favourite. For some reason, as we exited the stalls, the normally sure-footed Goldie stumbled, lost his footing, went right down, and I was nearly catapulted over the top of him. He recovered and was soon back in stride, but we lost a length or two. I was just relieved we didn't end up together in a heap on the ground.

We were third entering the straight, and held on to that in the six-runner field, 13 lengths behind the favourite, named Paddy's Luck.

All of a sudden, I felt that I was starting to achieve something – and not just my ten per cent of my horse's place winnings (of £116.50!) on top of my riding fee. Just two days later, I was back at Newbury to contest the Polar Jest Apprentice Handicap on a horse named Guffaw. Not that it was a laughing matter to get down to 6st 13lb to ride him.

To explain, my mount was allotted a weight of 7st 7lb, less my claim for never having ridden a winner of 3lb. That meant 7st 4lb. From that could be deducted another 5lb to allow for the saddle. This was the first, but by no means the last, occasion that weight was a serious issue.

Trying to keep your energy levels up when you've been starving yourself and dehydrating is no simple matter. There were no protein bars then. At around 7½ stone, I was fine to ride work on the yearlings, but I knew that now I could be asked to do weights of 7st or less on the racecourse.

Losing pounds when you have excess fat is one thing. Doing so when you're down to muscle is not so straightforward – as I will detail later. I was aware when I first approached Bill that he needed a lightweight jockey. Whatever his regard for my riding talents, if I was unable to make low weights, I wouldn't have a job.

The relative strengths of men and women had long been debated, but the feeling in physiological quarters was that at ultra-low riding weights, any difference between the sexes was not significant. An article in *The Times* in 1977, regarding the relative strength of men and women, suggested that the difference was narrowing in track athletics, swimming and cycling, due to improvements in the standard of training for women – although men's superiority because of greater average proportion of muscle to total body weight meant the gap was unlikely to close completely.

Significantly, in racing, however, it was believed that, although the difference in average body weight would always present a problem in mixed amateur races, it should, in theory, work out to the benefit of the girls in professional racing.

Thankfully, I made the weight on Guffaw, and we finished sixth of ten, but only beaten by about seven lengths. I felt I was making progress. If I wasn't partnering favourites, at least I was being paired with fancied runners. I sensed that I was impressing Bill sufficiently.

That said, it would be another two frustrating months before I raced again, back on The Goldstone, this time at Salisbury, in the 1-mile Netton Apprentice Handicap on 11 August. No problems this time with weight! Goldie was allotted top weight of 9st 8lb, less my claim of 6lb for not having ridden a winner.

It was a very pleasing run. Paddy's Luck (yes, him again) inched home by a neck from a horse named Galadriel, with whom I would do battle again the following season. Goldie finished third, with the *Raceform* comment: 'Headway 3 furlongs out, every chance 2 furlongs out, not quicken final furlong.' That would be my fourth and final race of 1977.

I was progressing slowly, but surely, and Bill had kept his word. I had made it on to the racecourse. I couldn't complain. Surely, it was now just a question of time before I rode that elusive victor …?

In fact, that 1977 season, one in which Bill recorded 47 winners, was an excellent one for the yard; a superb record, given the numbers he trained and that racing then had no all-weather or floodlit meetings, and no Sunday meetings. The next year, my aim was to become one of the winning statistics.

I was not to know this at the time, but progress for women had been much swifter abroad. I've already mentioned the United States, but it didn't end there. By 1978, Eileen McGuffey had ridden over 50 winners as a professional in Canada. She came over here to ride for the Classic-winning jockey-turned-trainer Duncan Keith.

Clearly, the UK had a long way to go.

Chapter 16

A Romantic Entanglement

SUMMER 1977, and for months I'd lived an almost monastic life. No doubt the nuns of my schooldays would have approved.

Work, sweat, work, ride, sleep: that was my routine. No time for vices. And certainly no time for socialising – until one evening in August my cousin Mandy insisted that I *must* attend her party, to celebrate her 16th. She was desperate to get me away from racing, if only for a night.

'You're mad to carry on like this,' she admonished me. 'You really must get out more.'

Like everyone else I came into contact with outside racing, she simply didn't understand. 'I love every moment of it,' I explained, partly truthfully. 'Nothing else could give me the excitement I felt when I rode The Goldstone to third place a couple of days ago after all that work, training and riding. I felt fantastic.'

I didn't add that Bill Wightman had praised me highly afterwards, a rare event for anyone at Ower Farm. I knew I'd performed well. I was high on confidence and, when that happens, you're like a junkie – you're hooked. You cannot wait for your next fix.

Throughout my first months at Bill's, I was very definitely single and a relationship was not on my agenda. Not a chance. The only partner I was interested in was my next racecourse mount. The only date, that of my next race.

It was probably just about the worst time to fall in love. Possibly it was my unusually high spirits about life in general that allowed me to be persuaded to go to the party – if only to show my face for a couple of hours. It would demonstrate I hadn't completely disappeared from society and was able to still mix with other 'normal' young people – not that I felt much like an attractive young woman who would turn heads. Possibly there was an added incentive in that Mandy, daughter of my great supporter Uncle John, lived at Forest Lodge, a magnificent country house that had a good-sized swimming pool.

It had been ages since I'd walked into a party atmosphere, hearing pop music blaring, shouts and laughter. I felt slightly like an alien intruder. I certainly couldn't enjoy the sumptuous food, or drink alcohol. Surveying the spread enviously, I was munching on a stick of celery when my eye caught that of a handsome stranger. He reminded me a little of Robert Redford. Yes, I know. It's a cliché, but it happens to be true!

That said, I didn't quite see myself as Mia Farrow's Daisy Buchanan to Redford's eponymous character in *The Great Gatsby*, and I assumed he'd be attached, anyway. Also, what my life definitely didn't need at that precise moment was a romantic entanglement.

But we got chatting. His name was Mike Burras, a friend of Julian, who was a close family friend of Mandy's. I soon learned he was a few years older than me and about to start the last year of a degree in civil engineering. Mike had a summer job in the New Forest and he knew nothing about racing or horses. Later, he asked what I did for a living.

'I'm a jockey,' I replied matter-of-factly. He did a double-take. He'd never met a jockey before, let alone a woman jockey. Perhaps – in view of the eventual upshot – he didn't appreciate quite how absorbed I was in my career, although when I explained more he appeared quite impressed.

Mike suggested we went for a swim. By now it was 1am, and I didn't have a swimsuit. Mike offered to drive me home in his Maserati to get one (having initially been impressed, I discovered his car was actually a battered Mini Estate).

My mother was still up, and clearly unable to believe her eyes, that I was here *with a man*, and a seemingly eligible one at that. Was her daughter actually enjoying herself? And with a human rather than an equine partner?

Before the night was out, Mike had invited me to another party the following week. I agreed, but emphasised that because of my dedication, I could never be a regular party-goer, despite my love of dancing. The lifestyle of Mike and his friends – parties, meals out, dances, drinking and late nights – was clearly not something I could contemplate enjoying on a regular basis. But my feelings for him tended to persuade me that I could cope with such a social whirl.

And so, we started going out. He was my first serious boyfriend. In one sense, it was good for me to have met a man who could put my life in perspective, someone who could converse about subjects outside the realms of *Sporting Life* coverage, but from the start it created conflicts for me. Mike was very gregarious and loved socialising. He was constantly inviting me to parties – but that meant a continual battle with temptation during a time, as they say, of sex, drugs and rock 'n' roll, a time when anything went. He enjoyed a lifestyle that was simply not conducive to my life as an aspiring professional jockey. It also meant I was out of synchronisation with everyone. On my social travels with Mike, I never met anyone else who had to get up at 6am, or earlier, seven days a week. I never met anyone who knew anything about horseracing. So, I was constantly retelling my story and, though flattering in a sense, it would have been easier to have just invested in a tape recorder and switched it on each time I was asked.

As for a relationship at this time, my career came first and I had no intention of getting seriously involved with even the most eligible man, which – on the surface – he was. But for a lot of men, a woman playing it cool and keeping her distance is a challenge that cannot be ignored. Mike was one of those men. Perhaps he was attracted to because I wasn't like all the others. Whatever it was he saw in me, it was clear that, from early on, Mike regarded me as marriage material. That was far from ideal.

I attempted to strike a balance between my developing romance with Mike and my everyday labour of love at the stables, and it wasn't easy. I simply could not afford to be suffering from a hangover, or fatigue from a late night. It was a psychological tug of war between two worlds, and it created nervous tension, which was exhausting.

Naturally, I'd be asleep at 9pm, but at least three nights a week I'd force myself to stay awake when Mike and I socialised. I needed strong coffee as a stimulant and plenty of sugar to keep me going. By 10.30, I could stay awake no longer. Mike wasn't happy and occasionally there were arguments between us. I couldn't blame him. What kind of girlfriend was I? I have to admit I was very keen on Mike and didn't want to lose him, so I agreed to go to an occasional party even when dropping with fatigue, often meaning I had only a few hours' sleep.

This was incompatible with my responsibilities at the stables, which now included helping to break in the new bunch of yearlings that had arrived. Now I was expected to be involved in the procedure right from the start. This was even more perilous than merely riding them – which explains why I hadn't been involved in my early weeks at the yard.

The process started in one of the loose boxes, a short walk across from Bill's house. They were roughly 12sq ft. Each yearling was introduced to a bridle, firstly without a bit and then a mouthing bit, the equivalent of a baby's dummy, to keep the horse happy.

As I described in Chapter 10, the yearling would first be walked around in a circle on a lunging rein, being all the while quietly encouraged, before some heavy sacking would be laid across him – so they became accustomed to a weight on their back. Then a saddle was added. We riders would then lean over the saddle while the horse was being held. All this required extraordinary patience and could take four or five days. Finally, we'd gradually put one leg over before we could properly sit in the saddle.

A human weight was a different matter for the horse – the aim of his game was to have the unfortunate rider on the floor as soon as possible. This I discovered when Bill Nash instructed me to lie across the back of one. I had walked in very calmly and, without making any sudden move, leaned over the horse's back, head down and eyes closed. So far, so good. I thought I had succeeded. Not a chance. He reacted violently to having something new – 7st-plus of me – on his bare back and kicked out, squealing his fury. I rolled on the floor before expeditiously exiting the loose box, doing my best to avoid the flying hooves.

There was nothing for it but to go back for more and repeat the procedure until I was able, very slowly and carefully, to slide one of my legs over the yearling's back and assume a precarious sitting position. The battle was not yet won, though. Despite my determination to assume control, I found myself on the floor once more.

As can be imagined, it can take days before the apprentice jockey can sit quietly on a horse's back while he is led round the box. Indeed, it could require another four or five days, depending on how the horse progressed. Finally, we would walk around the box mounted but without any other person present. At that stage your charge is adjudged by the head lad ready to enter the schooling ring – the previously described 'bull ring', the area surrounded by high straw bales. The horse in question may not share the head lad's opinion, of course. Yearlings still have as their prime motivation to get the jockey off as often as possible.

The yearling would have already been introduced to the bull ring on a lunging rein, but without being ridden. Now, we would follow an older, experienced, 'lead horse' into the arena. We would follow the lead horse around for the first day and then enter the bull ring without any other horse. First, we'd walk, then trot, and then canter around it.

In theory, once you give a horse confidence, you'll do anything with him. In reality, that's not necessarily the case. Irritated by the restriction of being introduced into the ring on the lunging rein, the youngster may be bucking and leaping and try to leap the bales despite their height. I had watched my friend Richard Newman in the bull ring during my early weeks and seen him being flung around mercilessly.

I suspect our contingent of yearlings behaved worse because Bill Nash made sure they were 'oated up' (had a high proportion of oat content in their feed). It gives them extra energy but also an increased tendency to become over-excited.

By January, last autumn's contingent should have all been broken. You'd be out of the bull ring, and the yearlings, who were by now two-year-olds (as I've mentioned, all racehorses become a year older on 1 January) would start out on the roads and then progress to cantering. It became no safer. In icy conditions, they could slip up or rear, falling over. Not until February would they start the more serious aspect of galloping. As can be imagined, this passage from raw yearling to race-ready two-year-old was pitted with hazards. People don't appreciate just how dangerous work-riding young horses can be, and what it takes to bring one to the racecourse.

So, it was especially important that my senses were alive and sharp. I had to be sensitive to each muscle twitch if I was to avoid suffering regular falls. The yearlings were like bucking broncos, and anyone lacking total concentration could expect to find themselves tossed aside like a rag doll. I was so looking forward to the 1978 Flat season and didn't want any injury to derail my career. Also, if I was tired, it would be obvious to the guv'nor and Head Lad. That meant I had to be fully alert and undistracted by other events, particularly social and romantic ones.

Chapter 17

A Marriage Proposal out of the Blue

CHRISTMAS 1977 and, as the New Year approached, Mike invited me to stay with his relations in Aberdeen for Hogmanay. Bill Wightman agreed to my having a week away. They would be my first full days off, apart from Christmas and Boxing Day, in 14 months. How my exhausted body needed that break.

We travelled there in Mike's £45 Mini Estate and first toured the Highlands. What a blessed relief. No onerous routine; no being told to 'hurry girl' by Bill Nash; no being thrown by assorted yearlings. I enjoyed the sense of freedom, which would be all but brief.

As I was driving from Ullapool in the Highlands to Aberdeen on a snow-covered route, I went to turn into a layby on the opposite side of the road, only for Mike's car to be struck broadsides by an overtaking sports car.

Our Mini was a write-off but somehow we survived with just bumps and bruises. Mike was amazed at my coolness at dealing with what could have been a very nasty incident. I explained it wasn't that different from dealing with a fractious yearling. Stay in control, assess the situation, brush yourself down, and start all over again. No time for tears or hysterics. I think he believed me.

We completed the journey by train. Settling into our seats, Mike told me he loved me. 'That's a strange thing to say when I've just written off your car!' I replied.

A romantic, Mike said he didn't care about the car. What he did care about, he said, suddenly staring into my eyes, was what I'd think about being Mrs Burras. I was speechless for a while, and finally said, 'I think I'd like the idea.' Even as I said it, a voice in my head warned me to tread warily. There was never any suggestion from Mike that I should give up my career. But the thought persisted: would our respective lives be compatible?

I didn't want to jeopardise my relationship with Mike, so I went along with it. However, I was not completely committed to the concept. As I discussed earlier, I had signed an absurdly outmoded apprentice contract which, amongst other things, stipulated that I couldn't get engaged without my trainer's permission.

In the circumstances, I decided not to make our engagement public, at least not immediately. I couldn't be sure of Bill's reaction if he thought my mind was on other matters, such as wedding arrangements. Would he continue to give me rides? I didn't want it to jeopardise my chances. Bill had to be sure that I was dedicated. On no account did I want him to think that I might be getting married.

It was another example of inequality of the sexes, of course. Would he have been concerned if one of his male apprentices had become engaged? Of course not, but this was the 1970s.

Mike assumed I'd be delighted that we were getting married, and he began talking about fixing a date. I went into delay mode, and replied, 'I can't think about that at the moment.'

With no wedding date fixed, I saw it as no threat to my career. I could look ahead to 1978 with great optimism.

Chapter 18

My Week of Wasting Hell

I HAD put on weight through the winter. No doubt about it. That was the consequence, in part, of a week of substantial Scottish cooking throughout New Year, and later indulging myself on a February break in Barbados with my parents.

Now, as can be imagined, that destination confirmed to the boys at the yard everything they thought about me: how the 'posh, spoilt bird' from Hambledon was spending her winter in the Caribbean. I should stress that for business reasons, my father and mother always took their holidays around that time. I wasn't going to turn down their invitation to join them – not least because I felt I'd earned it.

I was enjoying blue skies, warm seas and the popular rum-based banana daiquiris; a drink introduced to me in a bar by professional jockey Shaun Salmon and Willie Higgins, an apprentice, both from the UK. Shaun had been a top apprentice with Bill Elsey and had made an immediate impact on the racing scene in 1974 when riding 37 winners in his first season. But after losing his claim – the weight advantage given to apprentices – he had found it more difficult to get good rides as he had to stand comparison with experienced riders, some of whom were popular, household names – the likes of Piggott, Carson and Eddery. Many jockeys fell by the wayside at this point, particularly then, when there were far fewer opportunities than now.

Along with other British jockeys, Shaun and Willie were riding in Barbados then, because it was the close season for Flat racing during the British winter. They showed me around the Barbados Turf Club track at Garrison Savannah. Their companion was a Barbadian trainer. He looked at me in disgust when I said I was also a jockey, and had had four rides last season, with hopefully many more to come. 'We wouldn't even allow women to work as grooms in our stables,' he growled sneeringly. 'Racing is a world for strong men, not women.'

I told him in no uncertain terms that I found this a strange attitude considering how close he was to the US, where women jockeys were increasingly finding success. Maybe the intake of daiquiri loosened my inhibitions, but part of me felt like demonstrating to him that women jockeys were far from being demure little ladies. I resisted the temptation.

On our last night, I bade Shaun and Willie farewell with the words: 'See you on the racecourse.' This caused both of them great mirth. As *if* they'd meet me again on the track, they were obviously thinking. I was aware that there was a view in some quarters that Bill Wightman had given me a few mounts, and I'd had my bit of fun. But that was it. They didn't want me competing against them. That summed up the attitude of many male jockeys and those lads at the yard, like the previously mentioned Jack.

Back home, my intake of alcohol and a return to a normal diet in Barbados had, worryingly, caused the scales to touch an ominous 8st. Returning to the yard, I set to work building solid muscle steadily through a combination of the heavy workload, breaking in and riding the yearlings in their early work, and dieting. At the end of each day, I was always exhausted and frequently cold, wet and muddy.

I could happily have feasted on a meal sufficient for two grown men, but had to focus on a sensible diet. I had let myself go, and I knew I had to deal with this. By the start of the 1978 Flat season in March, with sensible dieting, I was down to a more acceptable 7st 8lb.

That was my weight when Bill Wightman approached me one morning in mid-April, and said: 'Karen, I may have a ride for you next week, on Sweet Caress.'

My spirits soared – until he added, with a wary glance at my heavily muscled thighs, 'Can you do 6st 13lb?' He added quickly, 'See what you can get down to. If I decide not to run Sweet Caress, you'll be right for Trojan's Centenary at Chepstow. It's about the same weight for both races.'

That meant 6st 10lb, taking into account even the lightest (3lb) saddle. I didn't betray my concern to Bill, but inwardly I was in panic mode. This wasn't easy-to-shed flab but primarily solid muscle, particularly around my shoulders and top of the arms, which I'd built up over months and was continuing to develop with my stable workload. It meant losing the best part of a stone in seven days – from a body that had very little more to give.

It was to become one of the worst weeks I've experienced, ever. Down the years, down the centuries, 'making a weight' has been a perennial curse for jockeys; causing not just physical health problems but mental ones. Wasting brought about the early deaths of a number of Victorian riders, including Fred Archer who stood 5ft 10in and whose natural weight was 11st. Regarded as the greatest jockey of all time, his 2,748 winners – including five Derby victories – were accumulated from 8,084 mounts. His was a story of triumph, but ultimate tragedy. He committed suicide before he was 30.

Fred Archer had been riding in Ireland at 9st 4lb, but was asked if he could do 8st 6lb in the Cambridgeshire – a reduction of 12lb in less than a week. He achieved this by not eating at all for three days, taking doses of a purgative and confining himself to a Turkish bath. He failed to make the weight by a pound, and his mount lost by a head. He blamed himself. A few days later, he was found to be suffering from typhoid fever. It was also the second anniversary of his wife's death in childbirth. The same afternoon, despite attempts by his sister to disarm him, he shot himself with a revolver, a victim of illness, depression and wasting.

Duncan Keith, mentioned earlier, quit in 1972 as No.1 jockey to the powerful Peter Walwyn yard in Lambourn, finally yielding to defeat in the battle of the scales. He was left with a thyroid gland that didn't function and a form of diabetes because of misuse of pills designed to get rid of body fluid. His life was dominated by pills and the sauna. He had undergone 13 years of sweating it out in saunas for three or four hours a day.

There were many highly unorthodox weight-loss practices. According to a turf historian of the early 1880s, numerous jockeys would 'subject themselves to the debilitating heat, fumes and steam immersed in a stable dung-hill for several hours'.

While successfully 'making a weight' can be regarded as an attribute, demonstrating competence and a disciplined approach to your sport and your life, I was acutely aware that there were also significant health implications – psychological as well as physical. Stress fractures were more likely after falls; regular dehydration can also affect the kidneys and apparently cause high blood pressure, something I've suffered from since my early 30s.

In addition, there has always tended to be a greater incidence of smoking and higher alcohol consumption among jockeys. Long periods of fasting can also have a detrimental effect on mental health, leading to depression, confusion and tension.

Steve Cauthen, who rode a stone under his natural weight, exhibited bulimic behaviour. Walter Swinburn, whom I would compete against, eventually quit the saddle because of bulimia, an eating disorder and mental health condition. Steve Cauthen, who rode a stone under his natural weight, has also admitted to being bulimic at times. Today jockeys receive sophisticated nutritional advice and also weights are higher. Not back then. We were instructed to shed weight quickly, and the means was left up to you.

So, I began serious calorie-counting.

My breakfast was cut down to 4oz of dried prunes (128 calories) and a cup of tea (13 calories). My lunch was supposed to be one Ryvita (55 calories), but craving more I had two Ryvitas and an apple (95 calories) and a cup of tea on the first day – a total of 218 calories. My only indulgence was a small grilled steak (160 calories) plus a lettuce leaf (10 calories) once I got home. (All figures are approximate.)

My dietary regime was accompanied by increased exercise. At lunchtime, when I might have been having a brief nap, reluctantly I donned my waterproof jacket and trousers to help me sweat, and pounded the country lanes around my home for an hour. I continued to wear my waterproofs at the stables.

There was no rest for a weight-loss warrior. The evening was spent at a local sauna, where I'd relax and count how many calories I'd consumed in total – 529. I felt pretty chuffed with myself until the scales the following morning revealed the unpalatable fact – I'd lost a mere 2lb. It didn't seem much for my efforts and already I craved food and drink.

I emptied my cup of tea as though I'd come across an oasis after three dry days. The dried prunes that I normally loathed tasted delicious. That week, my days passed in a blur of hard work, with my mind dominated by food and drink. Still clad in my waterproofs, I sweated until my throat burned. But I couldn't drink. How I envied the horses as they drained buckets of water.

On the third day, my nearest sauna being designated 'men only' for the evening, I headed for one further afield. I had no idea how much time you should spend there, and I settled down for a really long session to lose weight faster. I appeared to be the sole client that evening.

Saunas are still a familiar locale for jockeys as they bid to make weights. But few would have undergone what I went through that night. There was no way of checking the time, or knowing how long I'd been there as a I sat in the sauna, counting calories and dreaming of relaxing under a clear cold waterfall and consuming an enormous meal.

The temperature increased. Higher and higher. But I told myself I had to stick it out. Still hotter and hotter … I knew I had to shed every ounce in sweat – but how much more could I take? I vaguely thought: 'Where is everyone?'

I laughed to myself: 'You could die here and no one would know.' But still I stayed, as it became hotter and hotter. I didn't even know how long I'd been there. Ten minutes? Half an hour?

I started to doze off. The walls became blurred. I realised I wasn't dozing off, but gradually losing consciousness. I knew it was time to get out. If I didn't, no one would find me if I passed out. I was delirious, but knew this wasn't right. Semi-conscious, I managed to stagger dizzily to the door, fell out of it and collapsed on to the bench outside. Normality slowly returned, though it took nearly an hour before I felt fit enough to drive home.

I discovered that the temperature was at maximum. I should have adjusted it to suit myself, although why the proprietors didn't check on me, I shall never know. I'd been in there for well over two hours.

After that, I built up my sauna time gradually from half an hour to an hour and a half during the week, but this wasn't good for me. I was becoming dehydrated and I was concerned that I could be causing myself kidney damage.

This existence was absurd. I knew that. I'd had no promise that, even if I lost the weight, Bill would declare Sweet Caress for the race; he hadn't made up his mind about her fitness. If Sweet Caress didn't run, I would ride Trojan's Centenary at Chepstow. For that, I'd need to get down to *only* 6st 12lb. It may not sound much but those few pounds represented an extra day or two of almost total starvation and dehydration.

For the not-yet-confirmed ride on Sweet Caress I felt like I was slowly killing myself. Starvation and hard work – that had been my routine, and not without consequences. I knew that wasting was causing me serious health problems. I'd feel so weak, but more crucially, I was becoming anorexic.

The word was not in such common parlance then, but it means your body stops functioning properly. For a woman, it can mean you stop having periods. They may never come back, so it means that you can't have children. I had that in my mind. Also, women are more likely to become anaemic when dehydrating so I was always concerned about retaining my iron levels and took iron tablets.

And who knows about the possible strains on the heart?

Yes, it worried me. But the overriding drive was my desire to ride a winner. As I emphasised earlier, I was realistic enough to know my value to Bill was as a lightweight jockey. Yes, I was a talented horse rider. But that wasn't sufficient. 'Lightweight' was the crucial word – this was where I could compete with the male jockeys. Bill needed lightweights because he had horses running at low weights and there were only a limited number of lightweight men around at the time. I knew that if I didn't keep my weight down, I would not be considered.

How I suffered for it. You feel weak physically; there are no energy reserves. I also had difficulty concentrating and occasionally felt dizzy. Richard Newman still recalls how I used to come in complaining that I felt so weak because of all the wasting. You see, there comes a point when you have no more weight to lose – without making yourself seriously ill. If you haven't got a pound to lose, it's hard to lose weight. But mentally also, it really does affect you. You get more stressed out. You get moody. You're in turmoil. You can't concentrate. You get quite depressed with it, and it wasn't helped by the fact that you didn't know when your next ride would be.

Today there is much emphasis on mental health, and support mechanisms, but not then. You had to cope – male or female.

Dehydrating was an effective way to lose weight quickly and I went to extremes to lose pounds. But not as far as some. I would never have considered taking cocaine but was aware that it was a method other jockeys had adopted in Newmarket and Lambourn. Our yard – to my knowledge – was drug free.

As I've said previously, you become addicted to your sport. I needed, desperately needed, a race to look forward to, the sound of Bill Wightman saying quietly: 'I have a ride for you, Karen …' It's poetry to your ears – your reward for all the sacrifices.

Others could see the lengths I was going to in order to get that ride, and the effects it was having on me. Bill Nash confided: 'Now, Blossom [he called me this with affection, not condescension], you don't look well. Nothing is worth making yourself ill for, and these horses, they aren't winners, you know. They may be in the future, but for the moment, they're out for fitness and to gain experience. Even when you've lost the weight you aren't going to win these races.'

He was right, of course. Every word the head lad said was true. But it was all very well for Bill Nash to say that. For my career, I did have to neglect my health. Bill Wightman had made it absolutely clear at the interview that he wanted a lightweight jockey. I knew that was my value to him. I knew I'd have to do everything I possibly could to lose weight, even half-killing myself. I had to do it, otherwise I wouldn't even get on the racecourse. I regarded myself as lucky to have this opportunity. But no one would do me any favours.

As the pounds dropped away each day, a strange thing happened. My initial hunger left me. And all of a sudden, I didn't want to eat. In hindsight, this was a highly dangerous state of affairs. But in truth, I was beginning to feel that my entire career would end if I ate anything at all. Food was a threat to my future. I lost interest in it. Lack of food and drink plus considerable exercise made me feel sick. The mere thought of food made me nauseous. I went around like a zombie. But such a lifestyle (if that is the correct word) means you can't think straight. You can't concentrate. That's when it becomes hazardous to life and limb.

Indeed, that period has made me ultra-cautious to this day. The irony is that now if I put on weight, I can lose it quickly. However, I am still wary about not eating. That was the lasting effect it all had on me.

By the end of that week, I was having one cup of tea a day as my total liquid intake. I was grooming and mucking out in my waterproofs over thermals and in the sauna in the evenings I sweated more. I subjected myself to severe dehydration to the point where my throat felt as if it was on fire. I also felt so weak, with extremely low energy levels. I began to suffer severe, migraine-like, headaches. The only positive aspect of that was that I vomited without forcing myself (and there would be times when I was so desperate, I *did* force myself).

I consulted my GP for additional help with weight loss. He prescribed me diuretics (known as 'water' tablets) but told me not to take them unless absolutely necessary. They cause further water loss by increasing urination. I didn't use them because I feared that as soon as I mounted for work or a race, I'd need to rush to the loo. Many jockeys depended on diuretics, and continued to do so until they were banned in 1999 because of possible side effects: severe stomach cramps, nausea, weakness and disorientation, which could lessen a rider's concentration.

Some jockeys chose alcohol instead of food to restrict their calories, although that may explain why some of my contemporaries ended up with a drinking problem. As I've said, I drank very rarely – only occasionally at parties. I believe by limiting your drink at a young age you protect yourself from problems in the future.

By the Saturday before the race I was scheduled provisionally to ride in, I was so obsessed with my weight that the early morning appointment with my scales became a vital feature of my day. My mother, increasingly concerned about my state, did her best to make me eat something, drink something. She'd boil me an egg, grill me a small steak. But I had no desire to eat, and that upset her more.

The Sunday was the worst. I worked, and jogged, and starved all day and sauna-ed to lose the final 2lb. By Monday morning, I was 6st 11lb. I had lost 11lb in a week, and still needed to lose another 1lb. Early on Monday, I studied my drawn, lined face in the bathroom mirror. The haunted features that stared back at me showed no satisfaction; not even relief in that achievement. I'd set myself a target and done virtually what I'd set out to do. But now I felt nothing. I dressed and headed for the stables.

Bill Wightman approached me as I groomed my second horse of the morning. 'Sweet Caress has been withdrawn, Karen, so you'll ride Trojan Centenary at Chepstow on Tuesday. The weights have gone up, so you'll now be carrying 8st 1lb [7st 10lb with my 5lb allowance for not having ridden a winner].'

Bill added, perhaps attempting to assuage my disappointment: 'It doesn't matter that you've lost too much weight. I didn't phone you on Saturday because I wanted to see how much you could get down to. If you keep down to this weight, you'll stand the chance of a lot more rides.'

His tone was encouraging, and I appreciated that. But inside I was so angry, I could have shot myself. Why couldn't I have at least known on Saturday night and not put myself through that dreadful, destructive Sunday?

So, I prepared for that first ride of 1978 with my excitement severely diminished by the knowledge that I had lost so much weight to ride Sweet Caress ... only to end up partnering another horse, Trojan's Centenary, at Chepstow, in the Thistle Apprentice

Handicap (for three-year-olds). He would carry nearly a stone more than the weight I had fought so hard to achieve. Yes, I could ride with a heavier saddle, but it would also mean filling the saddle cloth with lead to raise it up to the required level. In racing terms, this is 'dead' weight; not human, galvanising weight.

Many will ask the question: was Bill Wightman being unreasonable? He didn't think so. I didn't at the time, either. Now, I think, yes – as much as I appreciated him giving me a chance that other trainers wouldn't, he was taking advantage of my ferocious desire to ride. It was becoming detrimental to my health and Bill would have known that. Today, such a regime would be considered completely unacceptable. But in the 1970s, when minimum weights were lower, such working practices were not exceptional in racing.

Bill would have regarded it as a way he could justify rides for me. Yes, there were one or two others in the yard who could do relatively low weights, but few could get down readily to below 7st. He would have rationalised that he was doing everything he could to get me on the racecourse. If that meant I had to lose that weight, that's what had to be done. It dominated everything. And, as I have explained before (but it's worth repeating), Bill looked at everything through a prism of his war suffering. His view was that the body can withstand anything, endure any suffering, if there is a will to survive, and in my case, a will to ride – and win. He was aware of how much I wanted it. His attitude was 'if you really want something, you'll do anything'. That was Bill's guiding philosophy – and at the time you didn't question it.

Oh, how I wanted it. Rides – and winning rides. I knew a professional girl had still to break the collective duck in the UK. Only later did I discover there was a good reason for that.

As the Lady Jockeys' Association newsletter of late 1977 reported: 'Alas we are still without a win by a professional girl on the Flat, in spite of the successes of Joanna Morgan over the water, and of girls in other parts of the world. The professional girls have had few chances, and most on very long-price horses.

'Now ten have ridden as professionals on the Flat this season, seven as apprentices. From a total of 32 rides, there have been three thirds [two of those thirds belonged to me, incidentally!] and two fourths. Mostly they rode no-hopers, and more than half their rides started at 20-1 or longer.'

The LJA bulletin concluded: 'Sooner or later a professional girl will break through, but she will have a hard task …'

Chapter 19

The Most Embarrassing Moment of My Life

THE ICY air threatened to cut me in half as I made my way from the weighing room to the paddock to mount Trojan's Centenary. My silks clung to my body and heads turned to gaze at me as I walked in company with the male jockeys.

I heard someone, clearly thinking he was a comedian, shout: 'Hey, is that a boy with long hair?' Mike, who was there, the first occasion he had watched me race, swiftly told the enquirer: 'I should hope not – she's my fiancée.'

It didn't trouble me. In fact, as soon as I donned my silks, I'd instinctively shed my femininity and felt I was no different from the men.

I'd partnered Trojan's Centenary several times in work, and knew that this three-year-old was a very nervous mare – a characteristic she appeared to have inherited from her dam, Zugela. When she was a two-year-old, I remembered watching her bolt with her work-rider across a field. That image had remained with me. She was traffic shy and objected to having her mouth pulled about. It caused her to rear dangerously. Apart from that, she was the ideal mount. In truth, I believed she was a woman's ride, needing good hands and gentle coaxing.

Bill Wightman was uncertain about her optimum distance. At first, she was thought to be a sprinter, but he was now running her over 1 mile 2 furlongs in the hope and expectation she would prove to be more of a stayer.

I thought that Chepstow, being an undulating course and similar to the Downs on which she trained, would suit her. In the event, she ran pleasingly enough, making ground late on, and finishing in mid-field. I told the filly's owners that she had stayed on strongly towards the finish, and I suspected she would make a stayer, perhaps racing at 2 miles. My verdict would be vindicated later in the season (when she was placed at 1 mile 6 furlongs and 2 miles).

As I dismounted, I reflected wryly that, for that two-minute, 15-second experience, I had made myself ill with dieting, spent many hours in saunas, worked and jogged in oilskins and felt wretched and irritable. But I had raced, I was in my second season, and I persuaded myself this was progress.

Then as I made my way to the weighing room, Mike dashed out of the crowd, flung his arms around me and kissed me passionately. I was horrified, not least because there is a strict rule that no one must touch a jockey or the saddle before weighing in, to ensure there is no interference with the weights. Also, bearing in mind that this was the late 1970s, and attitudes were not as enlightened as they are now, it would have shocked people convinced they were watching a male jockey to see him embraced by a man in front of everyone in the unsaddling area. These were still my early days and with 'K. Wiltshire' on the board of runners and riders, and my determination to follow Bill's guidance and not to look like a girl, there would have been no obvious clue of my gender. Poor Mike. His action had been the result of sheer relief that I returned

My first ride! Aged just three, I'm lifted into the saddle by my Uncle John

On my first pony: the thoroughly unpredictable Rocket

Riding my first horse Umphy (Ambassador of Blashford) with the Hursley Hambledon Hunt. I'm pictured with my father and my friend Jilly on her grey, Flavia

Striding to the parade ring to mount Park Walk ahead of my first ride on 13 May 1977

Dismounting from The Goldstone after finishing third at Sandown Parl on Jubilee Day, 7 June 1977. It was only my second ride

Our string on the gallops, supervised by Bill Wightman (mounted) and head lad Bill Nash. I'm third from the front on Charlotte's Choice Photo credit: W. W. Rouch

Enjoying the good times with my fiancée Mike Burras at a 'Vicars and Tarts' party!

First past the post! The Goldstone storms home to give me a famous victory in the Winterbourne Handicap at Salisbury on 14 September 1978

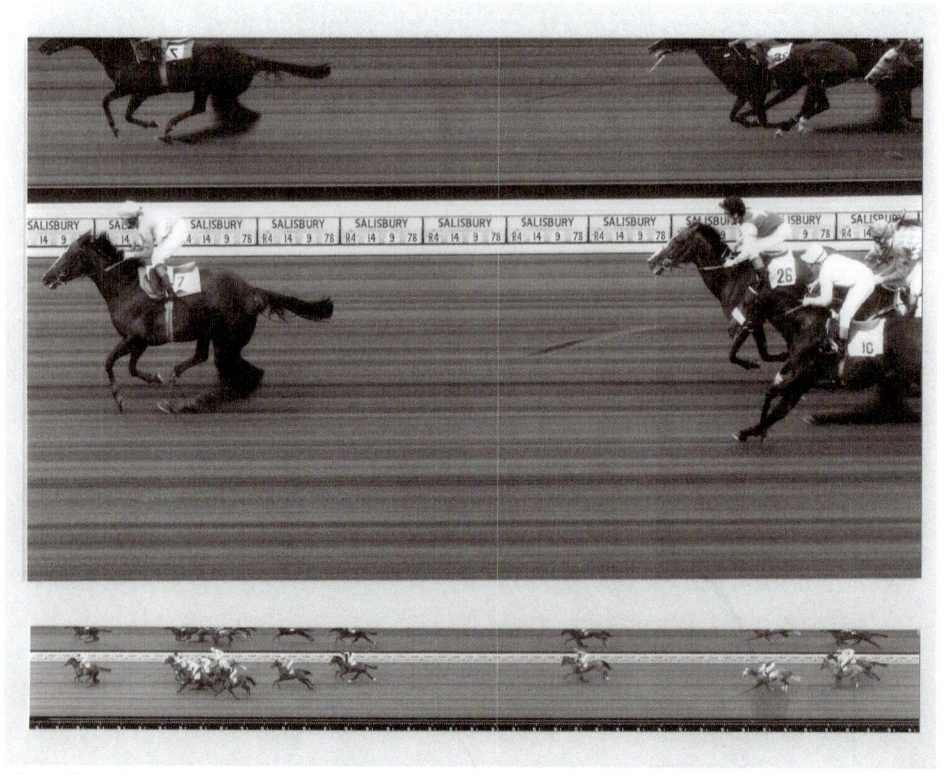

The official photo-finish print of my triumph at Salisbury – not that a photo was needed. We finished 2½ lengths clear of our rivals

The Goldstone and I are led to the winner's enclosure after our victory at Salisbury

Unsaddling The Goldstone after our Salisbury win, accompanied by Diana Roth, Bill Wightman's assistant

Talking to the press – I'm interviewed by the media after my Salisbury victory

I'm pictured with The Goldstone the day after my historic win, with his groom Laurie Bell and head lad Bill Nash (left)

At Newmarket on Cesarewitch day 1978 I receive my award for being the first British woman professional jockey to win a Flat race. Making the presentation is Joy Gibson of the Lady Jockeys' Association. Shortly afterwards she was crushed by a horse at the stables where she worked and was killed.

My mother Eileen and father Ronald relaxing in a pub the day after my wedding

My daughter Lara and I with my father on his 90th birthday in a photo taken by my mother

A humorous look at how women jockeys were perceived in the seventies! A Lady Jockeys' Association Christmas card from that time.

"I DON'T KNOW WHO WON, BUT MISS LUSHWORTHY FINISHED SECOND".

At Bill Wightman's 90th birthday celebration in 2004 – that's me, sixth from the right. Bill Wightman is the tall man at the rear, seventh from the left. In the foreground are Bill Nash (his former head lad) and Bill Anderson (Bill's former work rider who was at the stables when I was there) Photo credit: D.A. Chamberlain, Eastleigh, Hants

Me, with my mother Eileen and my daughter Lara.

without breaking my neck. But that was Mike all over. In his own way, he was determined to get involved in my racing life.

That Chepstow episode with Mike remains one of the most embarrassing moment of my life. I just wanted to be spirited away. All that struggle to prove myself a consummate, serious, professional jockey, and here was my fiancé embracing me in full view of everyone. Fortunately, Bill was away at another meeting and didn't witness this episode. Somehow though, I imagined he would hear of it – like a secret society, word spreads quickly in the world of racing.

Later that day, as I was making my way to find Mike, carrying my skull cap and whip, I felt a tap on my shoulder. Guessing it was him, I turned to find a complete stranger. Something about him – perhaps his grey suit, tinted glasses, well-built, well-heeled demeanour – made me assume he was not a punter but a bookmaker.

He was accompanied by another man, who put his arm around me and said conspiratorially, 'Remember my face well. If you give me a tip on a horse that you ride or from your stable, I'll see that you get a nice present. You understand dear, don't you?' He grinned in a way I didn't like, and opened a suitcase containing what appeared to be thousands of pounds.

It was like something out of a Dick Francis novel.

It only lasted a few seconds but it was distinctly unnerving. Did he think that, as a girl, I looked like an easy target? Who can say? What I didn't appreciate was being spoken to like that, and also I feared that someone might have witnessed the encounter and reported me – jockeys were forbidden to have any contact with bookmakers. It may have been assumed I had encouraged him.

I turned away quickly, and just muttered, 'Not interested.' I was horrified. I was shaking. Maybe all apprentices are approached in this way. Poorly paid, some must be tempted. Maybe it would make them feel more important.

I told my family who were there, but when I tried to point the men out, they had disappeared from view. 'I shouldn't have thought anyone would have noticed in this crowd,' said my father, trying to allay my fears. I never mentioned it to either Bill, Wightman or Nash.

Coincidentally, one of our rivals that day was partnered by Willie Higgins, one of the young riders I'd met in Barbados. He was an apprentice to Peter Cundell and was riding one of his horses, The Iron Lady. He was clearly taken aback to see me and gave me a lop-sided grin. I had hoped to beat him home, just to prove a point – of sorts – but that wasn't to be.

I cursed quietly to myself. It was utterly depressing to think of the mental and physical anguish I had endured in the last week, and all for absolutely nothing. It was an experience that was to be repeated often throughout my career.

I did have another conversation with Bill Wightman regarding my weight-loss regime, but as I wrote earlier, he had scant sympathy for me. Not for the first time, he put everything into perspective by comparing my issues with his own over 30 years earlier in Japan.

I also reported back on how the Chepstow race had gone and, though he appeared satisfied, days passed with no hint that I may get another ride. I just hoped he hadn't heard about either the kissing incident or my confrontation with what I was certain was a bookmaker. In hindsight, I probably blew both out of proportion in my own mind – but I didn't want anything to impinge on my short but burgeoning career.

Just when I was at a relatively low ebb, Bill Nash whispered to me one morning, 'Steve [Woolley] can't do the weight for The Goldstone this afternoon. I think the guv'nor may give you the ride. But don't let on that I told you.'

I maintained a straight face, trying to look as though I was taking this news in my stride – though I was silently praying to the heavens. 'This afternoon? Was it possible?' I asked myself. It would be The Goldstone's first run of the season, but significantly this was not a 'boys' race, as events restricted to apprentices were known. It was a race for professionals (jockeys with full licences) *and* apprentices – my first such ride.

I'd been used to riding in races worth £600 to £800. The 7-furlong Hurstpierpoint Handicap at Brighton was worth £1,668 to the winning owner. I'd partnered Goldie twice the previous season, and Bill obviously thought he should give me another chance on him rather than allow Steve to carry overweight.

Goldie was set to carry 8st 8lb, but that would be reduced to 8st 1lb with the 7lb claim of either Steve or myself, and the saddle would take it down to 7st 10lb. I could do that comfortably. Steve couldn't. His minimum weight was 7st 12lb.

I worked on in excited anticipation, but no confirmation came. Then I worried: what would Steve think? He was down in all the morning papers as the rider. This could prove embarrassing for him. He had been in racing since he was 16, and boasted around 12 winners from some 100 rides. I knew he wouldn't like the fact that I was challenging him for a ride. I was still a novice. But I had to ignore that factor. Getting rides was a highly competitive business, both at the top – the stories are legion of Lester Piggott 'jocking off' his rivals for major rides – and at my level. As my friend and fellow apprentice Richard Newman would remind me later: 'There was always the threat that you'd take rides off me. But then there was always the threat I'd do you out of rides. It was a very competitive game, but you accepted that.'

I recognised, even then, one brutal fact: if you couldn't cut it, whether male or female, as a jockey equipped to galvanise half a ton of equine blueblood, you have no career ahead of you. There is no 'fairness' about it; no equivalent of all-women shortlists in politics. A trainer or owner's sole criterion when selecting a partner for a horse valued at thousands, sometimes potentially millions, is whether their jockey will prevail at the end of a race.

There was a strict convention among apprentices at Bill Wightman's yard, as Richard has reminded me. You never asked for a ride, or said, 'Guv'nor, I deserve that ride.' It simply wasn't done. It could actually go against you. The same applied if you were 'jocked off'. There was no point in protesting. Bill may have just been testing you – to see what your reaction was to a setback. He demanded loyalty, and this was as harsh an examination as any of your character.

In general, Bill was exceedingly sparing in his praise – of anyone. If he believed you had talent, and displayed dedication and loyalty he was highly supportive, even if he didn't always show it.

Richard Newman once told me, 'You had to worry when Bill wasn't shouting at you. He was firm but fair. At times he came over as though he hated you. But he didn't at all. The guv'nor got on at me, but Bill Anderson [a former jockey in France, attached to trainer Marcel Boussac, and who became Bill's stable jockey after the war] used to tell me that if he did that, he was interested in you. He would see potential in you. When he stopped getting on at you, he wasn't interested.'

That was quite true. On occasions, Bill Wightman would swear at me, but Bill Nash told me that was a good sign. 'He's a perfectionist. He's just trying to improve you.'

Returning to my hope of partnering Goldie at Brighton, I was dismounting from a two-year-old when Bill Wightman said, 'Try another.' Then, as I went to switch horses, he added, almost as an afterthought, 'You'll be riding The Goldstone in the four o'clock at Brighton today. I'll be leaving here at 12.30, so rush home after you've finished, change, and I'll pick you up at The Bat and Ball [the Hambledon pub].'

'Thank you, Mr Wightman,' I managed, before he declared pointedly, 'Oh, and you needn't tell your whole family to come. It's a professional race. Not a picnic.'

God, he'd heard about Mike's kiss at Chepstow. That confirmed it, I thought. Or maybe he was aware that my parents had attended every race I'd ridden in so far. I think they'd been there less because they thought I'd win, and more because my mother, in particular, was terrified I'd be injured and wanted to be in close attendance if I was.

'I'll tell them, Mr Wightman,' I said quietly. Bill was very old-school and, quite rightly, was a stickler for adopting a professional approach. He wanted me completely focused and didn't want any distractions – and, I had to agree, certainly not an over-enthusiastic fiancé displaying his affection for me.

I dashed home and shouted to my mother that under *no* circumstances must she come down to Brighton. She immediately phoned my father and Mike, and they all drove down to the Sussex course.

Blissfully unaware of this, I travelled down to Brighton with Bill Wightman. In a firm tone he told me: 'This is a professional race, Karen. Watch the other jockeys. Act like them. Be business-like.' He was quite right, of course. How his jockeys rode, particularly his apprentices, was a reflection on his reputation as a significant trainer of his day, patronised by many illustrious owners. Bill wanted me to act professionally in every way. He was hard and demanding because he believed it brought the best out of everyone he dealt with. Luckily, my father was the same, so I could cope with that. Everything was for my own good with him – although possibly I didn't always appreciate that at the time.

In addition, it must be remembered, I was a member of an exceptionally rare breed. Professional girl jockeys were thin on the ground. Many in the racing fraternity were sceptical whether I could make it. Others were hostile to the fact that I was even getting the chance. My success, or otherwise, could have a profound effect on those who followed me.

I suggested brightly that Goldie could be placed. 'No,' Bill responded firmly. He was precise with his instructions, saying, 'Give him a good run. Do your best but don't push him too hard. Remember it's The Goldstone's first time out of the season, and he isn't fit. It's most important he doesn't have too tough a race.'

I realised that if a horse wasn't fit enough to win – this horse always needed time and racing to come to his peak during a season – what a trainer didn't want was him finishing too close to the winner after a hard race. That could adversely affect his handicap rating.

Bill also told me to ride him off the pace and not too close to his rivals. Goldie was a naturally competitive horse and riding him extremely close to other horses would release his competitive streak too early and risk sapping his stamina, resulting in a slower finishing speed and an overly tired horse. Bill knew best and was more aware of Goldie's fitness levels than I was. So, I had to remember the message pumped into me repeatedly by both Bills, Wightman and Nash: 'Ride to orders!'

It didn't make my task easy. You had to think about style while complying with orders, and doing so without incurring the wrath of the stewards. If you didn't ride to orders, you might not get another ride. That was the one thing that made me nervous.

As much as I had relished the prospect of being a jockey, I was still very naive about the ways of racing and not familiar with having to follow instructions. I found it strange to have to conform, as previously I had always had complete control over the way I rode my own horses competitively. This was all new territory for me: how a trainer like Bill, a man renowned for preparing horses for handicaps, would run his horses. It only became clear to me once I started to race. Within the limits of the rules of racing, he needed to have that control over his jockeys – it was not up to them to make decisions for him.

Of all the rules of racing, Rule 151, 'failing to run a horse on its merits' would certainly have incurred the scrutiny of the stewards. This stated that, 'The rider of every horse shall take all reasonable and permissible measure … to ensure that his horse is given a full opportunity to win or of obtaining the best possible placing.' The rule also stressed that it was the duty of a trainer to ensure that any instructions he gave to his rider didn't prevent this. It was the most important rule in the sport, and still is. As I discussed earlier, Bill was never hauled before the Jockey Club for transgressing this rule, regarded as absolutely crucial to the sport, because to infringe it damages the integrity of racing. The penalties for breaking the rule were substantially increased in 1998, while at the same time stewards were empowered to ask trainers to account for the running of their horses in cases of both improved and worse performances.

That day in Brighton, I contemplated what was being asked of me. Bill took me to the stands to watch the early races and to appreciate this most idiosyncratic, roller-coaster of a course, perched atop the hills above the town, to a background of the sparkling sea.

In the weighing room, there was a marked difference in the atmosphere between this professional race and my previous apprentice events. I went so far as to try and eavesdrop on the jockeys' conversations, and pick up any titbits of information that may help me. On this day, my rivals included Pat Eddery, who the previous year had claimed a fourth consecutive jockeys' championship; Greville Starkey, the former champion apprentice and Classic-winning jockey; Brian Taylor, who had won the Derby on 50-1 shot Snow Knight in 1974; Kevin Darley, then an apprentice but who would become champion jockey; and – I couldn't believe it – another of my Barbados drinking companions, Shaun Salmon. We had a good laugh, but this time not at my expense.

In the paddock, Bill reminded me again: 'You're amongst professionals now, Karen. You must look like them. When you go to the start, past the stands, think of your style.' That was so like Bill – he was so anxious to ensure that I wouldn't stand out from the men. I was thinking of his words when, uncharacteristically, The Goldstone, fresh at being back on the racecourse after a long winter, leapt in the air as I was led out on to the course. Fortunately, I quickly regained his and my composure.

Shaun cantered past me. 'Alright, Karen? Going to enjoy the race?' I merely nodded and smiled. Goldie was loaded into the stalls. He had to be blindfolded, but was no trouble. Pat Eddery, who would go on to win 11 titles, was on Balidon, a well-backed third-favourite. He was in the stall next to me. Pat was relaxed. But then, for a man who had already won the first of his three Derbys, on Grundy, this was a bread and butter race for him.

It was an intoxicating experience to ride against the top jocks – men like Eddery and Starkey, the latter a character with a humourless façade, on course at least. He had already won the Prix de l'Arc de Triomphe in 1975, and in 1978 would complete the Derby–Oaks double. They were household names. I'd watched them ride since I was a child. These men, at the top of their profession, didn't see me as any kind of threat. They clearly didn't think I'd get the opportunities to compete regularly with them.

It was different with the journeymen and the lightweights, who fought tenaciously for rides, and particularly those who rode for Bill, like Geoff Baxter or Taffy Thomas – who in this race was riding a lightweight for another trainer. They didn't want me taking the rides they considered should be offered to them. As I've written previously, competition for rides was far more intense then. There were considerably fewer races than now, before the advent of all-weather racing. Some excellent jockeys, all vying for rides, were fiercely competing just to get in the saddle, let alone win.

That afternoon would stay with me. Indeed, it still does. Nothing made me happier than racing against those top jockeys, the men I'd watched so enviously all those years before at Newbury. This, for me, represented what I'd always desired. I felt privileged to race against them. To me, it was everything.

Yet, such were the vagaries of my career that, before the day was out, I would be telling Bill that I was ready to quit …

Chapter 20

A Confrontation with the Guv'nor as I Threaten to Quit

ALTHOUGH MY natural instinct would have been to do my damnedest to try to beat the seasoned professionals amongst my Brighton rivals, I stuck diligently to orders and didn't test Goldie's fitness to extremes. The Goldstone was a big horse and took a while to get fit, or, as they say, 'come to hand', each season. As usual, he wasn't fast out of the stalls, anyway. I kept Goldie covered up at the rear, close to the rails and then let him have his head as we freewheeled downhill before the final climb to the finish.

It was satisfying to overtake other jockeys – including Shaun Salmon, one of my Barbados companions, I noted afterwards – as I kept my mount going steadily but not over-exerting him on his seasonal debut. We finished fifth behind the winner, Pat Eddery's mount Balidon, in a field of 14.

Bill was delighted with the way I'd paced Goldie and pushed him through some narrow gaps. This, I knew, would stand me in good stead. 'I'm confident he'll go through anything,' I told Bill. 'I feel as though I'm riding a tank.' And meant it.

As I walked away, I overheard Bill remarking to another trainer: 'Didn't she ride well? Did you see her?'

It was some commendation. I was so relieved that I hadn't let Bill, or myself, down in this first race against many senior professionals. I knew that, for all the anguish I had suffered, I was extremely fortunate to be employed by one of the few trainers to allow a female jockey to ride – and now in a race not confined to apprentices. I was aware that, at home, he had pointed me out to owners as I rode work on the gallops. He maintained they wouldn't be able to tell the difference between me and the boys. Yet, the point remained that, compared with the progress of women in many countries abroad, and particularly in the United States, the girls here overall were getting nowhere fast. My belief was that because of the low esteem in which amateur lady jockeys were held in the profession, I was being discriminated against. I had not only to prove myself as a competent jockey, but just as importantly, to demonstrate there was no difference between me and the boys.

The experienced male jockeys would take a lot of convincing, too. From that day onwards, as I began to race against the professionals, I detected from the men an attitude of 'Oh, you think you can do it, do you? You think you can be as good as us?'

It is often said that when you're in a sport like racing where serious injuries can occur, and even – thankfully rarely – fatalities, it does mean that, deep down, there is a rapport with each other. That contrasts it to sports where life-threatening injuries rarely happen. However, as I was to quickly learn, professional races in those days were tough and rough. No quarter was given. You had to survive. There wasn't the same accent on safety as today. They'd be pushing you, blocking you in and tactically you had to be aware of everything around you. In a ladies' race, you just galloped, and that was it.

The senior professionals would have liked me to have been restricted to ladies' races. If you were riding something they reckoned had any kind of chance, they'd become hostile, screaming and swearing at you – as I recalled in Chapter 1. They simply didn't want you there.

Maybe there was another explanation for this unacceptable behaviour. There was talk, and I'm only recalling what I was told then and later, that some jockeys had been drinking or had taken drugs. Riding under the influence of either was not made an offence until 1994.

What was certain was that it was a dog-eat-dog world, with every rider voraciously seeking potentially winning rides. One of the hungriest was the freelance Taffy Thomas. The Welsh lightweight had enjoyed his best season numerically with 98 wins in 1977, when he was sixth in the jockeys' table.

I should explain the hierarchy of jockeys:

- Those retained by a particular (usually major) stable which had first claim on them, but they could also ride for outside trainers.
- Freelances, often connected to a particular trainer, and with lightweights particularly in demand.
- Apprentices, attached to a stable.

At the beginning of 1977 the pair that were best placed to make low weights were Taffy Thomas and Richard Fox, who could both do 7st 7lb. Others who fulfilled the lightweight criteria were: Ernie Johnson (7-8), George Duffield (7-8), Willie Carson (7-9), Kipper Lynch (7-10), Geoff Baxter (7-11), Mark Birch (7-12), Paul Cook (7-12), John Reid (7-12), Philip Waldron (7-12) and Ron Hutchinson (7-13). In addition, Pat Eddery was listed as being able to ride as low as 8st 1lb.

After the Brighton race it was Taffy Thomas who approached me in the weighing room. Our conversation was rather tense. I already knew that he enjoyed a close association with Bill Wightman, and would be one of my principal competitors for rides on horses allocated low weights. Some of the jockeys were a bit lairy, and Taffy was one of them. A nice guy, but lairy. He clearly just wanted to put me in my place.

'He went well, didn't he?' declared Taffy who, along with Geoff Baxter, often rode The Goldstone when the horse was fit and thought ready to win. I concurred.

'He looks as though he could win next time,' continued Taffy, who had won on Goldie the previous season and clearly assumed he would be riding him when he was expected to do the business. I understood that this was just a preparatory run, but I didn't want to be used just to get a horse fit and then be 'jocked off' by a senior rider when it had a winning chance. I could see where this conversation was going.

'Then I hope I'm on him when he does,' I replied sharply, and departed.

In hindsight, I'm glad he said what he did, because the exchange infuriated me. I thought, 'There's no way I'm going to let that happen.'

On returning to the stables in the horsebox, I strode immediately to the house to confront Bill Wightman. I was furious and told him what Taffy had said. I told Bill in no uncertain terms that if Taffy got the ride when Goldie was fit and ready to win, I would hand in my notice.

Bill was at his conciliatory best. He explained to me that it depended on the owner, and it was out of his hands. He more or less confirmed that Taffy would get the ride. Bill was always very honest with me, and added: 'It's difficult enough for me to get you rides, let alone winning ones.'

I came as close as I ever did to raising my voice to Bill. I felt bad at having a go at him. He didn't deserve it. I knew he was doing everything he could. But I felt I had to put that pressure on him.

I told him: 'I can see what the situation is now. I'm going to be used as a work-rider and for getting horses fit on the racecourse. This is no good for me.' I wanted to win and make a career for myself as a jockey.

Apparently making no progress, I told Bill: 'Right, I'm going now,' and stormed off. I headed for my car, thinking, 'What the hell am I doing here?' and decided to find someone else who would give me rides. Bill came running after me. He wasn't angry. In fact, I think he admired my spirit. He would have known it took a lot for me to issue that ultimatum to a man of his standing in the sport. Bill calmed me down, told me to be patient, and promised to do what he could.

During my time with him, Bill constantly told me that, despite his best efforts, he struggled to get some owners to put me up. However, he said if it was purely up to him, he certainly would, because he considered me to be more than capable.

'I can't give you races unless you're as good as the men – actually you're going to have to be better,' he said. He didn't want anyone saying that I'd got a ride because I was something of a novelty. The fact was that if they'd watched ladies' races, an owner wouldn't even have considered putting one on their horse. Bill admitted to me that they had a bad name and that made it more difficult for him to convince the owners that I was different. Bill had to overcome that substantial hurdle, and convince them that I was a real professional jockey, at least as talented as the male apprentices.

I couldn't fault Bill. He tried all kinds of ploys to get owners amenable to the idea of me riding for them at a time when, as I have said, there was still ingrained prejudice against women riders. In particular, I knew Bill liked to have me speak to the owners about their horses after they'd watched them work. As I mentioned previously, he thought they'd appreciate the fact that I was well-spoken and from a good background.

Sometimes, I felt, he'd even try to play the sympathy card. Bill would bring them into the stables when I was carrying out really hard physical work, as if to say, 'She's not used to this, but this is how committed she is to getting a ride.'

Occasionally, later on, he'd ask me to come up to tea and meet the owners, but this had to be done discreetly so it didn't aggravate the lads. They would never go up to Bill's house. I didn't want the lads to know I was treated any differently.

Frankly, I had expected a lot more progress by now in racing generally. I had really thought the same judgement would be applied to racing as it was in showjumping, where you would be assessed purely on your ability. I was still young, and had gone into racing with a rather blinkered approach. I had misunderstood how the business worked. In retrospect, I hadn't truly understood most trainers' and owners' attitudes at the time. Probably it was a good job – otherwise I'd have been even more frustrated and angry than I was.

But I understood already that it was not sufficient to just be a talented rider. There was nothing fair about the system. You had to fight to win the right to partner good horses. Success would not come naturally to me. I was more assertive than many of the boys. But then I felt I had to be. Bill was confident that most of the lads would stay. His attitude was that they were fortunate to have a job at such an efficiently run and successful stables. I always made it clear that, in my case, he couldn't take it for granted.

He respected me. He could see my point. Maybe that's why he thought to himself, 'I've got to give her a chance sometime.'

I think it's always been true about male-dominated sports and businesses; you do get respect when you show that you are not prepared to accept the status quo. Bill, being a businessman, respected that.

Chapter 21

I'm In Despair – I Need to Ride Better Horses

BETWEEN RACES, I'd continue to work hard in the stables, and soon put some weight back on. It would have been impossible, with my frame, to stay permanently below 7st without causing myself serious illness.

Yet, as soon as a possible ride was broached by Bill Wightman, I'd ask: 'What weight is he carrying?' If it was a low weight, I'd groan inwardly – but I refused to countenance the prospect of rejecting the ride.

Knowing what lay ahead, each time I had to diet was tougher than the last. There was the occasional sympathetic voice. Once when I had to lose around half a stone in a few days, I averted my eyes as the majority of lads ate and drank normally during a break. I was back to the tea and dried prunes (breakfast), two Ryvitas (lunch), two lettuce leaves and a tomato (evening meal) routine. I felt, and must have looked, terrible that day.

'It's never easy, is it Karen?' was the sympathetic reflection of fellow apprentice Robert Baker, who I mentioned earlier. 'I've spent whole afternoons in saunas. It makes you feel terrible. We all go through it.' It was good to hear an empathetic voice, but it gave me little comfort. While on this diet, I had to maintain my onerous duties in the yard and riding out for hours a day, seven days a week.

As the body weakens, the danger is that your control over a horse decreases. The rider has to find extra strength from somewhere to compensate for this, and consequently becomes even more tired and weaker as a result. It's a vicious negative spiral, and potentially dangerous to ride in a race in this state.

Meanwhile, my fiancée Mike did his best to support me. On some evenings, he would drive me to the sauna. Afterwards all I wanted to do was go home to sleep, but he'd be determined to carry on and spend the evening socialising. Some fun! I couldn't even empty a glass of orange juice. My irritability increased, but Mike was patient with me, initially at least.

I did eventually get to ride Sweet Caress in my seventh race on 13 May. 'Yes, I can make the weight,' I told Bill with more positivity than I felt when I discovered she carried 7st 12lb, which, after taking into account my allowance and the saddle would mean I'd have to do 7st. Turning down a race – any race, any weight – never crossed my mind.

It meant I had to lose 5lb in a couple of days. On the second of them, I had agreed to pick up my parents, who had been away on a break, from Heathrow. They were keen to stop at one of their favourite restaurants on the way back for a hearty meal. They thought it would be a treat for me.

'I can't eat anything,' I insisted, surveying a menu on which everything from tasty starters to rich cream desserts sounded tantalising. Despite my mother's protestations, I sat and watched them eat. I had nothing. It didn't create a great atmosphere. Again, I wondered whether these kinds of sacrifice would ever be worthwhile.

Sweet Caress totally belied her name. There was nothing sweet about her. She was mad – headstrong and known to try to bolt with anyone. The day before the race, Bill Nash, concerned about the effects of my wasting, told me to take her up on the Downs to make sure I could hold her. She was in high spirits as we cantered off under the watchful eyes of the head lad and trainer. She fought against every muscle I possessed as I tried to control her. 'I must stop her … must stop her,' I mouthed repeatedly to myself, feeling my arms failing to pull with their usual strength. Somehow, with sheer bloody-minded determination, I gained control over her. Bill Wightman was suitably impressed.

Sweet Caress's race was a 5-furlong sprint, the Chapel Farm Handicap, for three-year-olds at Bath, again a 'professional' race. When the day arrived, I was weak from dieting. The fact that my mount was a strong horse with a hard mouth, who, I discovered, had previously bolted with one strong jockey all the way to the stalls – it does happen, even to the best – didn't exactly fill me with confidence.

It was also her first run of the season and she would be fresh. It occurred to me that I could be committing suicide. Not that I confided this to anyone. In the weighing room, Robert Street, who was riding one of our rivals, Burglar Bill, in the same race, confirmed my worst fears.

'I know what your horse is like – she bolts,' he said, offering to give me a lead up to the stalls. 'I'll go at a slow pace, and you keep her head right against the tail of mine,' he advised. Given that I'd never met Robert before, that was very decent of him.

In the paddock, Sweet Caress's owners were as worried as I was. I told them I'd ridden her in work several times. 'Has she run away with you?' they asked, evidently more concerned about us getting safely to the stalls than the race itself.

'No,' I respond truthfully. *Not yet*, I thought.

As I mounted Sweet Caress, I told her lad Scott to make sure we were behind Burglar Bill. She was fine going past the stands and I kept her close to the rails, but then she pulled herself out from Burglar Bill, and she was off, past the stalls, scattering the other horses, before finally she stopped about 3 furlongs further on. The physical demands of attempting to restrain her didn't do much for me, either, following my attempts to make the weight. I was so dehydrated and my throat was parched, dry and burning. This really worried me. I was desperate for a drink.

Sweet Caress had been placed previously, but was not seriously backed for her seasonal debut. Punters had it right. She'd run her race, was blowing hard – and we weren't even in the stalls yet. We joined the other runners, by now all installed. This was my first sprint, and a new experience. In longer-distance races you start at a controlled speed and have time to position yourself, everything is in slower motion, but in sprints it's fast out of the stalls and a good pace from the start while still reserving your top gear for the finish. Pace is paramount in sprints.

In the event, Sweet Caress lasted 3 furlongs before blowing up. She lacked fitness anyway, and those pre-race exertions had drained her. The tank was empty. I just about managed to avoid finishing last, but that was the only saving grace.

Another race run, for which I had dieted and dehydrated myself, and a win still remained an illusion, or should I say a delusion?

Twelve days later, I was back on The Goldstone, again in a 7-furlong race at Newbury, the London Apprentice Handicap – coincidentally the same event in which I had made my debut a year earlier on Park Walk. Thankfully, there would be no weight problem this time. Goldie was set to carry 8st 11lb. The instructions were similar to those at Brighton: keep Goldie covered up, on the rails, look to produce him late on.

Unusually, he broke well, and rather than ease him back and come with a late rattle, he remained in a prominent position. We finished just over five lengths fifth to a horse named Versailles Prince in a field of 12. Admittedly, Goldie was still not considered to be at his peak in terms of fitness, although he was one of the more fancied runners in the betting. I had high standards and felt I'd failed by not even securing a place. I ran the race over and over in my mind, depressing myself in the process. At times, your own post-race analysis can be a dark place to dwell.

As early June 1978 approached, the thoughts of most elite trainers were on Epsom and their prospective runners in the two 1-mile 4-furlong Classics, the Derby and the Oaks. As I've stated previously, as a rule Bill Wightman rarely trained charges considered to possess genuine Classic potential. However, there was a frisson of excitement in the yard this season because it was known that the guv'nor planned to run William Douglas-Home's Goblin in the Derby.

Costing only 3,600 guineas as a yearling, the son of Sun Prince had won a 23-runner 7-furlong maiden at Newmarket in October in a course-record time. Partnered by Lester Piggott, Goblin had defeated a horse named Rhineland by three lengths with the remainder of the field strung out behind. It was regarded in the yard as a highly propitious performance though for the colts' Classic, Goblin was regarded as very much an outsider as he was opposed by horses who had won or performed well in Classic trials.

As for me, the yard's focus on the Derby brought to mind Joanna Morgan, whose career I've broached previously. Wales-born

Joanna began her riding career in Welsh point-to-points but in 1974, aged 21, moved to Ireland, where she rode for trainer Seamus McGrath. The following year she partnered her first winner for him on Alla Capella, at Tipperary. It had been only in 1972 that the Irish Turf Club first licensed women to ride at all. Like me, she encountered an 'ingrained prejudice', as an *Irish Times* article put it, against women riding racehorses. But like me, she persevered. In 1976, she had become the first female professional to ride at Royal Ascot and in the same year had been the first woman to ride in an Irish Classic, the Irish Derby.

I had long kept a beady eye on Joanna. I regarded her as a rival – albeit she was generally riding in Ireland and had started her career before me. However, my competitive instincts were stimulated by headlines about Joanna hoping to be the first female to ride in the Derby – the Epsom version. In the event, she didn't, but the prospect of it galvanised me into action. I was determined that the distinction of being the first female to ride in such a historic race as the Derby should be mine, and emphasised my feelings to Bill Wightman.

I applied a lot of pressure. I knew he was a great friend of William Douglas-Home, and it tended to be easier for him to persuade owners he knew well to let me ride their horses. A week later, Bill told me the owner favoured having his regular jockey ride, but added: 'I think I can persuade him if you want to take the risk of being ridiculed – but I wouldn't advise it.'

Clearly, he believed that deterring me from pressing for the ride was for my own good. Bill felt the possibility of my being tailed off on a 200-1 shot – his eventual starting price in the Derby – would do nothing for my career. I had my own doubts about Goblin's intended Derby participation. Yes, he had won a

7-furlong maiden at Newmarket superbly, but would he get home in a race nearly twice the distance, even allowing for the fact that he was now a three-year-old? I just knew I wanted to be in the saddle. However, as an apprentice, I very reluctantly took Bill's advice. Goblin had no chance of being in contention and I suspect that, had I ridden, the focus on me by the press would have given Bill the kind of media attention he could well have done without.

Instead, Taffy Thomas rode Goblin, and the pair finished tenth, behind the victor Shirley Heights, ridden by Greville Starkey and trained by John Dunlop. The going was soft after a surfeit of rain and, while other horses weakened in the prevailing conditions, Goblin stayed on stoutly and made progress late on through tiring horses.

I had to wait until July for my next race. It was in a 1-mile 1-furlong event at Kempton, the Kenilworth Apprentice Handicap, on a horse named Tervey Boy, who had never achieved much. He'd had an operation on his back, and that caused him stiffness.

Once again, I had to adopt my wasting regime. Having been told I'd be riding two days before the race, I fasted and spent two evenings in the sauna, but was still 2lb overweight when I weighed in. Bill Wightman wasn't happy. I'd assured him I'd make the weight. It didn't do too much for my ego, either, when the PA announced that: 'Karen Wiltshire is carrying 2lb overweight.'

Kempton had a much more formal, businesslike atmosphere than most of the courses I'd raced. Bill told me he wanted Tervey Boy to be prominent, and see how long he lasted. We did just that, broke fast, ran well for 7 furlongs, before dropping back and finishing in mid-field.

The race was won by Paddy's Luck, partnered by a certain Walter Swinburn, the 16-year-old son of Wally Swinburn, the

Irish champion jockey. Walter would be known throughout his career as 'The Choirboy' because of his boyish good looks. We would meet again.

I was reunited with Tervey Boy in the Netton Apprentice Handicap, over 1 mile at Salisbury, but this time he felt stiff on the way to the start. He appeared to be fine for 5 furlongs, but then suddenly felt as though he'd gone lame, and we finished second to last. Not for the first time that season, I was in a state of despair. Being associated with a horse that had no chance could only be detrimental to my career. Gaining experience was one thing; bad experience was quite another. I needed to ride better horses.

I thought of Steve Woolley. He'd had many more rides than my five this season. Admittedly, he was more experienced than me, and he had ridden winners, but it illustrated the deep disparity between two apprentices from the same stables.

A couple of weeks passed, and no ride was forthcoming. My spirits could not have been at a lower ebb, so on an impulse after riding work, I marched into the office to challenge Bill Wightman. 'This isn't doing me any good,' I told him. 'I'm working here seven days a week, not for the money but to make a career as a jockey. I won't do that riding horses like Tervey Boy. Give me a decent ride and I'll show you how good I am.'

He nodded sagely, and heard out my tirade. 'Don't give up, Karen,' he said. 'Keep working well and I'll do my best for you. I have to get the owners interested.'

I needed a winner, *desperately* needed that first victory, to demonstrate my worth to owners. But by now I knew how competitive it was, with senior jockeys and apprentices fighting for rides. It can be expensive to own a racehorse. Such is the money involved in the sport, trainers can ill afford to make mistakes –

and that includes booking the right jockey, or at least one that receives the approval of the owners, when a horse is considered well-handicapped and ready to win. It could be that I'd have to rely on a horse owned by Bill, or one in which he had a significant interest, to give me a winning opportunity.

I knew my best hope of a winner lay with The Goldstone, whose owner had been happy for me to partner him. Could Goldie give me that elusive victory? I knew he usually went well for Geoff Baxter or Taffy Thomas. Bill would normally use either of them if the horse was considered fit and they were available, but I still hoped to persuade Bill to give me the ride when he next raced.

I reflected on Bill's most recent words to me: 'Don't lose faith, Karen. There will be something coming up before long.'

That advice was well-founded when The Goldstone was declared to run at Bath, and was thought fit enough, *and* well handicapped to do himself justice in a six-horse race. It was a valuable handicap – for a small course – and I knew there'd be several jockeys interested. I expected Geoff Baxter to get the ride in a race worth £2,135 in winning prize money, and there were some decent handicappers running: Chukaroo, Andy Rew, Ramadan and Taj Princess. But then it occurred to me that Andy Rew was trained by Paul Cole, and Geoff was his retained jockey. He would therefore be claimed to ride that horse.

Goldie was set to carry 8st 2lb in the Be Hopeful Memorial Handicap over 1 mile. If I rode him, my 7lb claim would take the weight down to 7st 9lb – a considerable advantage. 'You might have a chance,' confided Bill Nash.

Finally, the evening before the race, Bill Wightman confirmed that Bill Nash's optimism on my behalf was justified – *if* I could do the weight. I was 7st 11b and would need to lose 5lb, allowing for my saddle, by morning. It would still be hard work, and I told him I didn't want to go through that if he ended up booking someone else.

'If you do the weight, Karen, you'll probably get the ride,' he promised me. Hardly a ringing endorsement, but sufficient to get me to the sauna, and cease all food and drink intake immediately.

Bill Wightman phoned me when I got home to tell me that the local press boys hadn't reacted positively to the news that I may be riding Goldie. One writer had opined that, 'The Goldstone could go well, but that would depend on whether he had a strong rider.' In other words, not a girl apprentice. There had been strong pressure on Bill to put up Pat Eddery, who was without a ride. 'Why should the local press have any influence on the matter?', I thought. I told Bill firmly that I'd been in the sauna all evening, was dieting, and would do the weight. 'I want that ride,' I said. Bill finally concurred.

At least the *Birmingham Post*'s racing correspondent Stable Boy (traditionally, newspapers tend to use noms de plume for their racing tipsters and correspondents) was positive. After I spoke to Bill, a headline appeared in his paper the next morning. It read: 'Goldstone ready to pay off for Karen'. The article started: 'Karen Wiltshire spent the afternoon in a sauna yesterday, for at Bath today she gets the chance to win the richest race of her short career on The Goldstone.'

It added that if Eddery had been booked, 8st 2lb was his minimum riding weight, and he may have to put up overweight. Stable Boy concluded: 'I bank on Karen riding the race of her life to get The Goldstone home.' 'You bet!' I said to myself on reading this. Just a shame that Stable Boy and his publication was based far away in Birmingham rather than in my local area.

Before we left the yard, one of the lads remarked bitterly: 'Why couldn't Pat Eddery be up? Why does the jockey have to be a bloody woman?' This character was a real male chauvinist. There could have been few things worse in his life than a woman booked to ride a horse he knew was fit and had a good chance. It was complete anathema to him, and I knew other lads would have readily concurred. For months, I had ignored such pettiness – but it would have been nice to receive the lads' support.

Among my rivals again was Walter Swinburn. He was riding the lightweight Taj Princess and though he had a 7lb allowance as an apprentice (like me), he actually carried 7lb overweight, which meant he was riding at the same weight as a fully-fledged professional. That was a measure of the esteem he was held in, even then.

The bookies adjudged the race to be between two horses, Chukaroo and Andy Rew. The Goldstone was third-favourite.

Bath has a sharp bend turning into a run-in of nearly 4 furlongs. Bill Wightman gave me precise instructions, telling me to keep him balanced round the bend, take the shortest route on the inside rails, keep him covered up until the final furlong, and then produce him. All went well until we were forced to the outside, but then he found his usual late turn of foot. Three of us thrust for the line, behind the Walter Swinburn-ridden Taj Princess, who had gone clear and won by four lengths. We finished third, narrowly pipped for second in a photo finish with Geoff Baxter on Andy Rew, with Chukaroo a close fourth.

It had been a thrilling experience, to do battle in such a tight finish, with the whips up. I really felt like I'd been in a race. Being placed third, and involved in a photo finish, was a surprisingly positive experience; not least because I felt that I was being entrusted with a serious runner – rather than just one out to gain fitness.

I really felt a turn of foot from Goldie at Bath. I sensed he was ready to win a race if the conditions were right. But would it be for me? Bill Wightman appeared happy with the outcome, although he was more concerned that Goldie may have suffered a kick on a leg in the late scrimmaging.

Changing in the ladies' room, an owner came over to me. She looked wealthy, smart and successful. The woman looked around, and then whispered: 'You are a lucky girl. If I had my time over again, the one thing I would want to be is a jockey. You young girls can do anything these days. Good luck.'

Lovely to hear, though possibly premature …

I drove back with Bill Wightman and Steve Woolley, who had also had a ride in a fillies' maiden for Bill but had finished unplaced. No one said much en route, but when Steve got out to open the gate, I quickly said to Bill: 'Do you think I should have finished second?'

'It was a good race. I'm very pleased,' he said in his typically noncommittal fashion.

Back at the yard, my principal detractor Jack, of course, said nothing, but Grant Eden shouted: 'How's the maestro then?' That made me smile.

The following morning, I was relieved to be told by Bill Nash that the guv'nor had been very satisfied with my riding. That was just about the highest praise anyone at the yard was ever likely to receive from either!

But that didn't prevent me replaying the race in my mind. I knew I might have done better, and felt perhaps I should have nicked the runner-up spot. But I still hoped I could get another chance.

Chapter 22

Head Lad Tells Me: 'Win it for Me – You've Got to Prove a Lot of People Wrong'

WEDNESDAY EVENING was traditionally 'mash night' at the stables. On 13 September I stood with the other lads around the mash bin in the covered way between the two tack rooms. The talk – inevitably – was races and form for the next day as Bill Nash mixed the linseed oil into the bran. Jack sidled up behind me and gave me a painful kick in the calf. 'Hey, are you riding The Goldstone tomorrow?' he demanded, accusingly. 'He's definitely running at Salisbury but there's no jockey listed in the evening paper. Geoff Baxter'll be at Doncaster, so it looks as if you'll get the ride. Just our f****** luck.' With a glare, he added: 'He'll never f****** win with you on his back. He needs a real jockey.'

His words stung, and my hackles rose, but I refused to rise to the cheap jibe. 'I haven't been told anything,' I shouted back at him, rubbing my calf. 'I don't know if I'm riding Goldie – but then I never know until the last moment.'

'Could it be true?' I thought.

Almost instantaneously, Bill Wightman strode past me, and without turning his head, barked: 'Karen, you ride The Goldstone tomorrow.'

My features creased into a grin. 'Thank you, Mr Wightman,' I acknowledged, acutely aware this was a fine opportunity to win my first race. Goldie had demonstrated he was fit and in form two weeks previously at Bath. And there wasn't a more confident rider in the yard.

The Winterbourne Handicap, a 1-mile event for three-year-olds and upwards, was a race for professionals – it was *not* an apprentice race – and was worth £1,912 to the winning owner. My spirits soared. I knew from the evening paper the form of the other 12 horses running and we were in with a definite chance. I felt supremely confident. I knew Goldie, and he had responded well to me in the past. Salisbury, a right-hand loop, with a run-in of 7 furlongs, was uphill and testing for the last half mile, and I felt that would suit him. And there was no Taj Princess (winner by four lengths in Goldie's last race) in opposition this time.

After finishing the evening feed, Bill Nash confided in me: 'Now Blossom, you have an early night. You'll need all your strength tomorrow. It's a jockeys' race, and you've got to win it for me. We've got to prove a lot of people wrong.'

He paused and looked me in the eyes, before declaring: 'If I had one wish, it would be that you win.'

I felt quite emotional at his kindness. I desperately wanted to win for him – but that put added pressure on me. How could I let him down?

I discovered that Bill Wightman would not be at Salisbury. He would be travelling to Doncaster with another of his fancied runners. After the contribution he'd made towards my career, I felt disappointed he wouldn't be there to see me. Yes, it was a handicap and they are invariably tricky to call, but I had a feeling about the following day.

That evening, Mike was as excited as I was. 'Are you going to win?' he asked.

'I've got a good chance,' I replied, and left it at that.

By now, Mike was an informed companion. He'd been to nearly every race I'd ridden in and would spend ages with me, leafing through *Raceform* to check the form of my rivals.

That night I had a nightmare. I dreamed I'd been held up in the most awful traffic jam. By the time I arrived at the course, the horses were in the stalls ... Admittedly, such events do very occasionally happen – a jockey is delayed and has to be replaced. But on this day it was an unlikely scenario. Mike was driving me, followed by my parents. He had left plenty of time, and it was only around 45 miles to the course. I had to do a morning's work first, riding out two horses and cleaning three stalls.

On the way to the races, I picked up *Sporting Life*. On the front page, under 'LATEST (riding news)', it read: '3.45 Salisbury. The Goldstone, K Wiltshire (7)'. It felt good to see that. Inside the paper, there was a tipping box, in which three of the national newspaper tipsters – the *Daily Mail* (Robin Goodfellow), the *Daily Telegraph* (Hotspur) and *The Sun* (Templegate) all tipped The Goldstone. The remainder went for Galadriel, which was also the verdict of the Man on the Spot, who analysed my race in the *Life*. His opinion was that Galadriel 'holds probable market rival The Goldstone on their July Ascot running when she landed a hefty gamble, with The Goldstone back in fifth [and not ridden by me on that occasion].'

The item added: 'The Goldstone failed to quicken inside the final furlong when third to Taj Princess at Bath last time [when I *had* partnered him] and may again be tapped for finishing speed.'

'Huh!' I thought. I didn't bother to read the rest. It put me in a fighting mood. We *had* to beat Galadriel this time.

At the stables I had seen Bill Wightman before he had left for Doncaster. He issued his instructions: 'You know the horse well, and I have faith he'll run well. Don't worry if he breaks slowly. Keep him covered up and remember, when you decide to make a move, do it quickly and don't hesitate. The horse must feel you are confident and in command of the situation.'

He paused before continuing: 'I think it would be best if you came up the rails as you did last year. Don't hit the front too soon. Don't panic. Just wait your time and make sure he's running his best at the finish. Now, have you any questions?'

'No,' I replied. 'It's all quite clear. I'll do my best.'

Bill Nash overheard and added: 'You *must* follow the guv'nor's orders. You can't do any better than that. But please win – for me …'

His words echoed in my ears as I drove out of the stables. It was a great fillip – and also negated the comments from the stable lads I'd overheard. They'd been discussing the form of the horses in my race and their opinion was that they couldn't back The Goldstone – they couldn't put money on a horse *being ridden by a girl*. I knew they'd been scrutinising me all morning, hoping to detect any signs of nerves. But I remained cool, talking and joking as normal. I'd long ago ceased being fazed by their scepticism. Of course, there were odd doubts and fears as I drove home to change. But for all my determination to win for Bill Nash and prove the lads wrong, I tried to place everything in perspective. There were worse things in life than losing a race.

I changed into smarter clothes. Normally, I would never have worn a dress to the races – somehow I felt it would have been insulting the male jockeys, emphasising the difference between them and myself and inviting attention. I had always tried to be a chameleon and go unnoticed on the racecourse. Normally, I just wore corduroys and a sweater. But today, unusually, I opted for a pink silk blouse. It made me feel good.

Mike and I laughed our way to Salisbury. It helped to relieve the pressure, though he was a little concerned that I could be intimidated by the crowd.

'The few races I get are reward for all the hard work I've put in over the last two years,' I told him. 'I have to make the most of them, to enjoy them. If anything, it gives me a lift, knowing that the crowds are there, their eyes fixed on me. I'm proud to be out there among the men. I have a lot to prove to them, and I want plenty of witnesses when I do.'

As we drove into the jockeys' and trainers' car park, the steward cast his eye over Mike and me and enquired, partly in jest: 'Who's the jockey?' I'd heard something similar many times. I showed him the daily paper with my name on the racecard. He recognised me. 'Good luck, Miss Wiltshire,' he said smiling, while waving us on. In the weighing room, I found John, my valet, who'd always been cheerful and supportive when things hadn't been going well and I had blamed myself. Sometimes I arrived at a course panicking about being a pound or two overweight. He'd say: 'Don't worry. I'll give you a light saddle. You'll make it.' These saddles were so light, you could almost have been riding bareback.

On this day, there would be no such problem. Indeed, even with a 7lb saddle, I'd still need plenty of lead in my saddle cloth to bring it up to the weight allotted. The Goldstone was set to carry 9st 5lb, less my 7lb allowance, which meant 8st 12lb. That said everything about Bill Wightman's belief in me – with The

Goldstone set to carry that weight, he could have opted for a heavier, senior experienced man.

'What do you think of his chances?' John asked.

'Pretty good,' I replied. 'The last race I had on Goldie at Bath showed he's ready for a win, and I certainly am.' I laughed. 'So that makes two of us.'

John grinned as he handed me my silks, so familiar now – Sue Pakenham's navy blue with a white sash – and my boots.

'You show 'em, Karen,' said John.

I departed the milling crowd of jockeys, valets and lads, and made my way to a first aid room that, on this day, doubled up as my own changing room. After the bustle of the weighing room, it felt like being in an isolation chamber. It was something with which I'd had to become familiar. Would there ever come a time when female jockeys were commonplace? The thought flickered across my mind. 'Of course, there will,' I said to myself. 'Eventually.'

I left my gear there and walked the course, familiarising myself with the going, which was 'good', and the contours. I sensed we could do it.

I watched the first race, the 2.15, from the stands, imagining myself being involved in 90 minutes' time. Butterflies fluttered in my stomach, but also a feeling of impending excitement.

Back in my makeshift 'changing room', an elderly nurse was clearly more worried about my welfare than the possibility of my victory. 'You make sure you go careful and keep out of danger,' she said. 'You're a brave girl, so don't take any risks.'

As I left to go in search of John to finish dressing me, I told her politely but pointedly, 'If I was worried about my safety I wouldn't be here. That's the last thing a jockey can think about. I'll go out there to win and if I break my neck trying it's just too bad.'

She obviously considered me to be quite mad.

I returned to the weighing room. The hands on the big clock on the wall moved so slowly. As I glanced round, I noticed Shaun Salmon. We had ridden against each other several times, including at Brighton when I had finished fifth on The Goldstone.

'You make a good partnership,' he said. 'Good luck, Karen. This is a hard life for a girl, and you deserve some success.' It was unusual to hear such encouraging words from another jockey.

'If only a few more people thought the way you do,' I said gratefully. 'But where there's big money involved, it's difficult to persuade people to take a chance with a girl. I am incredibly fortunate that Mr Wightman has such faith in me.'

John fastened my silk cap, navy blue and white hooped, to my helmet, checked the elastic bands round my wrists that kept the sleeves tight and reduced wind resistance, tightened the scarf around my neck and gave a final tug on my breeches as they felt a bit loose.

I weighed out, sitting on the scales with my saddle and weight cloth filled with lead, and then handed the saddle and cloth to Geoff Yates, who was travelling head lad and representing Bill that day in the guv'nor's absence. I liked Geoff. He was a genial northerner with a good sense of humour – the type of character you needed on your side.

'Everything's OK, Karen,' he said, assuring me that there'd been no problems with The Goldstone. 'I'll see you in the paddock – there's nothing more I can do for you now – except wish you luck.'

The bell rang and I walked with the other jockeys to the paddock.

'Ladies first,' one remarked, with a grin.

'You all remember that when the race is being run,' I retorted, leading the way.

Geoff was waiting for me. The owner Sue Packenham, confined to a wheelchair, was at the course, but had to observe from a distance. I caught sight of The Goldstone, circuiting the paddock with the other 12 runners, led by his groom. The horse was gleaming in the summer sun and looked superb.

'Just do as the guv'nor told you,' said Geoff. 'And remember, whatever you do, don't panic if you think you can't find a gap. Just bide your time and an opening will come. Ride him like you did last year and you can't go wrong.'

The bell rang for jockeys to be mounted and Geoff gave me a leg-up. It was all down to me now.

I heard later that The Goldstone had drifted in the betting, from his forecast 5-1 in the morning papers, to his starting price of 9-1. The suspicion afterwards was that his price lengthened because punters learned he would not only be apprentice-ridden, but partnered by a woman. What did I care? I never paid attention to odds, anyway – and certainly not that day.

Goldie felt keen. There would be no dawdling to the start. I took him to the stalls at a fast canter. My message to him was clear, 'We're here to work.' At the starting stalls, we were called to enter first. That was because Goldie had been known to occasionally cause problems before allowing himself to be introduced into the stalls.

Today was no different. In fact, all the other horses were installed, and he was still refusing to comply. Six stall-handlers were heaving him but he was proving frustratingly obdurate. They tried a blindfold – a typical stratagem with wilful horses – but he still backed away.

The starter called out, 'I'll only wait a couple more minutes ...'

I was horrified. Would my big chance be ruined by a horse, with which I had such an affinity, refusing to enter the stalls? Would he have to be withdrawn and take no part?

Just when I feared that ignominious end to my day, he decided to comply, and just walked into his stall. It was like he was saying to everyone, 'OK, I've had my fun – let's get on with this ...'

Chapter 23

Victory! I Thought: 'Now I'll Probably be Quite Famous ...'

THE STALLS opened. Predictably, Goldie was last to break. But this was how he liked to run, biding his time, and then gradually moving into contention. After a furlong, we began to overtake the back markers. I followed Bill's instructions and kept to the rails, moving smoothly.

Around the 4-furlong marker, we passed more rivals. We were now nicely positioned, in the centre of the field, but still 'covered up', his nostrils almost touching the horse in front. He was moving comfortably, without exerting himself.

I moved off the rails slightly, but found my way to further progress barred by horses clamped tightly together. For a second, I felt despair. But then I recalled what Geoff had said to me, 'Whatever you do, don't panic if you think you can't find a gap. Just bide your time and an opening will come.'

I started to push Goldie between two horses in front. 'Please let me through,' I pleaded silently. I knew it would come to this. Knew there'd be occasions when I'd have to be brave enough to urge my mount through a gap. You can't think about the danger. If you do, you bottle it. And no jockey can afford that. Then miraculously, the horse to our right moved slightly towards the rails. The gap would be gone in a second. I seized my chance and forced Goldie between the two horses – we were all so close, I could hear hooves clicking – but, with a furlong remaining, we were level.

Even then, I bided my time. I did not want to hit the front too soon. But in the last half furlong I asked him to show a turn of foot, and went for home. I could hear nothing behind me but I remembered the old rule: never look back.

We flashed past the post – alone, clear of our rivals.

'Good boy, Goldie – we did it!' I shouted in exultation, slapping him down the neck. Done it in style, too, by two and a half lengths.

It felt like I was in a dream – but I could hear the crowd cheering. This was real, wasn't it?

I pulled up Goldie – which was not easy as he still had plenty in the tank – and couldn't help grinning at the other jockeys as we made our way back to the paddock, the likes of Michael Roberts, Brian Rouse, Richard Fox.

A successful punter, someone who'd had faith in me, called out, 'Thanks for winning for me.'

Geoff met me, beaming his approval, though he did admonish me for slapping Goldie down the neck, saying it was unprofessional. That irritated me slightly – it was a celebratory gesture you see often from top jockeys when they win big races. This was *my* big race. It just took the edge off the win. I felt he was looking for any reason to criticise me.

Just for a moment I thought of Jack, back at the stables, and how he would react when hearing about my win. How long had I longed for this day – to prove a point to him? It was a moment of ecstasy, the best thing ever, and would remain so until the birth of my daughter.

It's not easy to adequately describe the pleasure of winning a horse race. All I will say is that it's an incredible high, and you just want more of it. I understood now why racing becomes so all-consuming, and many find it so difficult to retire.

Afterwards, it was all so rushed. I thanked the owner, Sue Packenham, before heading for the weighing room. It was vital to weigh in – to fail to do so or to return weighing less than you went out would result in disqualification.

The stewards and John the valet congratulated me. By chance, the race commentator was Robin Gray, who also rode out for Bill and was racing correspondent of the *News of the World*. He summoned me to speak to the press.

From anonymity, I suddenly found everybody wanted to fire questions at me.

'What does it feel like?'

'How long have you been racing?'

'Where do you live?'

'How long have you been at Mr Wightman's stables?'

'What does your father do?'

The adrenalin was still surging through me, and I answered as much as I could in five minutes. After all I'd been through, I wanted the world to hear about me.

Tomorrow the racing papers would inform all the doubters that a woman rider had won a professional race on the Flat here in the UK on equal terms with male jockeys. Never again would men be able to say it couldn't be done. The way would be open for other women to follow. In just over one minute 45 seconds of my life, I'd changed perceptions.

We all celebrated in the racecourse bar – my proud parents, Mike and me. Mike was almost as thrilled as me after the win, and was impressed by the amount of time the reporters had spent with me post-race.

'You've made history, Karen,' he said with pride. 'You must get a big write-up after all the fuss they made outside the weighing room.'

For the first time in my life I felt that everyone was staring at me, and rightly so. Tomorrow, I thought, when I go out and buy the papers, I'll probably be quite famous …

Chapter 24

A Piece of Sporting History that No One Wanted to Talk About

THE FOLLOWING morning, I awoke a winner. It made me feel I now had the right to call myself a jockey. I no longer felt an imposter in a man's sport. I dashed out to our local newsagent. As I did so, I enjoyed mentally writing my own headlines.

Appreciating that newspapers love alliteration, I considered, 'First girl past the post' or 'First female on the Flat'. Or maybe just: 'Karen comes first'.

I bought *Sporting Life* and the *Daily Mail*. Quickly turning the pages of the *Life*, I found nothing. As for the back page of the *Mail*, again nothing. No pictures, no headlines. Inside, next to that day's race card, there was this:

> Karen Wiltshire, the daughter of a Hampshire farmer ['Eh? Where did that come from?' I thought] rode her first winner when The Goldstone burst ahead 100 yards out and took the Winterbourne Handicap going away by two and a half lengths from the bottom weight, Hunting Willy.
>
> 'I cannot believe it. It's been my ambition for years to be a jockey and ride a winner,' said Miss Wiltshire. 'I had

my chance with the Equal Opportunities law two years ago. I applied to join Mr Wightman and he gave me a trial. I've had about 12 rides, about six on The Goldstone. He needs knowing and takes time to get going, but he's got amazing finishing speed.'

And that was it, and precisely the same report in all the other papers, all buried away. And most frustratingly, there was no reference to the real importance of what had taken place that day: not that it was *my* first win, but that it was the first victory by any professional female on the Flat in the UK. It was a piece of sporting history that no one wanted to talk about.

'Maybe there would have been more interest if I had posed seductively and revealingly next to Goldie afterwards,' I thought.

Perhaps I had expected too much. It was hugely disillusioning, ignoring the fact that they'd got my father's occupation wrong. I distinctly remember describing him as 'a property developer'. Perhaps it was too mundane and they thought 'farmer's daughter' somehow sounded more appropriate?

Anyway, suffice to say I felt the press had let me down – and other women who were to follow me. There always appeared to be plenty of photos and stories of women competing at Badminton Horse Trials, or showjumping, particularly if there was some gossip attached, but apparently little to no interest in a victorious woman professional jockey. Were we to ride unheard and unseen? I had hoped to change all that.

At the stables, Bill Nash's delight was palpable. He couldn't have been more proud of me if I'd been a member of his own family. 'You did it, Karen. You did it!' he exclaimed.

Which was a definite contrast to the feelings expressed by many of the lads. I was soon to learn that, throughout the yard, my victory had been greeted with emotions ranging from scorn to indifference.

Richard Newman would recall later: 'When you started racing, the feeling in the yard was "She won't last long." When you won, they were saying, "Anybody could have won that. This was fixed. The guv'nor set this up."'

I suppose my win defied all their prejudices and prophecies, so they had to attribute it to factors beyond my control.

Charlie Swift and another lad, Grant Eden who was in line to be an assistant trainer at the yard, both congratulated me. However, Grant added: 'There was a terrible atmosphere amongst the boys who went to hear the race at the betting shop. When you won, there was a long silence.'

I suppose I hadn't expected any better.

Later, back home, I received a phone call from Peter Thompson of my local paper, the *Portsmouth Evening News*, asking for an interview. It was pleasing to have some recognition – I was beginning to wonder if it had all been a figment of my imagination.

That evening, I was also contacted by Joy Gibson, treasurer and one of the founder members of the Lady Jockeys' Association. She did unstinting work for the stable girls. Joy shared my surprise at the lack of press interest, but told me that the LJA had always planned to present an award to the first female professional jockey to win a race on the Flat. She insisted that the award should be made at a time and place to give it maximum publicity and suggested Newmarket on the day of the Cesarewitch (the major end-of-season long-distance handicap), just before the main event, the Champion Stakes. My win had been 'a big day for lady jockeys', according to Joy. This really pleased me.

The following morning, I mentioned the call from the *Portsmouth News* to Bill Wightman. I had expected him to be delighted that his stable would receive some positive coverage. Instead he retorted sharply: 'Don't have anything to do with the press. If they won't take no for an answer, then refer them to me.'

I was profoundly upset. I felt like I was being punished for winning a race, an achievement that had attracted some – though not a huge amount of – publicity for his stable. This was ridiculous. What had been the point of grafting through the elements, undergoing muscle-building and wasting regimes, and the animosity and antagonism of some of my colleagues, to finally achieve my goal, only to discover that I was not allowed to talk about it? I knew Bill just wanted me to succeed on ability – not because I was a novelty. And, in fairness he always praised my ability to other trainers and owners. But at that moment, I felt let down.

According to my apprentice agreement, I wasn't allowed to speak to the press without my trainer's consent (apart from some immediate post-race comments). Bill just told me that the Jockey Club wouldn't like it if I did. I knew the guv'nor would never have wanted to upset that particular fraternity, which was all very much old school, but I found this a bizarre comment. After all, the owner of The Goldstone, Sue Pakenham, was the daughter of Lord Leverhulme, the deputy chief steward of the Jockey Club. I never understood this comment, and still don't to this day.

When I questioned Bill Nash about it, his argument was that, 'the papers would want you in a bikini and it would disrespect the sport'. He was worried it would 'sexualise' me, and thought it was important that I should be above all such interest and continue to look and act like a professional – not like one of the amateur ladies. They also wanted my mind focused purely on racing, not on being a celebrity.

Of course, I knew there was an element of truth in their arguments. Both the Bills were trying to persuade people to accept women as professional jockeys. That was their absolute priority. Maybe they took it to extremes, it has occurred to me since. This was, after all, a very different era, socially and politically, to today.

It was pointless arguing with Bill Wightman – he clearly felt very strongly about this issue. But I was determined to bathe in a bit of glory, and went ahead with the evening paper interview, anyway. I assumed that Bill Wightman would not see the article and, if he did, would be appeased by the gratitude I intended to express about his part in my success. Peter Thompson visited my home the next day, and the result was a page feature. Thankfully, I never heard a further word on the subject from Bill.

I settled back into my regular life at the yard, giving advice to the two Bills on the horses I was working on the gallops.

Coincidentally, the same year, 1978, the first international conference of women in sport was organised by the Central Council for Physical Recreation (CCPR). There, it was said that the gap in physical attainment (between the sexes) decreases as stamina is needed more. It was pointed out, for example, that the overall record for swimming the Channel both ways was held by a woman.

Diana Bissill and Dorothy Laird, who attended on behalf of the Lady Jockeys' Association, noted in the association's subsequent newsletter that there had been 'a fairly strong representation of women's libbers' present and 'much stick was given to the male of the species'. However, both had intervened to say that, on the whole, 'we had had a fair crack of the whip from men jockeys, administrators and the media'. Which is probably true when it came to amateur races. Not so for professionals.

For myself, that day at Salisbury gave me a real injection of confidence in my abilities. I had ridden a winner. It felt like a huge badge of honour that no one could strip from me, ever. And apart from some quiet encouragement from Bill Nash in the process, I had not been treated any differently from the men. That was equally important.

This surge in confidence was vital because some of the horses I rode on the gallops weren't the most compliant. Riding them held no fears for me.

That all soon changed.

Chapter 25

I Heard a Voice Say: 'Don't Move Her – She Must Have Broken Her Neck'

ONE MORNING, around a week after my win and after I'd ridden work on three horses, Bill Wightman called out to me: 'Karen, you ride Avon Salmon next.'

I refused to let my dismay appear too obvious as I mounted him. They were words that made me instinctively uneasy. No horse presented much more of a challenge than Avon Salmon. He certainly possessed ability – by the end of the season he would win a maiden event at Newbury, which was no mean feat – but he was a decidedly awkward character.

To be completely frank about this, he was a bit of a rogue, one of the most difficult horses in the stables. He was a strong colt and no one could hold him. Bill Wightman always harboured great faith that it was just a question of psychology with such horses. You just had to get inside their brains. Which was great in theory! Avon Salmon was definitely one who was resistant to persuasion, mental or otherwise.

I had ridden him before, and had been very fortunate not to have been dropped by him, a fate that had befallen some of the lads. I reminded myself that this was our *raison d'être* – to quell the worst instincts of such characters.

'Avon Salmon, go with Charlotte's Choice to the mile and a quarter stand [a white handkerchief tied to a fencing post],' Bill directed us. 'Set off at a steady canter, take it easy up the hill, increase speed when you turn into the straight. Do a steady half speed, and increase it if you see me wave you on.'

Charlotte's Choice, who was stacked with ability, but could also be a handful, would be partnered by Richard Newman. How I envied him. 'Was this the price of success,' I thought, 'being partnered with one of the yard's most tricky customers?' Conversely, I took it as a compliment that Bill had asked me.

All the way down the steep pathway to the bottom of the Downs, I was prepared for my mount to whip round, drop his shoulder and dislodge me. I'd roll all the way down to the bottom. To my great surprise that didn't happen. I relaxed in the saddle as we reached the straight ...

Immediately, Avon Salmon bolted straight across a field adjacent to the gallop. The furrows were deep, and would have brought most horses to a halt, but they didn't impede this individual's progress. I tried desperately to at least persuade him to decelerate by pulling against his mouth, but it had no effect. He was now galloping uphill, but if I expected the gradient to slow him, there was no chance. I shouted his name, and pulled on the rein – to no avail.

I mentally prepared myself for the inevitable moment when he would dislodge me on hard turf. Somehow, we remained a partnership as we breasted the hill. I felt I was in control again, and he was tiring. Out of the corner of my eye, I could see Richard on Charlotte's Choice watching it all from a safe distance. He couldn't help, and it would have been unwise for him to even try.

I tried to urge Avon Salmon to continue with his workout. The guv'nor was standing by his Land Rover, ready to signal, and I started to pull up. But as soon as I applied pressure on his mouth, the colt lengthened his stride for the second time and bolted across the Downs, heading straight towards a mass of 6ft bramble bushes and hedges. I felt a chill of fear spread over me as I realised if he succeeded in jumping through those bushes, we'd be straight out on to the Winchester Road. It was a fast and busy road, on which vehicles could be doing 60 to 70mph. In a collision we wouldn't stand a chance.

Avon Salmon jumped it at its lowest level of about 4ft 6in, but by then I had leapt clear. It was my only course of action. For a few seconds, I knew no more. I must have been briefly knocked out cold.

Richard had watched it all from a distance. His father Lionel, the gallops manager, also looked on. When they watched me disappear into the bramble bush they feared the worst.

I came to, hearing a distant voice declaring: 'Don't move her – she must have broken her neck,' before Bill Wightman arrived in his Land Rover. I regained just enough consciousness to hear Bill reassure me – and no doubt himself – that I hadn't broken my neck. Or was this wishful thinking on his part, I thought, as I struggled to pull myself clear of the thorns that were using me as a pincushion. Discovering just enough strength to crawl out of the bush, I attempted to move my left elbow and, as I did so, pain seared through me. It felt as if my shoulder was coming away from my body.

'You've broken your collarbone, Karen.' Bill took one look at me and swiftly diagnosed my plight like some veteran medic. It's a common injury for jockeys; he had seen it many times before. 'You'll have to go to hospital.'

Meanwhile, Richard's father called out brightly: 'The horse is alright. Not a mark on him.'

I thought grimly: 'That's OK then, as long as the cause of my suffering has survived intact, and is presumably quietly munching on grass without a care in the world.'

Bill drove me back to the yard. There was no alternative, though I can testify that being seated in one of the original Land Rovers, travelling at speed over rough terrain, was not an experience I'd care to repeat.

Pain, agonising pain, shot through me, seemingly to all extremes of my body. I refused to betray my discomfort. It was hard-wired into me that I should display no weakness.

Even now. 'Oh, it was nothing,' was the impression I was trying to give to Bill, who probably realised it was something of a charade. 'It's fine. Can hardly feel a thing,' I reassured him, even attempting a smile.

He transferred me to the Jag for the journey to Winchester's Royal Hampshire County Hospital, but even that relative comfort provided no analgesic effect to put an end to my misery.

For hours, I lay on a hospital bed, my injury not exactly being a priority, I assumed. The nurses had recoiled at the stench when they removed my filthy boots. There had been a split in one, and the muck from my labours earlier in the day had spread through to my sock beneath. A pungent whiff of the stable yard permeated the whole casualty department.

It may have been just my impression, but medical professionals, so familiar with witnessing gruesome sights throughout their working days and nights, were reluctant to venture anywhere near my cubicle. Certainly, the awful smell didn't improve my mood or constitution.

By the time my mother arrived, upset and shaken, I was turning yellow and was vomiting. She confirmed the obvious. 'Oh, Karen. You look terrible,' she said.

'Thanks, mum,' I thought.

I was taken for an x-ray. The technician inexplicably pulled me round by my broken shoulder to get me into position. I screamed. 'Don't worry, dear. You'll be alright,' he tried to reassure me. He then proceeded to line the machine up on the opposite side to my injured one. I said nothing. I assumed he knew best.

When he appeared with the images, he was smiling. 'Nothing wrong at all,' he said. 'You'll be pleased to know there's no break.'

'*Yes, there is*,' I pointed gingerly to the damaged side, on the point of passing out in agony.

'It *is* your right side, isn't it?' he sought to confirm it, with doubt creeping into his tone.

'No, the left,' I cried, tears welling in my eyes, from the agony and frustration.

He apologised, repeated the process correctly this time, and that confirmed that I had, indeed, broken my collarbone. My arm was put in a sling, but that did little to ease the discomfort. Neither did the news that it would take a few months to heal fully.

As my mother drove me home, I reviewed a day in which I had descended from a jockey at the summit of my career, my first victory behind me and the hope of some good rides to come – reward, I felt, for all my hard work, and the belittling I'd had to endure – to this: a period of bleak emptiness. I wouldn't ride for months, and was still in agony. What had I done to deserve this? But then I had to accept it was part of a professional jockey's life.

Bill Wightman phoned when I arrived back, to enquire after my health. I related the details: that the bone had split in half, one part was underneath the other, and was protruding. I added that my arm was now in a sling.

He was surprised by this. 'You ought to be in a figure-of-eight bandage,' he said. 'That's the normal procedure when jockeys break their collarbones.'

For a few days, I moped at home. I had been due to ride The Goldstone at Ascot. That was a huge disappointment – but of little consequence compared with the pain of the injury and a lengthy enforced absence from the racecourse. Unable to move my arm, I couldn't even lie down, and slept in a chair, sitting up. Increasingly, I felt that my shoulder needed further treatment.

My own GP confirmed Bill's opinion that I should have a figure-of-eight bandage. A nurse was consigned to do just that and duly inflicted pain on me I had not experienced before or since. Patients in the waiting room must have thought there was a murder taking place. Somehow the nurse managed to complete her task without placing any padding beneath the bandage, which meant that it quickly started chafing and left me with sores across my shoulder, back and chest. I was almost unconscious with discomfort as we drove home.

A week later, I was back at the hospital and, at long last, I received the correct treatment and bandaging. Admittedly, I looked like I had a hunchback, but at least there was an element of comfort, the only problem being that the only arm movement I had was in my elbows. I couldn't feed myself, reach my feet to pull on tights or put on shoes, and I certainly couldn't drive.

That was to be my life, from now, early October, until December. Attempting to be positive, I considered the saving grace: that the fracture would give me a break. The prospect of a rest, albeit enforced, was not without its appeal: it was a time to relax, enjoy social events, walk, eat a leisurely meal – something I eventually enjoyed once my bandage was eased a little. For a time, I could live life without constantly considering my diet. Pam Bosley, a close friend of Bill Wightman's, came to visit quite often, to update me with all the gossip. The two Bills phoned regularly. Financially I didn't suffer. The Racehorse Owners Compensation Fund paid me £50 a week, and to that could be added £9 social security benefit.

My only significant positive during my time away was a trip to Newmarket to receive the aforementioned award from Joy Gibson of the Lady Jockeys' Association. I was to learn later that, intriguingly, earlier in 1978, 'a male associate member' of the LJA had offered £25 as an award for the first girl professional to win a race on the Flat, so that is what I would receive. I much appreciated the gesture; not so much the money, but the recognition of my feat. However, Bill Wightman was concerned that if I accepted cash it could be considered a breach of the rules (jockeys were not allowed to accept money from anyone other than the owner of the horse they were riding – this was to prevent bribery). While I didn't see how £25, even then (worth around £190 today), would corrupt me, I arranged with Joy that I would exchange the cash for some kind of silver trophy immediately afterwards.

As a preview to that presentation, Southern TV, then ITV's regional broadcaster in the south, telephoned me to ask whether I would appear on their early evening magazine programme *Day by Day*. I agreed, although I was not really allowed to talk to the media. 'What if Bill saw the programme?' I thought. I answered the predictable questions easily enough. How had I felt in the final furlong when I knew I would win? What did my victory mean to me? It only became awkward when the popular, experienced presenter Barry Westwood asked why my arm was in a sling. I explained about being thrown by Avon Salmon but even as I did so, thought: 'This was the first professional female jockey to win a race on the Flat and yet here she was apparently falling off a horse on the gallops. What on earth must all the viewers think?'

I tried to explain that my mount had bolted, had jumped a bramble bush near a busy road, but I had bailed out before he jumped. However, all the time I was thinking: 'People will question how an experienced rider could let her horse do that.' No doubt, I worried too much. But even during this hiatus in my career, my professionalism was so important to me.

I was surprised that around a month after my victory, I received letters from the *Sunday Telegraph* magazine and another Sunday newspaper supplement requesting an interview with me. I declined both because of my loyalty to Bill. I regret my decision now as it would have brought my breakthrough to the attention of a wider public and hopefully would have proved inspirational to young women contemplating becoming professional jockeys.

On the day of the LJA award, I was driven to Newmarket by Mike, and we were accompanied by friends. Though my arm was in a sling, my discomfort was more than offset by the fact that the award, in front of a large crowd, would be tangible appreciation of what I had achieved. My sense of pride was enormous. I felt I was blazing a trail for women to come. I had proved we could do it.

Despite my misgivings about lady riders, and the quality of their riding in general, I had great respect for Joy, who had been an assistant to trainers Bill Holden and Peter Robinson. She rode in ladies' races and mixed amateur events, sponsored by Brooke Bond Oxo, and was 1975 champion, earning her an olive-green Mini. Not too shabby a prize!

Joy told me she was soon to start riding out for the Classic-winning jockey-turned-trainer Frankie Durr, to whom she was assistant. Durr was about to start training near Newmarket.

My presentation took place after the afternoon's apprentices' race. Joy announced: 'It gives me much pleasure, on behalf of the Lady Jockeys' Association, to present you with this award for being the first woman jockey in England to win a professional race on the Flat.'

She also told me: 'It must be very difficult for you. I hope you make your mark and lead the way for all the others to follow.'

The presentation was duly reported in the next LJA newsletter, though with this addendum: 'Our girl apprentices continue to get few opportunities.'

According to LJA records, in 1978 14 women riders (mostly apprentices) totalled only 37 rides, and achieved one win and five thirds. Bear in mind that it was already three years since girls had been allowed to become apprentice jockeys. Progress was agonisingly slow.

I really took to Joy; so generous in spirit and with an obvious love for life. So, when a few Sundays later, I was sitting eating my breakfast with our Sunday paper propped up against the marmalade pot, one headline couldn't fail to arrest my attention. It also had me in tears: 'Lady jockey killed in freak riding accident'.

The article suggested it was a bizarre accident when a yearling which was going out to the paddock for exercise reared up and somersaulted backwards, crushing Joy Gibson against a wall, which then collapsed on her. She was just 34. I felt numb with shock. All I could think of was her cheerful demeanour. Instinctively, I reached for the silver dish I had bought with the

£25 I'd been awarded by the LJA, and which had pride of place on our mantelpiece.

As I did so, a spasm shot through my still healing shoulder. It was a reminder that, unlike Joy, I had got off lightly. Very lightly. I knew her injury was no 'freak'. I had witnessed too many similar incidents at Ower Farm. None had proved fatal, but they could easily have done so, and others had ended with broken limbs, like that suffered, as previously-mentioned, by Grant Eden.

This devastating news was a distressing reminder that in my chosen career there was a fine line between triumph and tragedy.

Chapter 26

A Decision to Make: Marriage or my Career?

LATE IN November, I travelled to Camden Town for an appointment at the medical rehabilitation centre for jockeys. Bill Wightman had felt that correct exercise would help my shoulder to heal, and I should consult a specialist who represented the previously-mentioned Racehorse Owners Compensation Fund (financed by a levy on all riding fees paid by owners).

There I saw men on crutches, exercising their shattered limbs in an attempt to strengthen them. Somehow it put my broken collarbone into context – which is not to say that my injury hadn't been particularly problematic.

Normally, I learned, jockeys return from broken collarbones after around three months. I feared mine would require much longer.

The specialist was clearly not pleased with what he observed, and after consulting the x-rays taken after the accident, opined that the bone had not been allowed to knit together properly. 'You'll always have a bump there,' he said as he fingered the protrusion on my shoulder.

More crucially, the specialist advised me that I would never be able to have such a fall again. He warned me that if I fell on my collarbone again, that would be the end of my career. Today, with

A Decision to Make: Marriage or my Career?

all the advances in medical science, that wouldn't be the case. But then it was a salutary warning to me.

'No exercise,' he decreed, advising me to just take life quietly as the break was otherwise healing well. 'You can't hurry these things,' he added. I was also advised to do no heavy work or ride difficult horses when I returned to the stables in February.

That was still three months away – an eternity as far as I was concerned.

I was not great company for my parents. My mother in particular, who had been very upset by the accident, had taken on the thankless task of nursing and cheering me up ever since it happened. She was not happy at all at the prospect of me returning to work at the stables, and that was evident from her features, often creased with concern. She obviously hoped I might opt for an alternative, safer career.

'There's no more chance of being killed at the stables than being run over by a bus,' I airily tried to reassure her, though to little effect. She was well aware of the fate of the lively, happy Joy Gibson, who had probably held a similar view to me.

There was too much time to brood as I idled the days away, in stark contrast to the last two years of onerous activity at the stables, punctuated by the occasional ride. It became my personal winter of discontent! This period coincided with the actual Winter of Discontent, during which there were widespread strikes across the UK by public sector trade unions demanding larger pay rises, contrary to the pay caps imposed by the Labour government, led by James Callaghan, against Trades Union Congress opposition. It was a period of political turmoil that would culminate with Margaret Thatcher becoming prime minister in 1979.

For myself, there was more than a frustrating hiatus in my racing career to dwell upon. My relationship with my fiancé Mike was another union that had run into serious trouble.

Approaching the end of December, my figure-of-eight bandage was removed and replaced by a sling. I could use my arm again and, just as importantly, I looked normal once more after four months with a hump of bandage in the middle of my back. What a relief. Yet, even as the nurse removed the bandage, I realised that Mike and I had drifted apart.

Early on, while I was riding and on top of life, on a successful career path, albeit a hectic one at times, we saw a lot of each other and enjoyed a wonderful relationship. Admittedly, he was never totally happy about how I spent my days. I strongly suspected that this was because he believed – possibly correctly, up to a point – that my thoughts weren't sufficiently on him because I was so involved with my riding.

I remember one Christmas he sent me a china locket case. On it was inscribed the legend: 'When this you see remember me.' He had written a note to accompany it (rather pointedly, I thought). It read: 'Just in case you forget. Happy Christmas, baby.' (He used to call me that.) He meant 'Just in case you forget *me*.'

Mike never really liked me working with the lads and work-riders, and quite often would just turn up at the stables out of the blue. I could well have done without his presence. On one occasion, he brought with him a pink wheelbarrow bearing the words 'Keep your thieving hands off'. He didn't think it was right that I was having to heave heavy muck sacks around over my shoulders. 'You're using a wheelbarrow from now on,' he told me. But it was also a message to the lads with any romantic inclination towards me: keep your hands off my fiancée as well!

I can honestly say that only one of the jockeys, Steve Woolley, ever made a pass at me. Steve had seen Mike around, but wasn't aware I was engaged. One night he saw me out to the car after a stable lads' and jockeys' party at one of Bill Wightman's cottages at Dean, where the stable staff lived. It was during a time that Mike was pressurising me to give up racing and I happened to mention this to Steve. He took that as a hint that I was 'available', put his arm round me and tried to kiss me. It was something of a shock, particularly as we'd always been in competition for rides. I told him I was engaged, and nothing more was ever said.

You can imagine how cringingly embarrassing it was to have Mike show his face at the yard. Being well-spoken, he fitted the lads' preconceptions about the kind of boyfriend I'd have, immediately being placed in the category of a 'toff' by the lads. Both he and the wheelbarrow – which I didn't use, incidentally – became the butt of the lads' ribald humour.

Mike had been working as a site agent for my father, but he was always a proud, independent man, and by the time of my injury was busy starting a new civil engineering business. He needed all the focus such an initiative required. It did not make him very patient with a moody convalescent. Looking back, I don't completely blame him, although I thought he could have been more supportive.

What proved to be the fatal flaw in our relationship was that, essentially, he was looking to marry a housewife and not a career woman. And marry not just a typical 1970s housewife, either, but an old-fashioned one – the type that, like his mother, baked bread every Sunday. I just couldn't imagine such an existence.

I felt increasingly as though this marriage, if it went ahead, would be far too restrictive on me. Apart from anything else, marriage would be irresponsible, particularly if we had children. Riding those tricky yearlings and two-year-olds, I was aware that something could happen to me at any time. I could be paralysed, or worse.

Perhaps I shouldn't have accepted his proposal. As I've said, once we became engaged, he was pushing me to set a wedding date. But I thought, 'Actually, I don't like this idea.' I knew it could be years before I'd want to be in anything like that kind of life. Maybe I was different – for even the progressive 1970s – in the way I thought.

In December 1978 I was at my lowest, often in pain, and irritable – and yes, probably boring with it, and Mike tended to keep his distance. When we did see each other, our meetings were short-lived. It's a good test of a relationship when you're ill. I felt Mike wasn't there when I needed him. He wanted to be out with his friends in the pub. It was a bit of a shock because he'd always been so devoted. Looking back, I was probably expecting too much.

I didn't particularly want to be seen in public a lot. Which was just as well because, apparently, he didn't relish being seen out with me. At least, I assumed he didn't – he rarely took me anywhere. I admit I wasn't looking my best, with the hump of bandage under my clothes, hands that only had limited movement with elbows fixed at waist level.

By now, our wedding had been planned for June. I had been unable to prolong the inevitable any longer, but I had also had plenty of time to contemplate what Mike would expect of me as a wife. Was I ready to settle down and follow a 'normal' life? Was I ready for domesticity in the form of an unambitious housewife, as I viewed it? Cooking and cleaning were not for me. My efforts at the former tended to end up with me spending two hours clearing up the mess. The thought of including a 'Baking Sunday' in my schedule was my idea of hell. I simply never saw myself as some kind of would-be domestic goddess, laying on dinner parties, and the perfect wife to complement her husband's business life, a part my mother played to perfection.

One evening, Mike persuaded me to go out to a friend's party in Portsmouth. I donned a button-up blouse and cardigan, with a skirt, but felt my appearance could not compare with the slim, chic elegance of the other men's girlfriends. I eased into a chair, nursing my first alcoholic drink for months, and felt that all eyes were on me.

Mike came over. 'Finish your drink. We're going.'

'But we've only just arrived,' I retorted. 'I'll be fine – but I don't think I'll be dancing.'

'We're going,' he insisted in a tone of voice I didn't appreciate. 'Hurry up with that drink.'

'No, I'm not hurrying – and I'm not ready to go yet. For heaven's sake, Mike. It's the first time I've been out for months.'

'I'll go on my own then.'

And he turned, walked out and drove off.

He didn't come back.

I called my mother and asked her for a lift. 'What did you do to upset Mike?' she asked, not exactly sympathetic.

'I think it must be the way I look,' I replied. 'You can't blame him for not wanting to be seen with me.'

It was clear the fissures in our relationship were only going to widen.

Mike believed my injury was a defining moment for me. He made it clear that he regarded the prospect of me returning to racing as rank stupidity, and did his best to dissuade me.

'It's a good time to give it up now – you *will* break your neck next time,' he'd tell me, alluding to what was immediately feared to have been my fate on the gallops.

I felt he was jealous about me being in the limelight – and upset that I was prepared to put my career before him. Effectively, I was faced with an ultimatum. Mike wanted to get married and for me to be the mother of his children. I just wanted to carry on racing.

I think he thought I'd choose him. Taking everything into account, and particularly what I felt was Mike's dismissive approach to my injury, there was never a chance of that. Frankly, the prospect of marriage, and Mike's definition of the respective roles that would apply, didn't appeal to me one iota.

In one sense, I could understand his fears that the Avon Salmon incident could happen again. Yet, my overriding feeling was that he was using it as a lever to try to stop me, and instead adopt a domesticated lifestyle. I didn't like that attitude, and as soon as you feel that, it makes everything stressful. If a man wants to forge a career, a woman is expected to support him. But the same didn't apply in reverse – at least where some men were concerned. I thought he was being quite selfish.

He was so good-looking that some women would probably have conceded and been satisfied with their lot. But you can't change who, or what, you are. I knew I wouldn't have been happy with my mother's role in life. I simply wasn't cut out for that.

Once I returned to the stables in early 1979, it would be my last year as an apprentice and the end of the period when I would be able to use my 7lb claim to persuade Bill Wightman and his owners to offer me promising rides. I needed the time to enhance my reputation. Did I really want to get married in the middle of it?

During my weeks off, I jogged round the country lanes near my home in order to regain fitness. But I could not wait to get back to work. The Flat season would start again in March, only a month or so after I returned to the yard.

Yet, there was one lingering concern: had that incident on Avon Salmon caused me to lose my nerve? How would I cope with the yearlings?

Bill Wightman knew all about the look of fear. He had seen it many times in the Second World War. He had observed it many times after his lads had returned from a bad fall. I knew I had to be able to swing straight back into the saddle of any mount, without any qualms. The lads, too, would be watching me closely for any evidence that I was not the supremely confident figure I had been until that fateful day in September.

I returned in early February, mucking out with a pitchfork, raking out and grooming. Bill Wightman told me to bide my time, but I could not wait to get back on a horse. After restraining myself for a couple of weeks, I told him I'd like to return to the saddle.

'Tomorrow?' he said.

'Fine.'

That evening, I felt as excited as when I had started riding at the age of six.

The feeling was replaced the following morning by one of trepidation when I discovered my first ride was wearing a breaking bit. He was an unbroken yearling.

'What are you, a man or a mouse?' I asked myself as I climbed into the saddle. Fortunately, it was an incident-free ride.

I returned to my normal hectic routine – in bed by ten o'clock, up at six and back to being endlessly rushed, exhausted, concentrating on building up muscle and regaining fitness, without which I couldn't race again.

Meanwhile, away from the stables, Mike's mood did not improve. A new nightclub had opened near his home and he and his friends maintained their hectic social life. I couldn't keep up. I tried to stay out until two or three in the morning on occasion, but such hours simply didn't correlate with my stable schedule. Regaining my fitness was all-consuming with the new Flat season only days away.

Eventually, I refused to go out. Mike would phone me and we'd exchange our news. I knew I had let him down several times when he had wanted to go out, and that had annoyed him.

The night before we were due to attend a friend's wedding, I phoned him and we went to a pub. He was moody and quiet. We walked out to the car park, and I said: 'It's not much good going on like this, is it?'

Mike agreed.

'We might as well break off our engagement,' I added.

He agreed.

Sad as it was, one of us had to say the words. Not exactly the encounter between Humphrey Bogart's Rick and Ingrid Bergman's Ilsa in the final scenes of *Casablanca*, though still affecting enough.

The friend's wedding was on 25 March, which coincided with the first day of the Flat season. We agreed to attend the wedding as a couple, but then go our separate ways.

I'd spent the winter building up to this day, put so much into my recuperation and struggle for fitness, and succeeded. Pride was my overriding emotion. Yet, here I was, about to split from my fiancé. I was in tears the following morning, but my head ruled my heart. I still loved Mike, but I could not combine a life with him and my career. One had to go. And there was no doubt which.

It was a slightly surreal afternoon, sitting through the wedding next to Mike, still wearing my engagement ring, knowing that we were about to part.

As we separated, Mike held me and said: 'I hope your racing career proves to be successful this season. You've made history once, Karen, and I suppose you just want to carry on making history.' He paused and added: 'You can do it again.'

I have sometimes reflected that if I *had* conformed to the way of life expected of me and married Mike Burras, I would not later have found myself in more than one abusive relationship, with controlling behaviour (though I should stress that none of those involved are mentioned in this book). They are ones in which you become constantly aware that your volatile, unpredictable partner, often under the influence of excessive drink or drug-taking, or both, could overreact to anything you say or do. It will be apparent from my story thus far that I would never tolerate such unacceptable behaviour or allow myself to be controlled, by anyone.

By this stage, early 1979, Bill Wightman was aware of my relationship with Mike. Probably Bill Nash, who would have been worried that it would distract me, had told him. Bill Wightman had invited me to an owners' party at the house in 1978, and Mike came along, so they'd met. It was probably the first time Bill Wightman had seen me dressed up in my finest rather than clad in stable wear, so it gave him something of a shock. Bill admitted that it was the first time he'd seen me as a woman rather than a jockey!

After Mike and I split, I had a chat with Bill. I told him that Mike and I were separating principally because I wanted to put my career first. I made it clear I couldn't get married because of my riding. It made Bill even more aware of what it meant to me.

He was very sympathetic and said, 'Come up the house any time you want.' He added, 'I know what it's like to be badly hurt by splitting up.'

Later, I reviewed what had happened in my life in the past six months:

The pain and shock of my accident and debilitating recuperation.

The tragedy of Joy Gibson's death which had affected me badly.

The daunting task of preparing for the Flat season after months of enforced idleness.

And now the upheaval of my break-up with Mike.

That accumulation of events hit me hard. It was a lot to assimilate, to accept. Now I needed the inner strength to keep going. That would prove to be much tougher than the physical strength and fortitude I'd required to get through the earlier days at the stables.

Chapter 27

Encouraging Words for the Girls from the 'Kentucky Kid' Steve Cauthen

AT WORK, I did my best to keep a smile on my face and maintain normal relationships with people around me. I pulled that off successfully. Yet, when I was alone, I would uncontrollably burst into tears. The worst time was at night, a period when, normally, I'd sleep contentedly from sheer fatigue. It was a normal human reaction, of course, and the fact that I hadn't returned to my old self was not lost on those around me, notably Bill Wightman.

'Cheer up, Karen,' he said. 'I've got a ride for you tomorrow.'

Those words made me feel alive again.

'Caught Again is running at Leicester,' continued Bill. 'It's a handicap sprint. I just hope her legs stand up to it.'

Instinctively, I wanted to phone Mike and tell him. But I couldn't. And didn't. For the first time in ages when I had a ride he wouldn't be there at the course to discuss my chances and those of the opposition. It would not be the same without him there. I choked back tears.

'Caught Again?' My thoughts turned back to Bill. 'How do you rate her chances?'

Caught Again was a three-year-old, owned and bred by Bill. She had problem joints, but had been sound throughout the winter, and Bill wanted to give her an early-season run when the ground tended to be easier. The going was soft, so Bill decided to take advantage of it, although the blacksmith had inserted a leather pad between her hoof and shoe to reduce any discomfort. Though she had not won, and had no form to speak of, this was a strong little filly. Bill wanted to establish if 6 furlongs would suit her. It was a maiden race, the Keythorpe Maiden Stakes, confined to horses that had not won. Colts carried 9st in these races and fillies 8st 11lb. Though I had put on weight during my enforced absence, I was still only 7st 11lb, so could make the weight comfortably, even allowing for my 7lb allowance which would mean the filly carrying 8st 4lb.

Because a lightweight wasn't required, I was acutely aware the guv'nor could have booked a senior jockey. It felt good when I glanced at the daily paper and realised I'd be up against some of the leading riders of this generation. They included Joe Mercer, a great stylist, who had secured his first Classic triumph, the 1953 Oaks on Ambiguity, while still an apprentice; and Greville Starkey; as well as Edward Hide, Brian Rouse and Geoff Baxter.

I also noticed that, following heavy rain, the ground was so atrocious that there'd be a flag start for our race – similar to that used all the time for jumps races – rather than stalls. It was so muddy it was impossible to tow the stalls into position and a flag start was something I'd never experienced before. With a long-distance race, it would be no problem. But this was a sprint. With a poor start, you could be out of contention even before you'd seriously got into your stride.

I travelled up with Bill Wightman and Steve Woolley and, having time to kill, I wandered into the restaurant at the course. I found Bill tucking into a roast lunch. How delicious it looked and smelled. He looked up enquiringly, and with a sympathetic smile, asked, 'You're not thinking of a four-course meal before the race, are you?' I assured him I was just looking for a bar to get myself a light snack. 'You want to go that way then,' he said, directing me to the exit. I departed quickly, but the aroma of roast beef, potatoes and Yorkshire puddings stayed with me as I consumed a small egg sandwich.

Here, at Leicester, the loo was my changing room and I then joined the other jockeys in what, unusually, was a small, cosy weighing room on a bitterly cold day. Hail began to beat on the roof. Jockeys ride in all weathers, all underfoot conditions, but none of us appreciated the elements on this day. As the first race approached, my fellow riders were reluctant to leave the warm intimacy of the weighing room.

Willie Carson, the 1978 champion jockey who later that season would storm home on Troy at Epsom – the first of his four Derby victories – asked the stewards if there was a chance racing could be abandoned. He spoke more in hope than anything else.

'He's a cheeky so-and-so,' I heard one steward mutter to another as they reassured him that racing would, indeed, continue. That was typical Willie, whose audacity would make him such a popular TV personality after he retired from the saddle.

The 2.15 started on time, the jockeys arriving back absolutely saturated and covered with mud. So much for the 'glamorous career' everyone assumed I had sought. This was about as far removed from the image of the sun blazing down on champagne picnics at Royal Ascot and spectators viewing races worth many thousands as you could get. Today's race was worth £850 to the winning owner.

My silks clung to my goose-bumped, shivering frame as I strode to the paddock to mount.

Bill Wightman had told me: 'Without stalls, you must make sure you get a good break at the start. Keep her well-balanced. See if she can keep up with the pace.' I focused fully on the race ahead – anything to distract me from the rain and chill. Achieving a satisfactory flag start with 19 runners is no easy feat – for the starter or the jockeys, and particularly with keen three-year-olds, most inexperienced.

The starter shouted: 'Make a line with that Land Rover.'

What Land Rover? I thought. I couldn't see a thing.

'Not yet, sir. Not yet, sir,' shouted back the jockeys as they attempted to coax their charges to face the right way. The usually ripe language was exchanged for deference where officialdom was concerned. Horses were wandering in all directions, but I was determined to make my way towards the front of what, laughingly, could be described as a line.

'Not yet, sir. Not yet, sir,' the jockeys continued their chorus.

'Sir' dropped his flag, and we were off. We were in third place and went well until the 4-furlong marker. Then she just died on me, dropping from sprint speed to a canter. We finished towards the rear, but I already knew she had gone lame. Bill inspected her hoof. The heavy going had pulled away the leather pad that had been intended to ease her joints.

It was another race I could not have won, I reflected, as cold, muddy and miserable, I returned to the toilets to change.

On the drive back, Bill tried to console me. 'Your style was very good when you cantered past the stands,' he said. I felt damned by his faint praise. 'Thanks for nothing,' I thought. I was not being ungrateful, but I knew I could do without many more rides like that.

My next race was a different proposition entirely. I would be reunited with my old friend The Goldstone at Kempton Park on

Easter Monday. It was too early in the season to expect another victory, but it felt good to be back on Goldie, now a seven-year-old.

Beforehand I had a good chat in the weighing room with Steve Cauthen, the American teenager who had arrived over here with a huge reputation and was the focus of much media interest. The previous year, having just turned 18, he had become the youngest and last jockey to land the American Triple Crown on Affirmed.

Weighing under 7st and standing only just over 5ft – how I envied him! – he won 487 victories and become the first jockey to win $6 million in a calendar year. Steve had become a national TV sensation in the States. He was on every show from *Good Morning America* to *Johnny Carson*, but then had upped sticks to come over here, primarily to ride for Robert Sangster and trainer Barry Hills. There was more money in the US, but a different class of racing here, over completely different terrain to America's standard tracks.

It was a challenge that attracted a number of foreign riders. Another notable American to visit here at that time was Bill 'The Shoe' Shoemaker, all 4ft 11in of him. The prolific jockey, who developed such an affinity with horses, came desperately close to winning the 1978 Derby, defeated narrowly on Hawaiian Sound by Shirley Heights.

It was an enormous thrill to speak to Cauthen, a man who, nine days earlier, had partnered Sangster's Marquee Universal to victory at Salisbury in his first race on British soil. The following month, just four days after his 19th birthday, he would secure our first colts' Classic of the season, the 2,000 Guineas, on Tap On Wood at Newmarket.

'Hello, how are you?' he enquired. 'I haven't seen many girl jockeys around.' Perhaps that was because I was one of very few,

I thought, but didn't say it out loud. He added: 'I do hope that women can take off here like they have in America.'

I told him I'd been trying to base my riding on his, to copy his streamlined style, which I think pleased him. He was very approachable and engaging. For such a big name in the US, he was so humble – a contrast to too many of the British and Irish riders I had encountered.

'I love it here in England. I like the people and enjoy the racing scene,' he responded to my obvious question: what was he doing here?

Eight years later, Steve would land the 1987 Derby on Reference Point. But the year following that triumph, he damaged vertebrae in a fall at Goodwood. Reportedly, it was centimetres from being a neck-breaker. As Brough Scott, my fellow work-rider and jockey-turned-broadcaster and journalist, would write later:

'When he flew in to Britain that April Steve Cauthen was to make a greater impact and leave a finer legacy than any jockey at any time. He set a new standard for race-riding by fusing the best of American poise and pace with the traditional strength and horsemanship of the British method.'

Being a Bank Holiday, Kempton was a vibrant scene, and packed with racegoers who were invariably attracted by the presence of Steve, the charismatic American, but as I walked out to the paddock, to my astonishment people demanded an autograph from *me*. Perhaps they'd already had their fill of collecting the signatures of Steve and the leading Brits. Nevertheless, I was pleased that they still remembered my win on The Goldstone the previous year. The other jockeys looked at me, slightly bemused by the attention I was receiving. 'Who the hell does she think she is?' they were probably thinking. But I relished my brief moment of celebrity.

Also in my race, the Bendigo Handicap, over 1 mile, was the irrepressible Willie Carson, one of my long-time heroes. He would always crack jokes, accompanied by that famous cackle. He'd do his best to calm me down, and was very considerate and caring. He was one of the few who was really nice to me and not at all chauvinistic, such good fun and still is. I've bumped into him in later years at awards dinners and he mimics us riding against each other upsides.

The only problem was that, this day, I was concentrating intently on my instructions, trying to look and act professional, and thinking, 'Why's he chatting to me and cracking jokes at a time like this?' But that was Willie.

Goldie was slow out of the stalls, made progress amid some nasty bunching in which horses clicked heels and jockeys shouted and swore at each other to keep out of their way, and we finished in mid-field, alongside Steve Cauthen's mount. Willie Carson won the race comfortably on Black Minstrel, a name I would encounter again.

Bill Wightman was delighted with this seasonal pipe-opener and, driving back from Kempton, told me he had decided to run a horse name Ardtully Lass in a 1-mile handicap race at Warwick the following day.

'Could you do the weight, Karen?' he asked. 'Yes, of course,' I responded quickly. Then added: 'What is it?'

Ardtully Lass would be carrying 7st 13lb, less my 7lb. I contemplated the reality: I had to weigh in at 7st 6lb which, with the saddle, meant I would have to get down to 7st 2lb. I was then 7st 7lb, and the race was less than 24 hours away. I had a problem – one that Bill could foresee.

'I'll have to put up a professional if you can't make the weight,' he added. 'Are you sure you can do it?'

'Of course, I can,' I cried. What was 5lb in a night and a morning? I was dieting in my mind already.

I wanted to ride, in part because Ardtully Lass was owned by George W. Martin, a friend of a friend, who I'd met at a party when my arm was still in a sling. He was enthusiastic about women riders. 'I'd like to see you girls get a chance,' he'd told me. 'I'll definitely follow your progress.'

'The trouble is actually getting owners and trainers to give us rides,' I told him, dropping him a rather obvious hint. It had obviously struck the intended target. I reassured Bill that I'd do the weight, and also that George was greatly in favour of women jockeys.

Sod's law decreed that I should arrive home with my mother threatening to cook 'a special meal' that night in honour of friends visiting from France. When I told her of my ride the following day, she mouthed two words: 'The sauna?'

'The sauna,' I responded.

I sat and watched them eat before driving to the sauna, remaining in it as long as I dared.

The following day I drove myself to Warwick. Remarkably, part of the weighing room had been sectioned off to provide a women's changing area. I felt like royalty. Progress indeed!

'Make it a win for the girls,' said Sue, Ardtully Lass's groom, with a laugh. She had a point – we were three females: the filly, her groom and me. I knew the horse well enough. She had won a maiden at the end of the last Flat season, and should have been fit from hurdling. But this was different. It was quite a valuable handicap. She had not been in this kind of company before, and the suspicion was that she would not appreciate the soft ground.

Bill had briefed me thoroughly. He had warned me that this could be a tough course to negotiate. Warwick is a sharp track with an emphasis on speed and adaptability and there was a likelihood of congestion, and I had to be wary.

'They will all be trying to get to the rails,' said Bill. 'The early part of the race will be a sprint, and then it's into a steep bend, with everyone looking for a good position. Imagine 25 runners coming out of their stalls at a sprint speed and all aiming for that bend and you'll see what you're up against.'

As I wrote at the start of my story, I discovered that what I was up against was far worse – obscenities being hurled at me and a whip-happy jockey who took liberties. Had it happened now, under the scrutiny of numerous TV cameras, the rider would have received a lengthy suspension. But back then it went unnoticed by the stewards. And what would they have made of the jockey who burst into my changing area and attempted to kiss me?

Despite my anger at the events of that day those two rides at Easter meetings had intensified my appetite for more and I waited on tenterhooks for news of another. I was rewarded at the end of the week when Bill Wightman called out to me as I was changing horses during riding work: 'Karen, I want you to do a 7-furlong half-speed on Somers Heir.'

Chapter 28

Riding at the Home of the Derby

I KNEW that Somers Heir was scheduled to run in the Crown Plus Two Apprentice Championship Handicap the following Thursday at Epsom. It was a prestige event and, having missed out on that Derby ride on Goblin the previous year, to finally get to negotiate the world's most famous racecourse would be a tremendous experience. It was also due to be televised as part of ITV's racing coverage.

And, mostly importantly of all, Bill Wightman's four-year-old was in with a major chance.

I also knew that Somers Heir was very strong, and had a will of his own. It would take all my strength to achieve the optimum from him. But this was my chance to impress Bill as never before. I had even started to diet just in case.

Somers Heir worked well on the gallops, and in the last 2 furlongs nearly pulled my arms out of their sockets in his determination to gallop. But I held him back to half-speed, and slowed him to a walk as Bill had asked.

Bill appeared satisfied. 'Can you do 7st 4lb by Thursday?' he asked, clearly noticing that I was slightly overweight – possibly a consequence of some fish and chips on the way back from Warwick.

'Of course, I can,' I assured him.

Bill added, to my surprise: 'If you put up on 1lb or 2lb overweight, you can still have the ride.'

'Thank you, Mr Wightman – I'll do the weight.'

Again, I'd have liked to share the news with Mike. Happiness should be shared, I've always thought. But those days were in the past.

I was 7st 7lb and needed to shift several pounds, but my worry was that drastic weight loss could weaken me. I'd require all my strength on such a strong-willed character.

I found it tough going. It was relatively cold and, in such circumstances, you don't perspire so much from working and riding, and by the day of the race I had only got down to 7st 2lb. I'd go to scale carrying 7st 6lb, which meant Somers Heir would carry 2lb overweight, with the saddle. At least I felt strong and fit.

As I travelled in the horsebox, I studied the form of the opposition. Black Minstrel was favourite, carrying 8st 2lb. I had raced against him on The Goldstone at Kempton on Easter Monday when Black Minstrel had won comfortably, partnered by Willie Carson. Today, he would be ridden by Walter Swinburn.

The going was very soft after heavy rain, and I knew this would be to Somers Heir's advantage. Live television coverage made me feel very nervous – I'd be scrutinised by everyone, including my harshest critics back in the stables. One of the lads bade me farewell with the kind words, 'Your arse will block the screen.' 'What a comedian,' I thought.

Steve Woolley called out: 'Don't forget to wave to your mother as you canter to the stalls.'

On arrival, I walked the course. It was a fascinating and valuable experience, surveying that historic piece of turf, and most notably Tattenham Corner, where the track descends and bends dramatically – a feature not all horses can handle – rather than watching it from afar on TV. The Derby course is 1 mile 4 furlongs. My race was only over 7 furlongs 11 yards, but it would be fascinating to negotiate those contours in front of what would be a decent-sized crowd. As I strode the course, I recalled the names of legends, equine and in the saddle, who had pounded this stretch of turf. Names like Never Say Die who, in 1954, gave an 18-year-old Lester Piggott the first of his nine Derby triumphs; Sea-Bird in 1965; Nijinsky (another Piggott victory, in 1970); and Mill Reef the following year.

However, it was also a moment to dwell on the fact that tragedy had struck here on 4 June 1913 when militant suffragette Emily Wilding Davison ran out in front of King George V's horse Anmer and died four days later of injuries she sustained.

Epsom was one of the country's leading courses, but still no thought had been given to facilities for women riders. My changing room was – no surprise to me – the first aid room, still occupied by paramedics. I changed behind a curtain.

I strode over to the weighing room. The sense of formality there was lightened by my valet, John. 'I'll be watching you on the telly today,' he said with a warm smile. 'You'll be a picture.'

Walter Swinburn approached me. He was polite, affable as always. I sensed and hoped he would make it as a big-time jockey – though at the time the horse that would be named Shergar with whom he would always be associated, was just a yearling. Being the son of Wally Swinburn, the Irish champion jockey in 1976 and 1977, was certainly a major aid in Walter's quest for greatness. He was also the beneficiary of instruction by two of the greatest jockey tutors at the time, Frenchie Nicholson and

Reg Hollinshead. His star was very definitely in the ascendant. How I envied him. But this, I knew, was the opportunity to, at last, get one over him.

I thought – and the betting confirmed – that his mount Black Minstrel, noted for a quick turn of foot in the final furlong, was Somers Heir's most potent rival.

When I weighed out carrying 2lb overweight Bill didn't appear too displeased. 'He should break well,' he told me after introducing me to the owner, Mr Duffield, a farmer who loved his horses. 'Make sure you're up there lying about sixth. But remember to keep your best in reserve for the finish. And keep him balanced in the final 2 furlongs.'

Bill made a particular point of the last sentence. Epsom notoriously has a camber towards the rails on the inside of the course, and many are the jockeys who have struggled to keep their horses balanced on such terrain.

Unusually, the owner intervened. 'Now, Karen, you get him up there – I think he likes to be right up with the front runners. Let him run free, don't hold him back.' It slightly conflicted with Bill's instruction, but I got the idea: keep him prominent.

On the way to the start, I managed to manoeuvre Somers Heir behind another horse and his head towards the rails, which deterred his inclination to bolt. Coincidentally, The Goldstone was also in the race, ridden by Karen Newman, the sister of Richard. Karen had come in and done some mucking out during 1978, the second year I was at the stables. It was another example of how Bill was trying to change attitudes in racing by encouraging women. Bill had asked me to mentor her, but that ride on The Goldstone at Epsom was one of only three she had, and none with a winning chance.

Somers Heir was one of the last of the 20 runners in the stalls, but one of the first out. We broke fast and were prominent at Tattenham Corner. I was on the inside, and fourth as we headed into the straight. I had never experienced so many close encounters, as rival horses cannoned into us in the search for the best position. The adrenalin was surging through me as I maintained my place. Beneath me, Somers Heir was striding out purposefully. I knew I had to hold my own. Not let them bully me.

There are few more satisfying, exciting experiences than knowing that the mount under you is full of running, with the finish post in sight. This was ours for the taking, I felt, as he made headway in the final 2 furlongs to take the lead. I could even hear the commentator over the PA, 'Here comes Somers Heir. Here comes Somers Heir. It's Somers Heir …'

But then, the commentator's tone changed. 'It looks like Black Minstrel is coming up on the stand rails with a late run. It's Walter Swinburn and Black Minstrel. Black Minstrel wins.'

Black Minstrel was out of my eyeline, but Walter must have thought the ground was better on the stand side. I had elected to run as straight as possible in the straight. I was devastated. Walter's mount had struck fast and late out of my vision on the other side of the course. Until those final moments I was certain I had won. But it transpired that Black Minstrel had won by a length.

My sense of supreme satisfaction at having ridden the world's best-known racetrack was halted abruptly.

After I weighed in, I was approached by Bill. Praise was not immediately on his mind. His features were grave. 'Karen, there's a stewards' inquiry for second place. Someone has said Somers Heir interfered with another horse. I will accompany you. Just voice your opinion and stick to it.'

I was in turmoil. After just being pipped at the post for first, now this. I was bewildered. What was I supposed to have done? If the objection referred to Tattenham Corner, then a lot of horses had collided. I'd certainly been bumped into.

We entered the stewards' room or, should I say, court room. That's what it felt like, as I was confronted by three officious-looking men who regarded me as though I was being charged with murder. Beside us stood another apprentice and his trainer.

'Look at the video of the race very closely,' I was instructed. 'Notice the blinkered horse and see Somers Heir move directly in front of him.'

The alleged incident took place just after Tattenham Corner, but for the life of me, I couldn't see who was encroaching on whose ground. I saw Somers Heir being pushed by a horse on the outside, but no one raised this point. And, indeed, the official *Raceform* comment later was that I had been 'carried left'. If we had moved left, it was only because another horse had forced me to do so. What I did know was that horses tended to drift towards the inside rails because of the gradient.

'Well, have you anything to say?' one of the stewards growled in an unnecessarily abrupt manner. I had a suspicion that, as I was a girl, they thought I'd break down and cry. Not a chance. I never felt less like it. I was annoyed about being in this position over what I felt was nothing of any consequence, and part of me wanted to give them a piece of my mind. But I also realised that I had Bill's reputation to consider. I couldn't embarrass him. Not in this company.

'I didn't realise I had galloped in front of the blinkered horse, and caused an obstruction,' I said in my most conciliatory manner, before adding more defiantly: 'I'm very sorry, but I myself was pushed by the horse on the outside.'

They conferred briefly, before the chairman of the stewards eyed me and said, 'We'll let you off this time, but don't let it happen again. Understand?' The impression he gave was that I was guilty, but there was insufficient evidence to prove any charge against me.

'Yes, sir,' I responded in a suitably humble manner, and left the room with Bill. What an afternoon.

My mood was already darkened by such a narrow defeat. The stewards' inquisition had left me furious.

'Smile, smile,' cried the photographers as I joined a line-up of the apprentices who had finished in the first three for a presentation. I felt like doing anything but smile. I was tempted to just glower my disapproval instead. That was my instinctive reaction to being the first women professional jockey to face a stewards' inquiry, possibly anywhere in Britain, but certainly at Epsom.

Already in position were Walter Swinburn and the third-placed rider. We were each given gift vouchers. If the photographs were published, I never saw them.

I took stock. Yes, I had been the first professional woman jockey to ride at Epsom, and around Tattenham Corner. Yes, I had lost by a narrow margin, and to a very good horse. However, on the way back home in the car, I received an extended ear-bashing from Bill. He said that the extra weight I'd carried made all the difference. It was true. That 2lb overweight could have been crucial.

I told Bill, 'You gave me 24 hours' notice. I can't lose that kind of weight overnight. Why didn't you give me more notice?'

Two weeks later, Bill asked me to ride a filly named Rockaway in the first at Salisbury, the Horserace Betting Levy Board Apprentice Handicap, a race for three-year-olds over 6 furlongs. My association with her had been a difficult one. On many occasions she had thrown me at home. She had been placed, and I had seen her once on TV where she had been a handful in the preliminaries, rearing and falling over. I was apprehensive, to say the least.

The filly was owned by Lady Georgina Coleridge, a fascinating woman, I would learn later. She was a journalist and for many years had edited *Homes & Gardens*. She became a director of IPC Women's Magazines until her retirement in 1974, and in 1978 wrote a book called *That's Racing*.

Lady Georgina had also been co-founder, in 1955, of the Women of the Year lunches, the aim being rather appropriately, where I was concerned, to celebrate the achievements of women in a 'man's world'. Presumably, she had no objection to her horse being partnered by a girl!

Bill wasn't at Salisbury, but had told me beforehand that this was an exercise to establish whether the filly could last 6 furlongs, having previously raced over five. While waiting to weigh out, I caught a glimpse of Rockaway, cavorting and leaping in the air, causing her groom Pat terrible problems. My parents had travelled to the course, and I could see my mother's expression. She was in a state of panic.

Geoff Yates, formerly travelling head lad who by now had replaced Bill Nash as head lad on the latter's retirement, was representing the guv'nor. He had saddled the horse and warned me, 'The filly's playing up a bit this afternoon.'

'That's putting it kindly,' I thought.

Geoff added, 'I think it would be best if you were one of the first to go down to the stalls – OK?' He also advised me to keep her covered up off the pace, and reserve her best for the final furlong.

Pat, who was walking the horse round the paddock, was definitely a relieved man when it was time to relinquish his control of Rockaway. Even as I mounted her, she put in a mighty buck before butting Pat into the railings as Geoff rushed to the rescue. He managed to lead us out on to the track, and I was away. My partner cantered furiously to the start.

Looking on was Richard Newman, who had been partnering Charlotte's Choice the day I broke my collarbone on Avon Salmon. Today he was riding for an outside trainer in my race.

'Are you OK, Karen?' he asked with concern, as I walked Rockaway round behind the stalls.

'Oh, fine,' I assured him, with a confidence I didn't possess.

The filly was no problem entering the stalls, but was clearly tense as we waited an eternity for the other runners to be loaded, with one refusing to go in. I tried to calm her, but when the stalls opened, she reared, flinging back her head, which hit me full in the face. Blood streamed out from my nose and mouth, soaking my silks and breeches.

The blow stunned me for a second as Rockaway was left several lengths behind. But having cleared my head, I pushed my mount past the back markers and into mid-field, which was where we finished. It was a promising run. With a better start, we could have been placed. She was clearly useful.

Later in the year, incidentally, the filly would win for Lady Georgina at Sandown, partnered by Joe Mercer – though I like to think I'd played my part in her progress.

But back to that Salisbury race in May: my mother was horrified by the spectacle of her blood-spattered daughter as we returned to unsaddle. I must have looked like the victim of a slasher movie. 'It looks worse than it is,' I just about mumbled as I was rushed to first aid. Quick dental treatment ensured that my teeth were just about intact but I couldn't eat, only drink through a straw. It would be a month before the swelling and scars finally disappeared.

Bill called me that evening to ask how I was. It was like talking through a melon, so swollen were my lips, and it required several attempts to make him understand that I was in some pain.

'Poor Karen – and poor Willie Carson,' he said, as if to place things in some kind of perspective. 'He broke his collarbone at Doncaster this afternoon.' Bill added that it was a shame I wouldn't be able to ride The Goldstone at Salisbury the following day.

'I'll be fine, absolutely fine,' I assured him, ignoring the fact that the course doctor had recommended that I shouldn't work for a week. Nothing was going to deprive me of a ride.

It was early in the season, and I knew Goldie wouldn't be fit enough to win yet. But I was overjoyed to be re-associated with him in what was a good-standard race, the 7-furlong New Forest Handicap, worth over £3,000.

Because of some technical fault, again we had a flag start. I kept Goldie off the pace, and, similar to my first ride on him, finished pleasingly enough just outside the frame.

What I didn't realise at the time was that this would be my final race.

Chapter 29

Facing up to the Continued Prejudice of Owners and Trainers

JUST BEFORE Easter 1979 I had received a letter from my Aunt Pat in San Francisco, inviting me for a long holiday. I ignored it, initially. I was preoccupied, working hard at the stables. I had no time for such trivialities.

But the idea of Californian sunshine, something I'd experienced three years previously, did have some appeal. The English weather was still inclement and, on days when I rode out six horses in torrential rain, it felt like an age since I had last been truly warm and dry.

This could be more than a break. It occurred to me that it could be a chance to investigate the racing scene in a location seemingly so far ahead in its positive attitudes to women jockeys. From what I knew, life there was far less arduous and more embracing of female riders.

I took stock, and considered what lay ahead of me in Britain. My record was good. From 18 rides, I'd rejoiced in that one win, been frustrated by that close second at Epsom when I thought victory was there for the taking, and had secured three thirds. I knew Bill Wightman trusted me with his horses – as much as he did his best male apprentices. But I also now appreciated that often I'd get rides on horses when Bill was seeking fitness, not a win, from them.

Also there was the perennial conundrum of doing the weight. I had struggled – and ultimately failed – to get down to 7st 4lb to ride Somers Heir at Epsom. To do even close to that weight deprived me of my strength in the saddle. Would I continue to record wins and places once I lost my claim, as I would in 1980, after having completed three years as an apprentice? Possibly, but probably not enough to make a long-term career out of it.

I had to face reality. I needed more than just rides on Somers Heir and The Goldstone – both owned by people highly supportive of women riders – to provide me with potential victories. And I considered it unlikely then that outside trainers would offer me mounts. There was simply no evidence that any would be forthcoming.

That said, I must stress that I had learned so much in those three emotion-charged years. My experiences confirmed I possessed the natural talent required and, to illustrate that fact, Bill Wightman had put me up on horses in maiden races, in which a low weight was not a factor – as I've said, colts carried 9st and fillies 8st 11lb – when he could instead have opted for an experienced professional. Bill's actions signified that I was as good as the men – and that meant everything to me. He once told me, 'I'd want you [riding my horses] as much as anybody.'

I knew he watched me closely in races, and if he'd ever considered me not up to the job, he'd have shown me the door, albeit in a very gentlemanly fashion. What had always been absolutely vital to Bill was that I wouldn't be exposed in a race as being a girl. That could have set things back for everyone. But, and it was a major but, without sounding too grand about my abilities, I needed wins, not just rides. I couldn't see those victories forthcoming – not while prejudice by too many owners and trainers remained.

It was with a heavy heart that I articulated these sentiments in a letter to Bill, who was away at the time. I thought it only fair to inform him as soon as possible that my time with him had ended, and I needed to look elsewhere – possibly in the more enlightened racing jurisdictions of the US – to further my career.

I discovered later that my letter had upset him. However, he had also been very understanding. There was no escaping from the fact – for either of us – that at that time, over four decades ago, as the 1980s approached, there was still a reluctance by many owners to entrust a girl with their horse. As Bill had repeatedly told me, he couldn't force owners to put me up. Owners pay the bills, and often like to see big-name jockeys on their horses. If a claimer was to ride, in order to bring down the weight, the majority still preferred a male.

Naturally, Bill did not want to lose a top work-rider after a three-year apprenticeship, but he wished me well in the United States. There, I already knew, women riders were a significant part of the racing scene, and received the kind of exposure that I would have relished in the wake of my historic breakthrough.

Before departing for California, on a Friday off, I watched the televised racing from Doncaster with a friend. Bill had a couple of runners there. Between races, Walter Swinburn, who was due to ride Black Minstrel in The Lincoln, the season-opening major handicap at Doncaster, the following day, was interviewed.

'Wow,' I exclaimed to my friend, explaining that they were the narrow conquerors of my mount Somers Heir at Epsom when we were caught late on. And seconds later, I relived the moment when they showed a clip of the race.

The presenter then turned to Walter and congratulated him profusely on a fine performance, in which he had made his challenge at precisely the right moment. This praise was thoroughly merited, of course. But it could also have been the opportunity to highlight what I had achieved as one of the then very few female professional riders. It slightly rankled that there was no mention of me.

Chapter 30

Some California Dreamin' Before I Wake up to Reality

AND SO, at the end of May, not without some misgivings, I walked out of my home and a secure job to cross the Atlantic for what I hoped would be a new adventure, heading for Bay Meadows racetrack in the San Francisco Bay Area. This was where Sea Biscuit twice won the Bay Meadows Handicap in the late 1930s. It was also where Bill Shoemaker began his career, exercising horses on the track in 1948. Like many American courses, it was a dirt track, and like nothing I had experienced before.

It may appear bizarre now, but I simply turned up and asked how I could go about getting work, as a jockey. The young woman at the front desk exclaimed in delight. 'The first English girl jockey – here! You must meet the press.'

And meet the press I did as I related my story to an intrigued media, who regarded me almost as an alien being. They couldn't wait for me to get in the saddle. 'What a story,' someone said. 'If you become the first English woman to win a race here at Bay Meadows, you'll get all the publicity we can give you, Karen.'

For a moment, I felt like a real celebrity. Not just an intriguing visitor. However, I got the impression that the story was rather more important to them than my racing career. I was a novelty. But once I started riding, I'd probably be forgotten.

One of the press men was an ex-jockey, who, having broken just about every bone in his body, had decided that life pounding a keyboard would be preferable. He said he knew a couple of trainers further north who would probably allow me to exercise their horses at their local racetrack. Why didn't I go to see them, and mention his name?

Afterwards, Jane Driggers, a female jockey to whom I had been introduced, showed me her room at the racecourse. It was like a plush, tastefully decorated private suite. Like me, she had been an innocent when she started out, originally at Portland Meadows.

In an article after her retirement in 1983, Jane said: 'I didn't know anybody. My mom said, "Walk up and down the shedrows [a row of stalls within a barn in a stable area] and introduce yourself and ask if they need any help." I just wanted to ride races, so I tried to be nice to everybody.'

Jane had her first mount in 1972 and became Portland Meadows' first female winner, prevailing in a three-horse photo finish. Her career prospered and by 1977 Driggers was a regular at Golden Gate Fields, Bay Meadows and on the Northern California 'fair circuit', as it's known.

A billboard and bus-sign campaign once announced 'Jane Driggers wants you at Bay Meadows'.

'This is all yours?' I asked her about her living quarters. I was incredulous.

'Of course,' she replied. 'I travel from racetrack to racetrack. I have to have a room.'

'You actually have one of these wherever you go?' I asked.

'Of course,' she said, adding – clearly mystified – 'Don't you?'

I laughed.

Jane had been riding since she left school. The operative word was riding. She was horrified when I mentioned that I'd got fit by filling muck sacks and running with them on my back. Jane told me that, in California, horses were exercised on the racetrack at 6am, not taken out on to grass gallops. Grooms performed the mundane tasks in the stables. Other riders broke the yearlings. Jockeys exercised horses, rode in races and were treated like celebrities.

Back in Britain, as an English jockey, I was very low in the hierarchy of the racing world; I occupied a lowly station in life. In contrast, Jane was one of the stars of the show. She knew it, too, and expected that everyone should come running. They generally did. I wondered what Bill Wightman and Bill Nash would make of such influence exerted by one of their jockeys!

My mind filled with images of a life of changing in ladies' toilets, of first aid rooms full of male paramedics who appeared reluctant to leave me alone with their equipment, and how I had to change behind screens. Of the partitioned-off end of the men's changing room in which one of the male jockeys had tried to kiss me.

A few days later, I travelled north to visit the trainers whose names I had been given. I drove up to the racecourse, but attempting to gain entrance was as difficult as breaking into Fort Knox. It took me about an hour to persuade the security guard to allow me in. Finally, I got to see the racetrack head and repeated my, by now well-rehearsed, life story. He said I would have no problem getting rides.

For a fleeting moment, I could envisage myself relaxing in my private suites on California's racetracks in breaks between mounts on horses primed to win.

My great American dream dissolved when I discovered it would take six months to get the formalities of a licence and adequate insurance sorted out before I could even begin exercising horses. I had hoped to at least be earning money by doing that before I was granted my race-riding licence.

I stayed for a couple of months, but then decided to leave. My older cousin Gary, who lived in Santa Cruz, used to take me out with his friends in the evenings, but I didn't like the hippy culture and drug-taking.

However, I had been inspired by what I'd seen and experienced. Although there weren't that many girls racing out there, at the time the ones who did appeared to be put up on a good number of mounts. There was also much more emphasis on publicity for jockeys, with female riders featuring in TV commercials – all glowing with health and vitality, of course – advertising a wide variety of products. This exposure can only have helped persuade owners to give girls rides on their horses.

In racing terms, it was overall a very positive experience, one which provided me with an injection of renewed encouragement. I arrived back home more optimistic and met with Bill Wightman to discuss whether I did have a riding future in the UK after all. However, he was always very honest with me and emphasised that he couldn't foresee owners in the UK being willing to give girls more rides, as they did in California, for many years. How prescient his view was. Although he wanted me back working for him, he couldn't guarantee me more than a handful of mounts a year and most wouldn't be quality rides.

Purely by coincidence, at that time my father asked me to take up a management role in his property development businesses, so I compromised. I worked for my father and continued to ride work on the gallops at Bill's in my spare time. I was wary, though – with my vulnerable collarbone in mind – about partnering the yearlings when they arrived in the autumn.

In the back of my mind, I suppose I always harboured a belief that Bill's prophecy was wrong and that it was going to become easier for girls while I was still young enough. If so, I planned to take out a licence again. In reality, it would be decades before that happened, though I have never ceased believing that girls are just as capable of race-riding as boys, particularly in my time at the lightweight level, and if they have 'good hands' and tactical nous as I did.

Of course, working conditions within stables have now vastly improved, but certainly in my time the long, onerous hours and a trainer having control over so many facets of an apprentice's life was not one relished by all girls, even horse-mad ones. I was a rarity in accepting such an existence.

Unlike the US, we didn't operate a meritocracy. The contrasting lives of jockeys in the American West and here continued to astonish me. To illustrate that fact, in November, 1980 I was sent a copy of the *San Jose Mercury News* by someone I'd met in California. One page was filled with photos of young men and women riding work at Bay Meadows. 'Here,' wrote the journalist, 'was the near side of paradise for the few dozen men and women who rise at 5.30 to earn their day's pay by exercising thoroughbreds.'

Their 'day', he emphasised, lasted barely more than three hours. 'It's a great job for the gals because they can be finished by nine,' Neal Silva, who owned ten of the thoroughbreds boarded at the racetrack, was quoted as saying.

Another owner declared his preference for women 'exercisers': 'Girls seem better able to gallop with a horse than guys. They relax them.' There was plenty of work for the exercisers and for three hours a day a good rider, man or woman, would average $1,000 a month. Today, that would be equal to about £38,000 a year.

That article said it all. At this time, an apprentice here was being paid £53 for a full-time week (around £17,000 p.a. today), with extra for weekend overtime, though that was largely obligatory.

As the autumn of 1980 approached, I departed Ower Farm, this time never to return – apart from social visits to Bill.

There was, however, one intriguing postscript to my story.

Out of the blue, in December 1982 I received a letter from Karl Zivna, a trainer in Vienna, asking me to be his first jockey, presenting me with the opportunity to race in Europe. Herr Zivna wrote that the Racing Club in Vienna had 30 racing days a year, and 230 races. But he also sent horses to contest events in Milan, Merano and Budapest. He promised 'interesting possibilities, both from the sporting and financial point of view', and offered a nice apartment on the stable grounds.

Herr Zivna added that, in the previous season, he had been fourth in the 'trainers' list' (championship), and had 25 horses, ten of which were three years old, in training for the coming season which lasted from the end of March to the beginning of November.

At the time I repeatedly re-read the letter and maybe in hindsight I should have at least investigated this opportunity and met Herr Zivna. In my heart I had desperately wanted to continue a career in racing and felt honoured by this approach from a prominent Austrian trainer. It wasn't an easy decision but reluctantly I declined his offer. Of course, when you don't allow your heart to rule your head you spend the rest of your life thinking 'What if?'

However, the letter had arrived just as my father finished renovating a large commercial property he had bought for leisure activities in Havant, Hampshire. He saw me as an asset to his expanding business and he wanted me to manage a snooker club there. Twenty years later, we turned the snooker club into a gym and fitness/dance studio which I continue to manage today.

As much as I would have loved to have ridden for Herr Zivna in Europe or alternatively moved to California, a pro-women state, where trainers and owners would have been keen to give me rides, I accepted my father's offer.

Here, I had been the right woman and Bill Wightman had been the right trainer. But it was the wrong time. Very wrong. I had been born at least 20 years too early. I was not optimistic about an immediate improvement for women – not in British racing, anyway. This is not to denigrate British racing in general – just that one aspect of it, but one that was crucial to me. After all, it attracts some of the finest jockeys from around the world to ride racecourses as varied as the near flat lands of Newmarket to the gloriously scenic Goodwood.

I had to face facts: to develop from a male apprentice was tough enough and many of those I raced against fell by the wayside – Walter Swinburn was one of few who made the breakthrough in my time – but for a woman, then, as my story amply attests, it was all but impossible.

British racing, it was clear, was not yet ready for professional women jockeys. It was not ready to treat us seriously.

That said, I achieved what I set out to. Get rides. Against the male professionals. And win. Bill would have put me up on the occasional winning chance. But had I stayed in the game it would have been frustrating to witness my male counterparts being offered more and better opportunities. Indeed, it was only because I had a killer instinct that I got as far as I did. I sensed that my friend Richard Newman didn't possess that. I thought he was too worried about keeping Bill happy. He was too nice a character – unlike me. I demanded that ride after that race at Brighton and gave Bill an ultimatum. Richard won't mind me saying that I was a lot more forceful than him!

In life, sometimes if you believe you should attain something strongly enough, it happens. If I'd gone in thinking, 'perhaps I shouldn't be here', or deferring to the boys, I'd have failed. Maybe that's why I had more rides than Richard at that time.

He recalls that the boys, as well as the girls, had an extremely tough time and faced huge challenges in the 1970s and 1980s. He soon realised that being a good jockey was not enough to secure promising rides on the racecourse. Other trainers – not Bill Wightman – used him to prepare horses for races, but when those horses were believed to have a winning chance, a well-known professional jockey would be given the ride, making it impossible for Richard to progress in his career.

I didn't think about gender when it came to getting rides. I knew I could boast a better level of natural horsemanship than any of the male riders when I arrived. I was fortunate because Bill Wightman placed great store on that quality. He had a huge regard for talented women riders. He believed that I would learn to ride a finish, employ the correct tactics, and hone my style.

In retrospect, I must admit I was shocked by the reception I received from the lads – with some notable exceptions – some fellow jockeys, and what I'd describe as an owners' and trainers' wall of prejudice. In the mid-1970s, I had innocently believed that, with the passing of that 1975 legislation, everything would happen.

That the world, including racing, would change dramatically. It did not.

Perhaps my naivety was a good thing. It meant I always harboured hope in my heart and that was what sustained me. I simply hadn't appreciated the kind of world I was entering, and how attitudes were so ingrained when I wrote to Bill Wightman all those years ago. Otherwise, I'd have become even more frustrated and angry than I did.

My desire to race, and win, never diminished. As a woman who was the first professional to win a race against men, you become a challenge to any competitive man on horseback.

Maybe I should have taken the West End singer and actor Mike Sterling, of *Phantom of the Opera* fame, more seriously when he offered to race against me long after I retired. We raced on a disused railway line at Soberton, close to my home. Mike, who had been a family friend since he was 17 (and who years later became a boyfriend), and I were both riding unfamiliar horses from a livery yard. To his chagrin – because he treated every challenge with deadly seriousness – I still managed to get the better of him.

You never lose that passion to prove yourself and years after our race together I couldn't resist reminding him that he had met his match ...

I would have relished the chance to race against another singer, Davy Jones of the 1960s pop group The Monkees, who, at one time, lived near me. Like me, Davy had also started out as a jockey (in Newmarket, with trainer Basil Foster) and his addiction to race-riding never left him. I understand he was quite impressive as an apprentice: a brave rider.

Later, Davy and I got to know each other because our daughters went to the same prep school. He was keen to race again but I kept telling him he needed to be fitter. He proudly showed me his racehorse, stabled at his Hambledon home, during a party there, while singing 'I'm A Believer', one of The Monkees' best-loved songs. I must add that he made a pass at me in the stable, and we had a passionate kiss – probably not unconnected with the combination of him getting divorced and me going through a difficult time in my marriage! The kiss came as something of a surprise, but certainly wasn't an unwanted one. He had been my childhood crush, and his picture had taken pride of place on my bedroom wall, amongst all my horse photos. Davy later moved to Florida, where he owned racehorses, and rode work on them, but sadly died of a heart attack at 66 in 2012.

Fans of The Monkees will know that 'I'm a Believer' contains the line: 'I thought love was only true in fairy tales ...' and that leads me neatly on to my own romantic involvements once I'd retired from racing.

Yes, I did eventually get married, but not to Mike – and it happened after my third engagement! My second was to a yachtsman named Greg who was very supportive when it came to my business interests, particularly my nightclub. But I still didn't feel ready for the constraints and commitment of marriage.

When I did get married it was to Arthur, a farmer's son. He had spent his childhood riding, but, being tall, was more suited to yacht racing, a passion I shared and which was my only form of competitive sport after retiring from horseracing.

Our daughter Lara and I shared a sailing coach and raced at Cowes Week and Dartmouth Week. Lara and her friend Kate were sought-after racing crew, but I wasn't. I was only invited to crew because they desperately wanted Lara and Kate!

Arthur took sailing very seriously, winning events in Cowes Week eight times and racing abroad, but unfortunately the owners of the competitive yachts he raced never wanted me as crew! He had worked as an engineer on *Kalizma* – the fabulous yacht bought by Richard Burton as a gift for Elizabeth Taylor – while taking a career break as a research microbiologist. He proposed to me in Elizabeth Taylor and Richard Burton's cabin and our relationship resembled theirs in many ways. Except we divorced just the once …

Chapter 31

An Emotional Return to Ower Farm

IN EARLY 2020 I drove back to Ower Farm with Nick Townsend, my collaborator in the writing of this book. It was far from my first return since retiring from racing in 1980.

I would often visit Bill Wightman to talk over old times and check on his health and was also in attendance at a grand gathering at Ower Farm for his 90th birthday, when many old friends and former staff congregated.

My friend Richard Newman, who at the age of 15, started out at Ower Farm at the same time as me, became his devoted carer, until Bill's death in 2009 at the age of 95.

After I quit the saddle, Bill had continued training for another 13 years before he finally retired at the age of 79, having accumulated more than 700 winners. He was the longest-serving trainer in Britain and was unique in that he started training before the Second World War and yet continued for long enough to saddle a winner on the all-weather, which started in 1989. Bill also developed a stud as an appendage to the racing stable.

If he had one regret, it was probably not winning a Classic. But he achieved so much else in racing, and that included giving me a chance when the majority of his peers wouldn't have given me a second glance if I'd have pitched up on their doorsteps. I knew that gave Bill a huge sense of pride.

I would often join Bill and Richard Newman at the races when his horses were running. In the later years of his career, when Bill opted to stay home and watch his horses run on television, I would represent him at the racecourse and often be interviewed on his behalf by broadcasters Nick Luck and Mike Cattermole. They were both fond of him and happy to help. When discussing his horses it was so satisfying for me to feel I was giving something back to Bill after he had supported me so much.

At the time of writing, the Ower Farm stables were empty. But not of poignant memories. As I walked around, if I listened intently, I could still hear Bill Nash gently chiding me: 'Hurry, girl. Hurry.' And the 'banter' and ridicule of the some of the lads.

Evidence of Bill's legacy remains. Some of Bill's much-loved horses are buried in the garden of Ower Farm. They include Pneumatic and Chilcombe Bell, the dam of Bell-Tent. And, of course, Bill, dear Bill, will always have a presence there. His ashes were spread on the gallops.

I think Bill's rivals, men like Mill Reef's trainer Ian Balding, were all surprised by how I had managed to persuade him to even offer me a chance. As I've said, in other ways, he was quite the traditionalist. Many were amazed that I managed to get on the racecourse at that time – I recall owner Mick Channon was among them – and, what's more, secure my victory, a second and three thirds.

Bill always felt that I'd do anything to win. He could see I wanted it so badly. I see such drive today in women such as Hayley Turner, to whom I'll return. But my achievements, as proud of them as I am, were not enough in the end to sustain a career for me in the industry – one which would have consisted of riding work and having the occasional ride 'just to get a horse fit'.

Thankfully, what I will say is that I emerged from the late 1970s none the worse for my experiences. My health, both physical and mental, was unaffected long-term by those weight-loss binges. When you realise the barriers there are to furthering your ambition, when you see men the same age, with similar and sometimes less talent, getting opportunities that are not offered to you, it's frighteningly easy to descend into a deep abyss. There were times when I struggled to get through that period.

The subject of depression in the male-dominated racing environment of the 1970s was simply not a topic of discussion. This was long before the time when men and women in all sports felt comfortable talking about their mental health. It would have indicated a sign of weakness and men wanted to appear macho and strong mentally as well as physically. This meant it was important for me to adopt the same image to save myself from being referred to as the weaker sex and ridiculed for being, in their eyes, weaker mentally as well as physically.

But overall, those experiences at a young age did me no harm. They toughened me up and made me self-disciplined – and played an important part in my development to become the successful businesswoman I am today.

People often ask: 'Do you yearn to have been able to ride now?' To which my immediate response is: 'You bet I do!' How I envy women like Hayley Turner and Hollie Doyle.

Hayley, who started out in 2000, was joint champion apprentice in 2005, and in 2008 became the first woman to ride 100 winners in a year and is a three-time winner at Group 1 level. I first met

Hayley at the 2008 'Lesters' (the annual awards event named after Lester Piggott) when I was invited to present her with 'Lady Jockey of the Year'. That evening, coincidentally, the Professional Jockeys' Association also paid a tribute to my victory on The Goldstone at Salisbury on the 30th anniversary of my finest hour.

In March of the following year, Hayley suffered serious head injuries when putting a horse through starting stalls on the Newmarket gallops, and it was widely reported that she may consider retirement. I bumped into her in the loo at that year's Lesters, and urged her to continue in the saddle. 'You'll regret it if you give up,' I told her. 'You're lucky to have the opportunity. Never give up.' I then told her, 'I've always regretted it,' and I must admit I burst into tears.

She saw how it had affected me. Nothing had more effect on me in life than – as I saw it then – having to stop race-riding. Hayley looked at me, as if to say, 'Is it that bad?'

I think she was taken aback by seeing how hard it had hit me. Hayley reassured me that she wouldn't quit, and was true to her word. She didn't retire; not then, anyway. She did 'retire' in 2015 with a view to becoming a racing pundit, but returned to the track in 2018.

At the time of writing, Hayley, in her 24 years in the saddle, has amassed more than 1,000 winners. Yet, when I watch her today, she's stronger riding a finish than she's ever been. I suspect she'll continue while she's still fit enough – though perhaps not as long as Lester Piggott, who was 59 when he finally retired from race-riding.

Though she started out around 20 years after I quit the saddle, Hayley clearly faced the same challenges as me in her early years. In an article in the *Independent on Sunday*, written by my collaborator Nick Townsend in 2005, she spoke of the antipathy in some quarters to female riders that still existed.

'My agent has said to me a few times that he knows which trainers to not bother ringing for rides because they won't have a girl on,' she said. 'A lot of them are of the old school. But luckily the percentage of them is going down rather than up.'

Fortunately, there were many who did support and encourage girl riders, notably her guv'nor, Michael Bell, who compared her style with that of the former champion Kieren Fallon.

But Hayley added wryly, 'It's not actually riding the horse that's the hard part. That's the easy bit, just riding round the track. It's finding the owners and trainers with the courage to put a girl on a horse.'

Hayley, who said that the American legend Julie Krone was her principal inspiration, added: 'Without blowing my own trumpet, a lot of people would say that you wouldn't be able to pick me out in a finish among the lads. It's making sure you're in the right position in the race at the right time, and getting a tune out of the horse. It's not all about strength. It's the horses who are the athletes. I just want to be making a good living out of riding racehorses – like any of the lads.'

And that sums it up really – Hayley has been experiencing similar opposition to that I had faced all those years previously, but she is one of the few who has overcome it and prospered.

Hollie Doyle has made her own imprint on the sport in recent years. In 2019 she set a new record for winners ridden in a calendar year in Britain by a female jockey with 116 victories. The previous record of 106 winners had been established by Josephine Gordon in 2017.

Her tally for the year reached 172 in 2021 and, two years later, Hollie became the first female to win three races at Royal Ascot.

It has been some career already – at the time of writing she was still only 27.

Hollie was named *Sunday Times* Sportswoman of the Year in 2020 and the same year took third place in the BBC Sports Personality of the Year award. This recognition is confirmation that her name has transcended the racing world.

I cast my mind back now and reflect on how I declined the offers to appear in Sunday newspaper magazine features following my victory on The Goldstone. As well as enhancing my riding career, they could have given me the publicity to become a role model and promote fitness and a healthy lifestyle to women. But I still maintain that, if someone gives you a chance in life, you should be loyal to them. My loyalty to Bill Wightman meant that I had to refuse offers from the press.

Today, as owner of a fitness club, I hope that I am a positive influence on women's lifestyles. I do feel I have a responsibility to keep myself fit, as those attending my gym see me as a role model and my Technogym toning circuit, which I promote by saying your figure will revert to resemble the one you had in your 20s, puts pressure on me to look young. As you lose muscle mass with age, it's not enough to just lose weight, you have to keep working out to retain the same body you had in your youth. I also give advice on weight loss – something I have certainly learned a fair bit about! I am well placed to state that a continuous strict diet can have a bad effect on you physically and mentally.

As I recalled in an earlier chapter, I became anorexic in a period when I had to diet and forego just about all food. All of a sudden, you can't eat, you can't think straight, you can't concentrate. That experience makes me very careful now. I make sure I eat, though it's easy to forget when you're busy.

Very rarely now am I reminded of the effects of the dehydration and dieting of my jockey days – only at times when I've deliberately wanted to lose weight rapidly for a special occasion (which I don't recommend to my members) and have taken high-energy cardio classes wearing thermal underwear to help me sweat off the pounds. By not drinking much and restricting my daily intake to less than 900 calories I can lose half a stone as quickly as when I was a jockey, but my weight is now normally around 8½ stone.

When Michael Turner became chief medical advisor to the Jockey Club in the early 1990s he treated jockeys as professional athletes and offered them scientific advice on nutrition and weight control. Jockeys now spend more time in the gym to help them lose weight and keep fit.

There is also coaching available, something that was lacking in my day. Saffie Osborne, whose remarkable progress belies her years – she was just 22 at the time of writing – has been coached by the former top jockey George Baker, winner of four Group 1s, the last of which was the 2016 St Leger.

Thankfully, never again will jockeys have to suffer like I and others did in pursuit of mounts. Minimum weights have risen and no longer are riders forced to adopt unhealthy lifestyles in order to obtain rides – though sometimes they still have to diet and dehydrate to do the weights.

However, the downside of this is that women have lost their most valuable asset, of being able to do low weights far more easily than men. Without this advantage I'm sure I would never have got on the racecourse.

Chapter 32

More Than 40 Years on from my Historic Win, There's Been Insufficient Progress for Women Jockeys

TODAY, YOU'LL still frequently find me on the racecourse and, when the opportunity arises, I do my best to further the cause of women jockeys through media and public appearances.

In the 1990s I was invited to participate in the media training element of the newly formed Jockeys Education and Training Scheme (JETS), a charity that was set up in 1995 to help current and former professional jockeys plan and achieve a secure future. It is an excellent scheme, funded by jockeys' prize money contributions and additional support from the Injured Jockeys Fund.

This really appealed to me because I was keen to seek broadcasting work on the racecourse, where I could promote women professional jockeys whenever I had the opportunity. My appearances included Royal Ascot in 2009 when I was offered the chance to work with broadcaster Rupert Bell (the brother of trainer Michael Bell, and father of racing presenter Oli Bell). I fulfilled a similar role with Rupert at Royal Ascot in 2012 and was also interviewed by Mick Fitzgerald for Sky's coverage of Shergar Cup Day in 2022. That gave me the opportunity to talk about the talent in the 'Girls' Team'.

There was one amusing moment – though one great for my self-esteem – when Mick initially failed to recognise me when I arrived at the course. He thought I looked too young to have been a jockey riding in the 1970s. Indeed, he thought I looked younger than him!

I'm still active in making appearances on the racecourse. More than 45 years on from my win, there is still fascination amongst many racegoers that there was a time when British racing rarely featured women professional riders – and, at one time included none at all. I even had lessons in public speaking from Sir Timothy Ackroyd, an actor and voice coach, whom I met in a coffee shop!

On one occasion, in the paddock at Newbury on the 40th anniversary of my victory, I was, by chance, overheard by Chris Cook, then writing for *The Guardian* but now with the *Racing Post*.

He tweeted: 'At Newbury, a good interview over the tannoy with @xgirljock, the first female professional to ride a winner on the flat in Britain immediately followed by the Best Dressed Lady Competition #irony'

We spoke and the following day an article appeared in *The Guardian* under the headline: 'Wiltshire Proposes Quota System to Increase the Use of Female Riders'.

He wrote:

> Racing's rulers should consider financial incentives and perhaps even quotas as a way of increasing opportunities for female jockeys, according to Karen Wiltshire, who was the first female professional to ride a winner in British Flat racing. This week brings the 40th anniversary of Wiltshire's landmark achievement and she is dismayed by the lack of progress that women have since been able to make.

'I thought at least a third of jockeys in races would be women by now,' Wiltshire said yesterday.

She has been impressed in recent years by the achievements of Hayley Turner and others but the latest figures show female participation varying from 10% in the least valuable races to 1% in the most valuable.

'I've been thinking of ways to change things. It's a big business, Flat racing, so there has got to be some incentive, like a cash incentive in handicaps, so the trainer and owner got a bonus in prize money if there was a girl riding.'

But Wiltshire concedes that in the most valuable and prestigious Flat races, an extra 5% or 10% on prize money is unlikely to change the entrenched habits of wealthy trainers and owners.

'Probably at Group level or in Classic races, it's going to have to come down to a quota system. Historically, when you go into a male-dominated world, whether it's politics or whatever, it takes a long time [to effect change], generations. The only way to fast-track that is a quota system. If trainers aren't going to give women chances at a higher level, perhaps that's the only way.'

While Wiltshire would like the sport to insist on female participation in the very best races, she does not deny the practical difficulties facing such a scheme, for which an inventive solution would be required.

'Do you say there has to be at least one woman jockey in each Classic or Group race? It's very difficult.' But she feels action is now required and is not in favour of the French solutions of a weight allowance for horses ridden by women, as she dislikes the implication that female jockeys might be less capable and in need of some kind of advantage.

Some may query my stance on this. And in general, as will be evident from my earlier observations, I believe that meritocracy should rule in the workplace. I must stress that my belief has always been that women jockeys do not require help once *in the saddle* through a weight allowance. However, they do require help to gain opportunities to actually *get rides* through the implementation of quotas and financial incentives to trainers and owners.

Another idea I'd like to see introduced is that there should be at least one ride a year guaranteed to both girls and boys when signing an apprenticeship contract. I should stress that, even if this was implemented, it doesn't mean they would get a ride on a horse with a winning chance; they would still have to negotiate with their trainer for this opportunity, as I did. But at least it would be a start. I still remember that moment of undistilled elation when Bill Wightman announced I was to have my first ride; I felt that all my hard work had been worthwhile.

A year after the *Guardian* article, I put forward my proposal regarding a quota system to Rose Grissell, the British Horseracing Association's (BHA) head of diversity and inclusion, at a 'Women in Racing' meeting at Ascot. Initially, she expressed interest in my ideas to incentivise owners and trainers to give rides to female jockeys and find sponsors prepared to support my plan. However, Rose eventually responded to say that their research had showed female jockeys felt incentivising owners to use female jockeys would indicate that they weren't good enough and be detrimental to the sport.

I have to admit that Saffie Osborne endorsed that view. She told me that the girls' attitude was simply this: 'If they're good enough, they get opportunities.'

I understand that stance. Yet, for all that, earlier, I lauded the achievements of such talented individuals as Hollie Doyle and Hayley Turner, the truth is that they are the exceptions. There are still too few women professional riders.

Let's consider the reality of how frustratingly slow progress has been for women since I made my breakthrough.

According to an item in the November 1987 Lady Jockeys' Association newsletter, Kim Tinkler had, for the second year running, easily headed the number of winners ridden by women professionals, in spite of that year being that notoriously difficult post-apprenticeship season when she lost her claim. Kim had won 21 races, three more than the 1986 season, though nearly all on horses trained by her husband Nigel.

That year, a total of 41 women professionals accumulated 43 winners from just over 600 rides. Other than Kim Tinkler, Dana Mellor recorded nine wins, Gay Kelleway and Jackie Houston three, and Wendy Carter two. None of the other girls mustered more than one victory.

It wasn't until 1997 that a female rider, Alex Greaves, won (actually dead-heated for first) a Group 1 event (these are the elite races and include the Classics), the Nunthorpe at York on her husband David Nicholls' Ya Malak.

Starting her career in 1988, Alex had become the first female apprentice to ride out her claim and in 1996 achieved what I'd yearned to do by becoming the first woman to ride in the Derby, on Portuguese Lil, a 500-1 outsider. It could be suggested that she received preferential treatment in that her guv'nor was also her husband. But that shouldn't detract from her achievement. She gave the six-year-old, an 11-1 chance, a fine ride to dead-heat with the Kevin Darley-partnered Coastal Bluff.

A similar observation could be applied to the dynamic Gay Kelleway, whose triumph on her trainer father Paul's Sprowston Boy in the 1987 Queen Alexandra Stakes was the first victory by a woman at Royal Ascot.

She remained for many years the only female jockey to have achieved that feat – until Hayley Turner emulated her in 2019, winning the Sandringham Stakes on Thanks Be.

According to the records of the LJA, Gay was the first recipient of a new sponsorship initiative by Heinz; the company having decided that they should link their reduced-calorie products with weight-loss and winning. That would have sounded very appealing in my day!

Even by the turn of the century, 13 years on from Gay's achievement, of the 40 professional female riders licensed by the Jockey Club, the majority were apprentices, with only four fully-fledged women jockeys.

On paper, yes, matters have improved since then. According to the Professional Jockeys' Association, in early 2020, there were 42 female apprentice jockeys licensed out of a total of 110.

The following statistics reveal a rather more relevant analysis:

In 2023, the exceptional Hollie Doyle finished fifth in the Flat Jockeys' Championship with 89 wins from 611 rides, her tally only bettered by champion William Buick, Oisin Murphy, Rossa Ryan and Tom Marquand (Hollie's husband).

However, the only other woman professional rider in the leading 20 was Saffie Osborne, at 20th. Saffie rides for her trainer father Jamie, but is also offered winning mounts by many other trainers. In 2023, her three most notable victories – in a Listed event, Group 3 race and The Chester Cup – were all for outside trainers, including Ed Walker, who regards her as 'a fabulous horsewoman'. As he told my collaborator Nick Townsend, 'At 22, she has already conquered two professions, having been a brilliant event-rider before becoming a brilliant jockey.'

Hollie and Saffie apart, the next female in the list was Hayley Turner at 61st.

As for British jump racing, that doesn't reveal a story that is any more positive for women riders – certainly not compared to Ireland where women like the 2021 Grand National-winning jockey Rachael Blackmore, who, that same year was leading jockey at the Cheltenham Festival, and Katie Walsh and Nina Carberry, haven't just progressed to compete but have done so at the elite level.

In Britain only Bryony Frost has made a real breakthrough, with her six Grade 1 triumphs including three on Paul Nicholls' Frodon – the 2019 Ryanair Chase, 2020 King George VI Chase and 2021 Champion Chase.

However, it is the Flat code that is my primary concern.

As I've suggested previously, I genuinely believed I'd be offered many more chances, much quicker. I harboured a staunch belief that an abundance of ability, utter self-belief and profound determination were all it required to achieve as much as the men.

Even when I retired, I was certain that, following what I had achieved, far more women professional jockeys would emerge and establish themselves.

How wrong I was. The position has improved but not sufficiently. Frankly, for all that Hayley, Hollie, Saffie and others have achieved, not nearly enough progress has been made in the four decades since I retired – despite attempts to suggest that it has.

I was intrigued to find that, to coincide with 2020's International Women's Day, Great British Racing (the sport's promotional and marketing body) decreed that the girls should no longer be referred to as 'female jockeys' and instead be called 'just jockeys'.

According to the GBR website: '#JustJockeys highlights the incredible achievements of women in the sport of horseracing and highlights the need for us to drop the term "female jockeys" and celebrate the sport as one.'

It continued: 'Women have an established and recognised standing in racing and the number of successes continue to rise. The total number of winners from [female] jockeys has increased by 76% from 2015 to 2019, despite a 2% drop in the number of [female] jockeys.

'Talented, determined, resilient and brave, all in a day's work for a jockey. Racing has no gender, it's your skill and talent that counts. They are: JustJockeys.'

Fine-sounding words, but as I've reflected in my comments already, the reality doesn't support them.

Yes, things have improved markedly since my time – when I had to attempt to disguise myself as *not* being female – but in my view, women still have to bear a heavy burden of discrimination as jockeys. It is a burden far heavier than any of the lead weights they've had to carry in handicaps.

I will conclude by saying that, when I departed Bill's yard, I felt that, in my own way, I had at least helped to crowbar open the door of opportunity for the next generations to benefit, and that it would not be too long before many other women demonstrated that they had every right to be there, fighting finishes alongside their male counterparts.

It's taken way longer than I ever could have imagined to reach even the stage we have, but I will continue to believe that in years to come more female jockeys will make their presence felt and, who knows, join the roll-call of champions.

But what no one can dispute is that I played a significant part in demonstrating that there definitely *is* a place for us girls in racing …

Bibliography

THIS IS one woman's story. However, it largely relates to a period not too far short of 50 years ago, and it has been a major task for the authors to conduct research and check facts, largely without online assistance. They would like to acknowledge the help of the following publications:

Alcock, Anne, *'They're Off!' The Story of the First Girl Jump Jockeys* (London: J.A. Allen, 1978).

Ayres, Michael, and Newbon, Gary, *Under Starter's Orders: A Guide to Racing on the Flat* (Newton Abbot, Devon: David & Charles, 1975).

Butler, Deborah, *Women, Horseracing and Gender: Becoming 'One of the Lads'* (London: Routledge, 2015).

Davidson, Scooter Toby, and Anthony, Valerie (eds), *Great Women in the Sport of Kings: America's Top Women Tell Their Stories* (New York: Syracuse University Press, 1999).

Walker, Alan Yuill, *Months of Misery, Moments of Bliss: The Biography of Hampshire Trainer Bill Wightman* (Lambourn: A & V Publishing, 1996).

Also the kind assistance of Tim Cox, whose magnificent library devoted to the thoroughbred horse has been invaluable.

Newsletters and other material of the Lady Jockeys' Association.

About the Authors

Karen Wiltshire

Karen Wiltshire wanted to be a professional jockey from the age of six and fulfilled that ambition when employed by distinguished racehorse trainer Bill Wightman, who owned a racing stables close to her Hampshire home. Against all odds and without having any family connections in racing, Karen became the first female professional jockey in the UK to win a professional Flat race, in 1978.

After her retirement from racing, she managed the leisure side of her father's property company: a nightclub, restaurant and boutique hotel at Northney Marina, Hayling Island – where she moored her first boat, appropriately named *The Goldstone* – and a snooker/nightclub in Havant which 20 years ago became a gym with fitness studios. Karen has been a licensee since her twenties, and six years after her triumph in the saddle was taking on the men in another male-dominated business, successfully selling beer. She was rewarded by the brewers Carlsberg with a trip to Copenhagen by Concorde.

She now owns the leisure premises in Havant and continues to manage the gym, fitness and dance studio and private parties at her licensed club. As a fitness instructor she enjoys teaching high-energy cardio classes and is passionate about promoting a healthy lifestyle and safe weight loss.

Karen has also worked part-time selling and valuing properties for the Countrywide group of estate agents, and others, and also founded her own property company, Mediterranean Homes, selling villas with pools and moorings in Empuriabrava, Spain, where her family had a villa.

Her daughter, Lara, an Oxford graduate, works as a trader in the City – like her mother, she was not daunted by entering a male-dominated workplace.

Nick Townsend

Nick Townsend has spent the majority of his career as a sports writer on the *Daily Mail*, as football correspondent and chief sports writer of the *Independent on Sunday*, and freelancing for publications including the *Sunday Times*, *Racing Post* and *Racing Ahead*. He has written on just about every sport in a long career and has covered Olympics, football and rugby World Cups and Ashes cricket; but horseracing has always been one of his specialist and best-loved subjects.

He is author of the best-selling *Sure Thing: The Greatest Coup in Horse Racing History* (Penguin Random House), which tells the story of the country's best-known professional gambler and former trainer, Barney Curley.

His other work includes the authorised biography of racehorse trainer Mark Johnston (Highdown, now Racing Post Books) and an updated version of this, titled *Phenomenon* (Welbeck) published in 2021.

He also collaborated with Barney Curley on his autobiography *Giving a Little Back* (Harper Collins), Sir Steve Redgrave on his autobiography *A Golden Age* (BBC Books) and Sir Ben Ainslie on his autobiography *Close to the Wind* (Yellow Jersey/Random House).

Nick also penned a self-help guide with Sir Steve Redgrave, *You Can Win at Life!* (BBC Books).

The authors would like to record their appreciation of editor Katie Field's meticulous work on their manuscript.